D0207966

KIERKEGAARD'S DIALECTIC OF INWARDNESS

KIERKEGAARD'S
DIALECTIC OF INWARDNESS

A Structural Analysis of the

Theory of Stages

STEPHEN N. DUNNING

PRINCETON UNIVERSITY PRESS

PRINCETON, NEW JERSEY

Copyright © 1985 by Princeton University Press
Published by Princeton University Press, Princeton, New Jersey
In the United Kingdom: Princeton University Press
Guildford, Surrey

All Rights Reserved

Library of Congress Cataloging in Publication Data will be
found on the last printed page of this book

ISBN 0-691-07299-x
Publication of this book has been aided by a grant from
The Andrew W. Mellon Foundation

This book has been composed in Linotron Garamond

Clothbound editions of Princeton University Press books
are printed on acid-free paper, and binding materials
are chosen for strength and durability

Printed in the United States of America
by Princeton University Press
Princeton, New Jersey

For my mother,
Kathleen Mulligan Dunning
In memory of my father,
Harrison Freeman
Dunning

CONTENTS

CHARTS

PREFACE

THIS BOOK requires a word of explanation. There are so many studies of Kierkegaard that one might justifiably question the addition of yet another. Moreover, there are now in America a substantial number of expert Kierkegaard scholars, men and women who have journeyed to Denmark, mastered the complexities and nuances of Danish, and bring many years of reading and reflecting upon Kierkegaard and his times to their writing. Why, then, this book from one who is a newcomer to Kierkegaard studies and who has never had the opportunity to study in Denmark?

The answer to both questions is that this book is the result of what almost appears to be a "chance" discovery. In the spring of 1980, while preparing to teach a class on *Either/Or*, I noticed that volume I is susceptible to a Hegelian dialectical analysis. I gave a paper on this finding to the Department of Philosophy at Villanova University, and an article, "The Dialectic of Contradiction in Kierkegaard's Aesthetic Stage," was readily accepted by the *Journal of the American Academy of Religion*. These responses encouraged me to explore the possibility that *Stages on Life's Way* might confirm my initial impressions about the aesthetic stage and also to begin to study Danish and the current state of Kierkegaard scholarship. The positive result with *Stages* received helpful criticisms when reported to the Nineteenth Century Theology Group at the 1981 Annual Meeting of the American Academy of Religion. Meanwhile, the National Endowment for the Humanities granted me a research fellowship for 1982-1983 in order to pursue the project in terms of Kierkegaard's other pseudonymous writings.

It is my belief that the resulting book makes a unique contribution to the understanding of Kierkegaard. I am painfully aware of its limitations and of how much it could be improved by more years of working with Kierkegaard's writings and the Danish language. But its time has come. Indeed, to augment it substantially with discussions of Kierkegaard's nonpseudonymous writings or of his actual readings of Hegel and the Danish Hegelians would require additional volumes. As it stands, the essay has a certain completeness as an immanent criticism of the major pseudonymous works and an interpretation of the theory of stages presented in them. It is as such that this work makes its entry into the crowded field of Kierkegaard studies.

ACKNOWLEDGMENTS

I WISH TO EXPRESS my gratitude to those friends and colleagues who have offered encouragement and helpful criticisms as this project has progressed: Robert Dostal, Gordon D. Kaufman, Robert A. Kraft, Robert L. Perkins, Michael Raposa, Mark C. Taylor, Frank Trommler, Sylvia Walsh Utterback, and Merold Westphal. Sanford Thatcher and Gretchen Oberfranc, of Princeton University Press, have been of great assistance, for which I am duly grateful. The book was written during a research fellowship from the National Endowment for the Humanities, and preparation of the manuscript was facilitated by a grant from the University of Pennsylvania Research Foundation. I also thank my wife, Roxy, for her support and patience throughout the months of research and writing.

NOTE ON TEXTS

THANKS TO the energy and industry of Howard and Edna Hong, English-speaking Kierkegaard scholars will soon have at their disposal a new, very much improved, and consistent set of translations of Kierkegaard's works. Of these, four of the volumes relevant to this study are currently available. Although the marginal page correlations in these new translations refer to the first edition of Kierkegaard's *Samlede Værker*, and it is the third edition (1963) that is readily accessible to me, correlation tables with all three editions are included both in the new translations and in volume 20 of the third Danish edition, to say nothing of the handy first volume of *The Kierkegaard Indices*, compiled by Alastair McKinnon, in which the second and third Danish editions are correlated with the older English, German, and French translations.

When I have found it necessary to alter a translation in some way more extensive than, for example, simply deleting unnecessary capitalization, I have provided the location in both the English translation and the *Samlede Værker* (and frequently the Danish words in question) in a note. References to the *Papirer* (second edition, 1901-1946) can be recognized by the use of Roman numerals for the volume in question.

In the following list of abbreviations for Kierkegaard's works, the date of publication is given in brackets after the title, except for works published posthumously.

CA   *The Concept of Anxiety: A Simple Psychologically Orienting Deliberation on the Dogmatic Issue of Hereditary Sin* [1844]. *Kierkegaard's Writings*, vol. VIII. Edited and translated with an introduction and notes by Reidar Thomte, in collaboration with Albert B. Andersen. Princeton: Princeton University Press, 1980.

CD   *The Concept of Dread: A Simple Psychological Deliberation in the Direction of the Dogmatic Problem of Original Sin* [1844]. Translated with an introduction and notes by Walter Lowrie. Princeton: Princeton University Press, 1957.

CI   *The Concept of Irony, with Constant Reference to Socrates* [1841]. Translated with an introduction and notes by Lee M. Capel. Bloomington: Indiana University Press, 1965.

CLA   *Crisis in the Life of an Actress and Other Essays on Drama* [1848]. Translated with an introduction and notes by Stephen Crites. New York: Harper Torchbook, 1967.

CorA   *The Corsair Affair. Kierkegaard's Writings*, vol. XIII. Edited and translated by Howard V. Hong and Edna H. Hong. Princeton: Princeton University Press, 1982.

CUP   *Concluding Unscientific Postscript to the Philosophical Fragments* [1846]. Translated by Walter Lowrie and David F. Swenson. With an introduction by Walter Lowrie. Princeton: Princeton University Press, 1941.

DODE   *Johannes Climacus or, De Omnibus Dubitandum Est and A Sermon.* Translated with an assessment by T. H. Croxall. Stanford: Stanford University Press, 1958.

E/O   *Either/Or: A Fragment of Life* [1843]. Vol. I translated by David F. Swenson and Lillian Marvin Swenson; vol. II translated by Walter Lowrie. With revisions and a foreword by Howard A. Johnson. Princeton: Princeton University Press, 1959.

FT   *Fear and Trembling: Dialectical Lyric* [1843]. *Kierkegaard's Writings*, vol. VI. Edited and translated with introduction and notes by Howard V.

Hong and Edna H. Hong. Princeton: Princeton University Press, 1983.

FT(L)   *Fear and Trembling: A Dialectical Lyric* [1843]. Translated with introduction and notes by Walter Lowrie. Garden City, N.Y.: Doubleday Anchor, 1954.

JP   *Søren Kierkegaard's Journals and Papers.* Translated and edited by Howard V. Hong and Edna H. Hong. 7 vols. Bloomington: Indiana University Press, 1967-1978.

PF   *Philosophical Fragments or a Fragment of Philosophy* [1844]. Translated by David F. Swenson. Revised by Howard V. Hong. With an introduction by Niels Thulstrup and commentary by Niels Thulstrup and Howard V. Hong. Princeton: Princeton University Press, 1962.

PV   *The Point of View for My Work as an Author: A Report to History.* Translated with introduction and notes by Walter Lowrie. Newly edited, with a preface, by Benjamin Nelson. New York: Harper Torchbooks, 1962.

R   *Repetition: A Venture in Experimenting Psychology* [1843]. *Kierkegaard's Writings,* vol. VI. Edited and translated by Howard V. Hong and Edna H. Hong. Princeton: Princeton University Press, 1983.

R(L)   *Repetition: An Essay in Experimental Psychology* [1843]. Translated with introduction and notes by Walter Lowrie. New York: Harper Torchbooks, 1954.

SD   *The Sickness unto Death: A Christian Psychological Exposition for Upbuilding and Awakening* [1849]. *Kierkegaard's Writings,* vol. XIX. Edited and translated with introduction and notes by Howard V. Hong and Edna H. Hong. Princeton: Princeton University Press, 1980.

SD(L) *The Sickness unto Death: A Christian Pshychological Exposition for Edification and Awakening* [1849]. Translated with introduction and notes by Walter Lowrie. Princeton: Princeton University Press, 1954.

SLW *Stages on Life's Way: Studies by Sundry Persons* [1845]. Translated with introduction and notes by Walter Lowrie. Princeton: Princeton University Press, 1940.

TC *Training in Christianity and the Edifying Discourse which 'Accompanied' It* [1850]. Translated with introduction and notes by Walter Lowrie. Princeton: Princeton University Press, 1967.

Unless otherwise noted, italicized words within quotations are italicized in the source from which they are taken. Biblical quotations follow the Revised Standard Version.

KIERKEGAARD'S DIALECTIC OF INWARDNESS

INTRODUCTION

"THOUGH our outer nature is wasting away, our inner nature is being renewed every day" (2 Cor. 4:16). The Pauline conviction that there are two natures in every person—an outer, transient nature that is opposed to or at least radically independent of an inner, eternal nature—has inspired and instructed Christians for many centuries. Only in the 1840s, however, in the pseudonymous works of Søren Kierkegaard, does the concept of inwardness as such become the central theme in the thought of a Christian philosopher. Many ideas are interwoven in those complex works, some appearing in one and some in another, yet it is the inner/outer relation that provides an Ariadne's thread, enabling the interpreter to find a coherent statement in the pseudonymous texts as a whole.

In addition to this comprehensiveness, several other features of this theme bear mention. First, because the inner/outer relation is discussed by all of the major pseudonyms, it is a focus that allows each pseudonym to speak for himself, in contrast to those many issues that are more germane to one pseudonym than to the others.[1] Second, close attention to the varying opinions expressed by the different pseudonyms discourages a dubious identification of any one of them with Kierkegaard himself.[2] This recognition, in turn, reduces the tendency to rank the pseudonyms hierarchically according to their alleged proximity to their creator.[3] Thus the dialectic of inwardness makes a really immanent criticism of the pseudonymous texts possible and is accordingly the primary focus of this study.

A closely related theme is Kierkegaard's individualistic concept of the self. Throughout most of this century, the existentialist belief in the self as solitary has dominated Kierkegaard interpretation.[4] Many contemporary scholars, including some whose work has in other regards profoundly influenced this book, continue to promote that idea.[5] Yet there are also those who have begun to challenge Kierkegaard's admittedly individualist rhetoric, especially on the basis of the social and political implications of his late, nonpseudonymous writings.[6] Only a few have discerned in the earlier, pseudonymous literature a relational concept of the self, and their discussions have been limited to what is possible within a short article or paper.[7] To that growing consensus this essay will add a great deal of evidence based upon detailed analysis of the dialectic of self and other in a number of the pseudonymous texts.

The dialectics of inner/outer and self/other also offer an excellent way to grasp Kierkegaard's theory of stages. According to James Collins, it is this theory that has earned Kierkegaard a place in the history of philosophy.[8] Yet scholars still do not agree on the number of stages[9] and whether the later stages represent distinct spheres or progressive developments of the earlier ones.[10] The analyses that follow will demonstrate that the theory of stages can be understood as a systematic development from the aesthetic through the ethical and culminating in the religious, and that the religious is to be treated as one rather than two stages. Thus there is a total of three stages, and they constitute a progression (although without any implication of logical "necessity"), rather than utterly discrete or diffusely overlapping spheres.[11]

The basis upon which I argue for this interpretation is close analysis of the dialectical structures to be found in a number of the major pseudonymous texts, as well as detailed discussion of texts that focus on the stages but do not reveal such structures. It is true that Kierkegaard's pseudonyms frequently castigate the systematic dialectics associated with Hegelianism.[12] It is therefore all the more startling that the very "systematic *ein, zwei, drei*" ridiculed in *Concluding Unscientific Postscript* (*CUP*, 319) can be discerned in many of the pseudonymous texts, *Postscript* among them! Such Hegelian structures are perfectly obvious in the first part of *The Concept of Irony*, so obvious that the claim has been made that Kierkegaard's apparent Hegelianism there is ironical.[13] But irony can hardly account for the other five works in which such systematic structures can be found, works in which those structures are neither acknowledged nor obvious. Indeed, to discern them it is often necessary to ignore the overt organization of the text, to dig beneath the surface in order to identify the layers that structure the terrain to be explored.[14] In contrast, irony always tips its hand, as it certainly must if it is to be understood as irony. Since such hints are totally absent from the vast majority of the materials under consideration, I have come to the conclusion that Kierkegaard was quite unconscious of the extent to which he continued, even after breaking with Hegelianism, to think in terms that permit—and often seem to demand—a Hegelian structural analysis.[15]

It is unusual, but by no means unprecedented, to interpret Kierkegaard's thought in systematic and structural terms. The plea, "And, oh, that no half-learned man would lay a dialectic hand upon this work," with which he closes his admission of authorship of all the pseudonymous works through 1846 (appended to *CUP* as "A First and Last Declaration"), has discouraged more than one well-meaning scholar.[16] Nevertheless, a number of fine studies have been published in recent years that are systematic or structural in approach;[17] one even employs the methods of poststructuralist literary criticism.[18] In this study, however, the bracketing of the question of authorial intention and method is used only in order to provide a more direct access to the texts themselves; it carries no ontological presuppositons or implications, any more than the discovery of Hegelian systematic structures should be taken as an argument for the truth (or falsehood) of Hegelianism as a philosophical position.[19] My hope is that these analyses will illuminate Kierkegaard's pseudonymous works and his theory of stages, and thereby provide the means for a more profound and critical engagement with his dialectic of inwardness.

ONE

Training in Dialectics:
The Structure
of Kierkegaard's Dissertation

In 1841, Kierkegaard submitted and defended a dissertation entitled *The Concept of Irony*. There is general agreement that this work has a clear Hegelian structure, at least in part one, although debate continues as to whether those elements are intended seriously or ironically. Those who treat them as ironical suggest that *The Concept of Irony* is really Kierkegaard's first "pseudonymous" work, for it does not, in their judgment, reflect the views of Kierkegaard himself.[1] I choose to begin with *The Concept of Irony* for another reason. As a text that embodies a clear dialectical structure, it is evidence of Kierkegaard's early talent for writing (whether in earnest or as parody) in a Hegelian manner. Thus *The Concept of Irony* provides an excellent opportunity to introduce the sort of dialectical analysis that I shall carry out in relation to the pseudonymous literature and the theory of stages.

The term "dialectical," which is justly notorious for its ambiguity,[2] is used in this study in two ways. One, which is familiar to readers of Kierkegaard and existentialist literature, involves the dialectic between the two distinct poles of consciousness in every individual: inwardness, subjectivity, and selfhood are understood in contradistinction to externality, objectivity, and social relations. The other meaning, which is associated more with Hegel, concerns the attempt to discern a holistic or systematic development within consciousness and experience. For Hegel, such an endeavor is mandated by the conviction that there can be no ultimate dichotomy between the inwardness of thought and the externality of being, that subjectivity and objectivity find their "necessary" unity in consciousness. Kierkegaard ardently disputes that belief.[3] Yet a number of his major works demonstrate the same sort of systematic structure that he deplores.

This analysis of dialectical structures does not, of course, exhaust the varieties of dialectic in Kierkegaard's thought. Perhaps the most obvious omission is "objective" dialectics, that is, the analysis of external reality as objectively dialectical. Although this view is normally associated with the historical evolutionism of Hegel and Marx, it is also evident in Kierkegaard's analyses of the paradoxes of such Christian concepts as the incarnation. But Kierkegaard's primary dialectical concern is with the relation of the subject to the object, not with the essential nature of the object as such.[4] It is this dialectic of inwardness—of concepts developing within consciousness—that I shall examine in this study.

Kierkegaard's use of pseudonyms, which he calls a method of indirect communication (and which is frequently called his "existential dialectic"), is another dialectic that I shall in large part ignore. There are no less than four ways in which this dialectic of pseudonymity has been discussed. Most common is the opinion that Kierkegaard himself expresses in a statement appended to *Concluding Unscientific Postscipt*, namely, that he hides himself behind the pseudonyms in order to free the reader to deal directly with the possibilities presented in the literature.[5] Significantly, a great many scholars take just the opposite tact, analyzing every shred of the pseudonymous works in order to find allusions and insights into Kierkegaard's personal history, hoping thereby to discern a dialectical relation between his life and works.[6] A third way is to seek a dialectic among the various pseudonyms, which leads into the fourth approach, a focus upon the dialectic within the total authorship between the aesthetic and the religious works.[7] These approaches, although no doubt useful in other studies, will not be employed here. Rather, I shall analyze the dialectical themes and structures within each text as it stands and relate them to one another only in terms of the theory of stages.

Although *The Concept of Irony* does not shed much light on the dialectic of existence in the theory of stages, it is an excellent place to explore the nature of formal dialectical structures. Such structures involve a series of opposed poles, and the way in which those oppositions are related to one another determines the character of the dialectic. When they simply negate one another, the dialectic is one of contradiction, and any sort of relief from the negative relation is denied. Such oppositions appear in various philosophical and theological dualisms, as well as in the bipolarities of structuralist and semiotic analysis.

A second type of dialectic goes beyond mere contradiction but does not really supersede it. Here there is a third moment in which a reciprocal relation between the opposite poles is affirmed, but in such a way as to preclude further development. An example of a dialectic of reciprocity would be contractual relations, or the *Do ut des* of Roman religion. In commenting on what it means to ask questions, Kierkegaard mentions the limitations of such reciprocal dialectics. Two people may discuss an object together, each granting the legitimacy of the other's opinion, but without attaining true unity about the object in question: "Although this relationship has reciprocity, it contains no moment of unity (neither the immediate nor the higher). Moreover, the true moment of duality is essentially lacking, since the relationship exhausts itself in mere reciprocity" (*CI*, 73).

Kierkegaard himself is justly famous for advocating a dialectic of paradox. Here a genuine unity is achieved, but one that accentuates rather than supersedes the contradiction between the two poles. The most famous historical example of such a dialectic is doubtless the Chalcedonian claim that Christ is one person in two distinct natures. Of Kierkegaard's pseudonymous works, *Fear and Trembling* and *Philosophical Fragments* both discuss and embody a paradoxical dialectic in a particularly clear and consistent manner.[8]

Hegel's dialectic of mediation offers still another possibility, for it conceives the third moment as more than a reciprocal stalemate or a paradoxical unity of two contradictory poles.[9] Mediation is a union in which a third step takes the opposites up into itself as aspects or moments within a new reality. In this process, each pole loses its negative character in relation to the other and is thereby fulfilled in its true nature as positively related to the other. Most important, the new third can now embark upon its own course, for it is a new entity that will in turn find itself in a new contradiction. Thus a dialectic of mediation never stops, never allows any dichotomy to reign supreme; its unities always lead to new, more complex dualities, until the entire process of a particular idea is complete. Whereas repeated paradoxical dialectics can constitute only a series, a dialectic of mediation will have a progressive, systematic character, for it aims at representing the totality of this process.[10]

Although the three moments of a systematic dialectic are best known as thesis, antithesis, and synthesis (terms favored by Fichte and sometimes used by Kierkegaard), I prefer as a technical shorthand the vocabulary of Hegel (also occasionally employed by Kierkegaard). His term for the first moment is *an sich*, in-itself, by which he means that first encounter with a concept or object in which it is posited by consciousness as an immediate, simple, abstract phenomenon.[11] It is immediate because there has not yet been any reflection about it, simple because there is as yet no awareness of opposition within it or between it and other phenomena, and abstract because it is at first conceived as a thing in-itself. The essential nature of the phenomenon is not adequately revealed in this first moment; it remains merely "implicit," which is in fact another way of translating *an sich*.

A presupposition of Hegel's dialectic is that nothing can be understood in-itself—everything becomes intelligible only when fully developed. Thus the first moment, in which an object passively appears to (or is posited by) consciousness as immediate, simple, and abstract, must give way to a second moment in which that object is revealed to be an active subject that is mediated, complex, and concrete. This is the "dialectical" moment par excellence, and it, far more than Hegel's notorious third moment, is actually responsible for much of the confusion that surrounds dialectical analysis. The reason for this confusion is that the subjectivity that emerges in the second moment is a self-consciousness that is both discontinuous and continuous with the consciousness of the first moment. The discontinuous relation is already clear in the new focus upon reflective mediation, complexity, and so forth. The continuity, which is sometimes exploited but more often overlooked in actual dialectical analyses, lies in the fact that the new self-consciousness itself takes responsibility for the inadequacy of the initial consciousness. In short, the moment of self-consciousness is the realization by consciousness that it, and not some external reality, determined that its object is merely immediate, simple, and abstract. The important shift here is that consciousness now has itself for its object, which is precisely the meaning of "self-consciousness." As self-consciousness, the object now appears as actively *für sich*, for-itself or explicit, and therefore negates the passively in-itself or implicit nature of the first moment.

The almost mystical heart of Hegel's dialectic appears in the third moment, in which there is a "negation of the negation." His term for this, *Aufhebung*, has no equivalent in English. Translators have used "abrogation," "annulment," "overcoming," "sublation," "transformation," "sublimation," "supersession," "reconciliation," "culmination," and so on. The difficulty lies in the fact that *Aufhebung* can mean either to perish or to preserve—and Hegel tries to make it mean both perish and preserve at the same time. For him, the truth of the third moment lies in its ability to take up the truth of both of the previous two moments into itself and thereby overcome their previously negative relation to one another. Thus the negation is negated, and the tension between the first two moments is internalized within the third as a distinction that is no longer a contradiction. This is called *an und für sich*, in-and-for-itself, and it alone, in Hegel's view, deserves to be seen as the truth of the phenomenon.

Other ways of characterizing this in-and-for-itself moment may help to clarify its meaning. As the *Aufhebung* of the immediate and the mediated, it is a mediated immediacy. Since the first moment is universal and abstract and the second is particular and concrete, their sublation appears as a concrete universal, as an "individual" in the technical Hegelian sense of that which is both universal and particular. When the philosophical issue of the one and the many is in view, the development is from unity to manifold to unity-in-difference. If the accent is on the development of consciousness in relation to a particular concept, that concept is first posited as theoretically or passively "given," then developed as an active, autonomous self-consciousness, and ultimately emerges as an active self-consciousness that is also aware of its own passive givenness. Such a unity of consciousness and self-consciousness can be called the "absolute" consciousness of reason, using "absolute" in Hegel's sense to designate that which embraces otherness or contradiction within itself.

This pattern then repeats itself, and, were it merely a sterile repetition of the pattern for its own sake, it would certainly be a tiresome parade. But it is much more. The dialectical structure of a Hegelian text is not simply the monotonous repetition of triads; it is the systematic development of an idea from a totally in-itself condition to a completed in-and-for-itself state, and each of the three moments includes within itself a further dialectical development according to the same pattern. Thus there are moments within moments, and the fascination of Hegelian dialectics lies in the potential such a system has for expressing complex relations among conceptual positions. For example, within the for-itself moment one will encounter another for-itself moment, and the pitch of negativity represented by that moment can be very intense indeed. This systematic architectonic is frequently criticized for a rigidity that it in fact rarely has in Hegel's own works. Indeed, the opposite complaint, that Hegel is loose almost to the point of arbitrariness with his systematic structure, would be a good deal more justified.

It is obviously confusing to use the term "moment" for each of the many possible levels of such a dialectical structure. Although Hegel does so, and Kierkegaard follows his example both with "moment" and with 'stage," I will do so only in direct quotations. I also wish to avoid the awkwardness of "sub-moments" or "sub-stages." Such devices are fine when used sparingly or in a short essay, but could create much confusion in a work such as this, where so much of the analysis involves working out the various dialectical levels and moments. Therefore I shall adhere to the following (admittedly artificial) distinctions: the highest level of analysis deals with *stages*, for that is how Kierkegaard's theory is generally known. Within each stage, the next level of analysis is treated as dialectical *movements*. In the case of texts that do not deal with the stages, the analysis begins at the level of movements. Within each movement, I identify dialectical *moments*. It is unfortunate to have to confine this characteristically dialectical term to one level, for every in-itself is of course a "moment" in relation to the subsequent for-itself. But I see no way to maintain that flexibility without constantly risking confusion. When a further dialectical development is present within a moment, I characterize it as consisting of *phases*. On those rare occasions where the triadic pattern reappears at a still lower level, I speak of dialectical *points*. The structures I shall analyze, therefore, have the diachronic character of progressive triads generally conforming to the pattern of in-itself, for-itself, and in-and-for-itself, and the synchronic character of multiple levels: stages, movements, moments, phases, and points.

This discussion of dialectical structure provides an introduction to the analysis of *The Concept of Irony*. Although Kierkegaard's dissertation is not by any means his most satisfying text in systematic terms, a careful look at its structure shows that the work possesses a coherence and development that has, to a great extent, eluded previous interpretations.[12]

A. Abstract Subjectivity

The Concept of Irony is divided into two parts, the first of which deals with "The Standpoint of Socrates Conceived as Irony." Here the origin of irony in the life and thought of Socrates is argued. The three chapters in part one bear titles reminiscent of Kant's dialectic of the categories of modality: the conception made possible, the conception made actual, and the conception made necessary.[13]

"The conception made possible" manifests an internal triadic structure that is not found in the other two chapters. It deals with the representations of Socrates in works by Xenophon, Plato, and Aristophanes. Kierkegaard justifies treating Aristophanes last rather than first (*The Clouds* was written twenty years before Socrates' death, whereas Xenophon and Plato were both students of the master and wrote about him in retrospect) by appeal to their differing relations "to the idea (the plain historical—the ideal—the comical)" (*CI*, 182n). This means that he considers Aristophanes' comical portrayal of Socrates to be the most adequate of the three in relation to the idea of irony. A closer look at the text will show how this is the case.

Like all commentators, Kierkegaard criticizes the superficiality and inaccuracy of Xenophon's understanding of Socrates. He faults him for "cutting away all that was dangerous in Socrates" (*CI*, 54) and portraying him as a thinker totally committed to the pragmatic and the useful. The dialectic in Xenophon is one of commensurability rather than irony (in which the external expression is incommensurable with the inner meaning). In "Xenophon's peepshow," Socrates appears as a Sophist rather than an ironist (*CI*, 63-64).

Plato is quite another story. According to Kierkegaard's interpretation, there are actually two types of irony and dialectical thinking discernible in Plato's writing. Owing to the convoluted style of his analysis, I will begin with a relatively clear passage in his concluding section:

> That irony and dialectic are the two great forces in Plato
> will surely be admitted by all; but it is no less obvious

that there is a double species of irony and a double species of dialectic. There is an irony that is merely a goad for thought, quickening it when drowsy, disciplining it when dissipated. There is another irony that is both the agent and terminus towards which it strives. There is a dialectic which, in constant movement, is always watching to see that the problem does not become ensnared in an accidental conception. . . . There is another dialectic which, since it begins with the most abstract ideas, seeks to allow these to unfold themselves in more concrete determinations; a dialectic which seeks to construct actuality by means of the idea. (*CI*, 151)

Kierkegaard characterizes these two types of irony and dialectic as negative and positive. Socrates employs negative irony and negative dialectic, for his goal is to assist "the individual paralyzed and weakened in himself to regain his original resiliency, protectively and attentively allowing the individual thus strengthened to come to himself" (*CI*, 66). In contrast, a positive dialectic is employed by Plato himself, for his speculative interest is in ascertaining the true content of the object or idea under discussion (*CI*, 77). Negative dialectic undermines ideas that hold the thinker captive, while positive dialectic leads the thinker to a fuller understanding of the content of an idea.

Kierkegaard vacillates on the role of the mythical in relation to these two dialectics, at one point commenting that it is neither one nor the other (*CI*, 151),[14] but he is quite clear about the relation between Socrates' negative dialectic and that of Hegel. The former is dichotomous: as a relation between two persons in dialogue about an object, the negative remains merely external, the question posed by another consciousness, perhaps quite arbitrarily. In contrast, the "modern" trichotomy achieves "the unity of successive conception and intuition" in the speculative development, for "with Hegel the negative is a necessary moment within thought itself" (*CI*, 69, 72).[15] As for Plato, the ultimate goal for Socrates would pre-

sumably be that silence in which all external, accidental questioning has ceased, whereas for Hegel the process of question and answer is a result of the relation between thought and its object. In a judgment on Greek thought that sounds remarkably (and un-ironically) Hegelian, Kierkegaard comments that the ancient dialectic achieves mere reciprocity—that is, neither true unity nor true duality—for it is merely a dialogue among the reciprocal parties, not the unfolding of the true relation between consciousness and its object (*CI*, 73).

Although Kierkegaard credits Plato with showing the unity of positive and negative moments in Socrates, he clearly believes that the negative has primary significance for the actual Socrates (*CI*, 67). This negative Socrates is thus the very opposite of the picture painted by Xenophon. Rather than "an apostle of finitude" (*CI*, 157) who defends mediocrity, usefulness, and the like, Plato presents Socrates as an opponent of finitude and the useful, that is, as an apostle of negativity. Commenting on the difficulty of uniting two such divergent interpretations, Kierkegaard suggests that only irony is equal to the task and then turns to Aristophanes' conception as one that "will provide the necessary opposition to that of Plato, and by this very opposition bring about the possibility of a new direction in our calculation" (*CI*, 158).[16]

Socrates is portrayed by Aristophanes as a Sophist whose empty thoughts are fittingly symbolized by clouds. The irony here is that of a "purely negative dialectic," a dialectic in which everything is renounced, "which remains for ever in itself and never ventures out into the determinations of life or the idea" (*CI*, 165). The result of this purely negative dialectic is "nothing at all." Whereas Plato's dialectic is positive and works to produce reality, and the negative in Hegel is internalized so that a positive work can again be achieved, Aristophanes portrays the Socratic dialectic as one that is utterly useless and comical—an "immersion in himself" rather than "an authentic philosophic dialectic" (*CI*, 173-175): "Whereas the essentially philosophic and speculative dialectic unites, the negative dialectic, since it renounces the idea, is a broker

always negotiating in a lower sphere, that is, it separates" (*CI*, 179).

Kierkegaard's only dialectical claim for this Aristophanic climax to chapter I is that there are "elements" of both Xenophon and Plato in it. The Xenophonic element is usefulness, but usefulness construed as the advantage gained by unscrupulous indifference to objective relations. The Platonic element is positive devotion to the idea, but this now takes the form of ineffectual immersion in self. Kierkegaard concludes: "In relation to Plato, therefore, Aristophanes has subtracted something; in relation to Xenophon, added something" (*CI*, 182). He argues that the concept of irony as a negative dialectic is portrayed by the Greeks as subjectivity, for by it the individual withdraws from actuality into "personal satisfaction" in the self (*CI*, 183).

Surely, however, the interest of Kierkegaard's account, and the justification for following a dialectical rather than a chronological order, is not simply that a bit of both Xenophon and Plato appears in Aristophanes, or that one is reduced while the other is increased in order to show the relation between dialectic and idea. Rather, Kierkegaard's analysis casts Aristophanes in the role of a genuine Hegelian *Aufhebung*, a culmination in which the portrayals of Xenophon and Plato are both annulled and preserved. On the most concrete level, the useful practicality of Xenophon's Socrates and the useless ideality of Plato's are united in Aristophanes' comic picture of a thinker whose advantage lies in uselessness. Less concretely, the empty diffusion in actuality portrayed by Xenophon is negated by the fullness of the idea suggested by Plato, and in Aristophanes' comedy there is empty fullness or full emptiness, for his Socrates is so full of himself that he is empty in relation either to actuality or to the idea. Finally, at the most abstract level, the development of the concept of irony as subjectivity can also be stated dialectically. In Xenophon, there is not yet any sense of an inner self that is distinct from the actual world of its environment. Thus usefulness and practicality are fitting ideals at this point. With Plato, a dichotomy enters in, and

an external dialectic of self and world is initiated. Here the negativity of subjective thought and pursuit of the idea emerges for the first time as the character of the self that is distinct from its empirical world. Aristophanes overcomes the opposition between the views of Xenophon and Plato, for his Socrates embraces the negativity of thought to the point where his subjectivity becomes his actuality. No longer either a function of external actuality or a subject standing over against it, Socrates now emerges as a man totally given over to subjectivity and irony, and thereby reconciling within himself the simplicity of Xenophon's Socrates with the ideality of Plato's.

To restate this dialectic in technical terms, Xenophon represents the in-itself phase, Plato the for-itself, and Aristophanes the in-and-for-itself, which takes the prior phases up into itself. But this is not all. Kierkegaard now steps back from the dialectic he has presented and announces that, as a whole, it constitutes "a conception of Socrates made possible." This passage (*CI*, 183-184) may well be a parody of Hegel's fondness for digressing from a dialectical analysis as such to a discussion of the relation that "we" as dialecticians have to that analysis—here Kierkegaard calls himself "the third," which is Hegel's technical term for the consciousness that mediates the unfolding dialectic in thought[17]—but *we* must not lose sight of the fact that at the same time a dialectical advance is taking place. Up to this point, Kierkegaard has dealt only with accounts of Socrates left by his interpreters. In chapter II, he turns to historical fact, the data through which the conception of Socratic irony—so far only made possible—can become actual. Thus chapters I and II constitute respectively the in-itself and for-itself moments within the first movement, which is the dialectic of Socratic irony.

"The conception made actual" (chapter II) traces the development of the concept of irony as a dialectic of opposition. Irony enters actuality as the contradiction between Socrates' daimon, which represents the subjective freedom of the individual, and the state, which is the objective substance of collective human existence. Kierkegaard insists that the daimon plays a purely negative role in Socrates' life: it warns him of danger (as in Plato), but it does not command him (as Xenophon claims) (*CI*, 187). Indeed, the daimon concerns itself only with Socrates' particular life. It is a subjectivization of the oracle, for only the individual subject can know what it says, and it has no interest in the laws and problems of the state. But the daimon is not yet "the full inwardness of freedom," because it remains external and unconscious in relation to the subject it addresses (*CI*, 190-192).

The most important aspect of the daimon is that it provides Socrates with a subjective or negative position over against the power of the state:

> When subjectivity with its negative power has broken the spell in which human life reposed under the form of substantiality, when it has emancipated man from the relationship to God just as it liberated him from his relationship to the state, the first form in which this appears is ignorance. The gods flee away taking with them all content, and man is left standing as the form, as that which is to receive content into itself. In the sphere of knowlege such a condition is correctly apprehended as ignorance. Again, this ignorance is quite consistently designated as human wisdom, for with this man has come into his own right: the right not to be, as such. (*CI*, 197)

Socratic ignorance, then, is a negative rather than a neutral or passive position. It is the courage to throw off the burden of a "substantiality" or "content" that has become oppressive, to choose the negativity of mere "form." Kierkegaard uses this opportunity to criticize Hegel for his frequent citing of the Greek aphorism "Know thyself." Its real meaning, he insists, is to separate oneself from the other, to assert the subjective self over against the state (*CI*, 202-203), a notion quite incompatible with what Hegel has in mind. For Kierkegaard, Socrates' irony is in fact the birth of subjectivity and the concept of the individual: here "we have an irony carried through to its utmost limit, an irony that allows the objective power of the state to crush itself against the rock-like negativity of irony" (*CI*, 221).

In the third chapter, "The conception made necessary," the task of analysis becomes more complex, for here Kierkegaard introduces the question of Socrates' significance in world history. This topic, of course, is ideal for ironizing Hegel, but beneath that irony it is possible to discern a genuine advance in the dialectic of irony.

The world-historical task for Socratic irony was to destroy sophistry; authentic subjectivity had to unmask and undermine arbitrary and unjustified subjectivity (*CI*, 224-225). The Sophists also used reflection to oppose the substance of the state; in an age when disillusionment with the immediacy of the state had fragmented knowledge in relation to morality, the Sophists met a widespread need with their offer of a "detached culture" (*CI*, 226). They taught people how to have a ready answer for every question, how to show that everything is true or nothing is true, and how to win every case without regard to matters of principle or substance. In their sophistry and casuistry, reflection atrophied. They sacrificed the negative freedom of reflection to their self-serving methods and goals (*CI*, 225-230).

In a possible allusion to Hegel's concept of the "cunning" of reason in history, Kierkegaard observes (*CI*, 231-232) that the encounter between Socrates and the Sophists demonstrates "the ingenuity to be found in world history."[18] They were, he adds, "made for each other," for they both taught the freedom of reflection and the negativity of the infinite, but in totally different ways. Whereas the Sophists sold their services as teachers, Socrates denied that virtue can be taught at all. Whereas the Sophists exploited the concept of infinity to win every case, Socrates insisted that it is a limit to human knowledge: "If the Sophists could answer everything, then he could question everything; if they knew all things, he knew nothing at all; if they could speak without cessation, he could keep silent, i.e. converse" (*CI*, 233).

The rest of the chapter consists of an extended and critical discussion of Socrates as a world-historical hero. This section is so Hegelian that it is hardly surprising to find it followed by a Supplement on Hegel's conception of Socrates.[19] Together, this last section of chapter III and the Supplement to it provide a very important insight into the dialectical structure of *The Concept of Irony*.

Kierkegaard's criticism of Socrates is that he lacked "the objectivity wherein subjectivity is free in itself" (*CI*, 233). His position was ultimately that of mere negativity; in no way did he put his reflection in "the service of the idea" (*CI*, 236). Although he was the means by which world history implemented irony and thereby created a transition from a previous development to a new one, Socrates was unable to offer anything positive. He "launched the ship of speculation. This entails an infinite polemic, a power to remove every obstacle that might hinder its course. Yet Socrates does not himself venture on board, but merely dispatches it" (*CI*, 239). His was the infinite negativity of protest against every aspect of the established order, against everything that might be received by the individual apart from subjective reflection. In Socrates, the concept of irony appears as an abstract, absolute subjectivity, a subjectivity lacking in the concrete, positive relations that give to life and the self their actual content and character.

Despite lavish praise for Hegel's treatment of Socrates, Kierkegaard does fault him on this one point. Hegel cannot let go of the idea that Socrates was committed to the positive conception of the good (*CI*, 252, 254), much as Plato had united the negative and the positive in his conception of Socrates. But Kierkegaard insists that this is a distortion of the actual Socrates, who never went beyond his irony and absolute negativity. He was not "the founder of morality," except insofar as morality is understood in the Hegelian sense as the negative freedom of the subject over against the state (*CI*, 253-254). But this is not the good, at least not in the sense Hegel means it. Thus the infinite negativity of Socrates is lost in Hegel's account. By relating Socrates to the good, Hegel obscures the fact that Socrates conceived his task as a divine mission to play the role of Charon, to ferry "the individual from reality over to ideality . . . ideal infinity, as infinite negativity, became the nothingness into which he made the whole manifold of reality disappear" (*CI*, 255).

At this point Kierkegaard returns to a bit of Hegelian jargon that he had introduced earlier in the Supplement. Interpreting a passage in Hegel, he had suggested that "Socrates has arrived at being-in-and-for-itself as being-in-and-for-itself for thought" (*CI*, 246). He clarifies this statement a bit later, in a long passage that sums up nicely a number of these themes:

> In the older Hellenism the individual was not at all free in this sense [of subjective conscience], but was implicated in the substantial concrete ethic; he had not yet taken himself, not yet separated himself from this condition of immediacy, did not yet know himself. This was accomplished by Socrates, although not in the same sense as the Sophists who taught the individual to contract himself into his own particular interests. Socrates, on the other hand, brought the individual to this by universalizing subjectivity, and to this extent he is the founder of morality. He asserted the significance of consciousness, not sophistically but speculatively. He arrived at being-in-and-for-itself as being-in-and-for-itself for thought, arrived at the determination of knowledge which estranged the individual from the immediacy in which he had heretofore lived. The individual must no longer act out of respect for the law, but must consciously know why he acts. But this, as anyone can see, is a negative determination: it is negative towards the established [*Bestaaende*] as well as negative towards that deeper positivity, that which conditions both negatively and speculatively. (*CI*, 248-9)

Here being in-and-for-itself for thought is clearly conceived as the alienation of the individual from a prior, naive immediacy. It is an advance in consciousness. So far, so good. But it is also true that this being in-and-for-itself is merely *for thought*. It has no positive or substantial relation to the individual's identity in a particular context. Thus this dialectical term expresses both Socrates' accomplishment in world history and his limitation and inadequacy. This conclusion brings Kierkegaard back to the analogy with Charon as one who ferries individuals from the actual world to the land of mere shades:

> He made the whole manifold of reality disappear. Insofar as Socrates continually caused being-in-and-for-itself to become visible, it might seem that surely here was his seriousness; but because he merely came to it, merely had being-in-and-for-itself as infinitely abstract, he therefore had the absolute in the form of nothingness. Actuality, by means of the absolute, became [*blev til*] nothingness, but the absolute was in turn nothingness. (*CI*, 255)

The term "being-in-and-for-itself" confirms how consciously dialectical the structure of Kierkegaard's analysis is. He defends the thesis that irony is subjectivity and therefore negative in relation to the objective realm. Thus the "being" here under consideration is that conception of irony. In good Hegelian fashion, that being has developed through a triad of moments. In the first such moment, the conception of irony was made possible on the basis of the interpretations of Socrates in ancient literature. Here subjectivity was merely posited; it progressively emerged in three phases from an embryonic invisibility in Xenophon through the tension of the tragic, dualistic ideality in Plato, and culminated in the comic ideality and negative irony of Aristophanes. Although Kierkegaard does not use the term at this point, this positing of irony constitutes the "being-in-itself" moment of the conception of irony as subjectivity.

The next moment can accordingly be seen as for-itself, a moment in which the initial subjectivity is qualified or negated. Here irony has an external relation to actuality, which is the contradiction between Socrates' daimon and the Athenian state. The daimon is not fully subjective, although only Socrates can interpret it; and the subjectivity of negative irony is here drawn into relation with the objectivity of the state. In these two ways it can be seen that the actuality or for-itself moment of the conception of irony is, relative to the in-itself moment, a moment of objective subjectivity, of subjectivity as objective opposition to the objective order.

In the third moment, the term "being-in-and-for-itself" is introduced, and it is now possible to appreciate its dialectical appropriateness at this point. For here the negation that took place in the for-itself moment (with the objectification or externalization of subjectivity) is in turn negated: "the conception made necessary" portrays an irony that is "infinitely abstract," and in which both actuality and the absolute appear to be nothingness. Thus the concrete objectivity of the second moment is overcome, not through a reconciliation with the actual world of substance, but by a total rejection of it (in the form of the repudiation of the Sophists, who used reflection to gain worldly advantage). Here the opposition between subjectivity and objectivity is internalized. The external is not just the daimon or the objective state—it is sophistry, which is the effort of subjectivity to exploit its negative position for objective gain. In defeating the Sophists, Socrates wins a victory for pure subjectivity and thereby completes the first movement of the dialectic of irony as subjectivity.[20]

B. Concrete Subjectivity

The dialectic does not stop with subjectivity in-itself, which Kierkegaard calls "the first moment," in contrast to the second, in which "this universality [of thought] must be known by me" (CI, 246). In order for irony as subjectivity to develop further, it must attain a higher dialectical degree of consciousness. The next such movement constitutes irony as subjectivity for-itself, which is characterized by Kierkegaard as "a subjectivity of subjectivity":

Should a new manifestation of irony appear, moreover, it must be insofar as subjectivity asserts itself in a still higher form. It must be a subjectivity raised to the second power, a subjectivity of subjectivity, corresponding to reflection on reflection. With this we are once again world historically oriented, that is, we are referred to that development which modern philosophy acquired in Kant and consummated in Fichte, and even more to those positions after Fichte which endeavored to assert subjectivity in its second potentiality. (*CI*, 260)

This passage occurs in the introduction to the second part of *The Concept of Irony*, where Kierkegaard shows how the concept of irony unfolds historically according to a dialectical structure. Socrates represents the first form of irony, in which "subjectivity received its due";[21] the post-Fichtean Romantics (Schlegel, Tieck, Solger) constitute the second form, a subjectivity so "intensified" and self-conscious that "it could only receive its due by being abrogated" (*CI*, 260). This *Aufhebung* is fittingly represented by Hegel, in whom irony is said to have "met its master" (*CI*, 260).

The abstract dialectical terminology also reappears in the second part, in a second section entitled "For Orientation." There, after observing that irony is the intention to have an outer appearance that contradicts the inner reality (*CI*, 269, 273), Kierkegaard returns to the theme of irony as a determination of subjectivity: "doubt is a conceptual determination while irony is the being-for-itself of subjectivity" (*CI*, 274). The meaning of this characterization is that, in contrast to the aggressive posture of doubt, irony tries to withdraw from the object and deny its reality (*CI*, 274). But the almost casual use of the technical term "being-for-itself" confirms that the "being-in-and-for-itself for thought" of the conception of irony in part one is really equivalent to the completion of subjectivity in-itself; and here, the Romantics represent subjectivity for-itself. Once again, the care with which Kierkegaard has constructed this complex dialectic is evident.

In a recapitulation of his interpretation of Socrates' irony, Kierkegaard stresses its for-itself (negative) character again: "irony in a strict sense can never set forth a thesis, because irony is a determination of the being-for-himself subject, who, with perpetual agility, allows nothing to endure [*bestaae*]" (*CI*, 286). In Socrates' case, however, there is a limitation on this negativity, for he negated only the substantial actuality of his own age and culture, not actuality in general.

It was Fichte who paved the way for overcoming that limitation. In reaction against the externality of Kant's concept of the thing-in-itself, Fichte internalized even that concept in the infinite identity of the I with itself. This I = I is an abstract identity that attains negative infinity at the price of all finite content (*CI*, 289-290). Fichte's purpose in doing this was to be able to construct the world; but, in the hands of the Romantics, that same I = I became the means for disposing of the world. Indeed, as Kierkegaard remarks in a footnote, irony is now synonymous with Romanticism (*CI*, 292). Romantic irony sets itself up as lord over actuality, to create and to dispose as it wills, having no respect for the validity of particular moments—a validity upon which Hegel always insisted (*CI*, 296). In the Romantics, the conception of irony that had been dimly glimpsed in Socrates—an infinite absolute negativity that is not at all in the service of the idea or anything positive—becomes actual in the form of individuality. This individuality (the I = I) "has a purpose which is absolute . . . to become *für sich* what it is *an sich*" (*CI*, 298). In order to maintain this individuality for-itself, the ironist must avoid every appearance of continuity in the actual world: indeed, the only suitable continuity for irony is the negative attitude of boredom (*CI*, 301-302).

Within subjectivity for-itself, Kierkegaard again structures his analysis according to three moments. This purpose is not immediately clear in the discussion of Schlegel's *Lucinde*, where Kierkegaard's primary concern seems to be a demonstration of the world's immoral character. Romanticism, he complains, "is different from Hellenism in that along with the enjoyment of the flesh it also enjoys the negation of spirit" (*CI*, 305). But when he turns to Tieck's work, Kierkegaard reveals that a structure is unfolding: "Schlegel lectures and attacks actuality directly. This is not the case with Tieck, however, who abandons himself to a poetical exuberance while preserving its indifference towards actuality. It is only when he does not do this that he comes near to attacking actuality, yet even then his attack is always more indirect" (*CI*, 317).

Although the usual dialectical order would be to proceed from indifference to opposition, here opposition constitutes the first moment of subjectivity for-itself (Schlegel), which establishes a negative relation between romantic irony and actuality in general. This "subjectivity of subjectivity" also lacks (negates) the abstraction of Socrates' infinite negativity, for it asserts not the ignorance but the total self-adequacy and infinity of the subject (I = I). The one justification that Kierkegaard can find for such autism (my term, not his) is that it constitutes a necessary remedy for "an age in which men had become ossified, as it were, within the finite social situation" (*CI*, 318). In their self-absorption, the Romantics are, by comparison, quite alive, even though they appear to be asleep and in a state of dreaming.

The third moment within Romantic irony appears in the philosophy of Solger. It was he who first became "philosophically conscious of irony," but at the same time "got himself lost in the negative" (*CI*, 323). Solger is a "metaphysical knight of the negative" whose aphorisms fail to offer "a coherent, progressive, and strictly philosophical account" (*CI*, 324). Thus, since "the negative only becomes visible through the positive," Solger's writings leave the reader "completely confounded" (*CI*, 323). However, despite his absolute negativity, "Solger seems vaguely to have grasped throughout this whole inquiry [that] the negation of the negation contain[s] in itself the true affirmation" (*CI*, 330). Yet his failure to develop that intuition and to place the negativity of irony as a moment within a positive context means that Solger never goes beyond subjectivity for-itself, and therefore can be regarded "as a sacrifice for Hegel's positive system" (*CI*, 335). Schlegel, Tieck, and Solger represent the three dialectical moments of irony as the determination of subjectivity for-itself. In Schlegel, the subjectivity of subjectivity is posited in-itself as an attack upon actuality in general. That aggressiveness is then opposed by Tieck, who finds that the infinity of the subject results in indifference to the actual world. Neither of them is fully self-conscious about irony, as is demonstrated by their satisfaction with such estrangement from all positivity. In Solger, the opposition between Schlegel's attack and Tieck's indifference is overcome by the consciousness that to negate a negation is to imply an affirmation.[22] In short, the negativity of irony cannot fulfill itself as pure negation; its very effort to do so negates itself as negation and thereby opens the door once again to affirmation.

C. Absolute Subjectivity

In the conclusion to *The Concept of Irony*, irony is presented as a "mastered moment." Since this section is both very short and totally lacking in any internal dialectical development, it might appear to be less serious than the theory of irony that has already been expounded. Out of irony as utter negativity in relation to external reality, irony suddenly appears as a mastered moment in the poetry of Goethe (*CI*, 337), which recalls the earlier remark that in Hegel irony had met its master.[23] Goethe's mastery of irony consists in the capacity to make his poetic existence "congrue with actuality" (*CI*, 337). Whereas the dialectic of irony has continually maintained an opposition between inner essence and outer, actual appearance, here that contradiction is abrogated: "Thus irony is here mastered, reduced to a moment: the essence is none other than the phenomenon, the phenomenon none other than the essence; possibility is not so prudish as not to betake itself to actuality, but actuality is possibility" (*CI*, 337-338). The role of irony, then, is not to negate the external phenomena of actuality but to promote a proper relation between the subject and actuality: "it teaches us to actualize actuality" (*CI*, 340), to respect the phenomenon, but without idolatry.

Kierkegaard then cryptically closes his essay by pointing toward humor as the key to "the 'eternal validity' of irony," for humor contains both a deeper scepticism and a deeper positivity than irony, because it involves not merely human but "divine-human" determinations.[24] His final remark is a polemical thrust at Martensen, a personal satire that is the basis for Capel's argument that Kierkegaard was "never an Hegelian" (*CI*, 428). It must be admitted that, in Hegelian terms, this last movement should be the culmination of all that has gone before, whereas in fact it seems to repudiate it by parody and polemics. If irony is simply the incommensurability of inner with outer and essence with phenomenon, then this final negation of the negation can easily be taken as an ironic overcoming of irony in which commensurability is restored. By implication, Goethe and Hegel would then represent a circular and meaningless return to Xenophon.

Such an interpretation, however, presupposes an abstract and undialectical definition of irony as incommensurability. When the entire structural development of the concept of irony is reviewed, with particular attention to the relation between irony and subjectivity, a very different picture emerges.

The first and most important finding of structural analysis is that the dialectic in *The Concept of Irony* is not a dialectic of irony at all—it is one of subjectivity. This interpretation is established by Kierkegaard's treatment of Socratic irony. He begins with Xenophon, for there he finds a portrayal of Socrates as a man without inwardness, a man who in no way distinguishes the self from the external world. Only with Plato does irony become a possibility, for Plato's Socrates has his own positive relation to the idea, which enables him to stand over against the world in an external dialectic of opposition. Irony, then, is the negativity and incommensurability of the thinking self in relation to the world. But, more important, it is also the birth of subjectivity as such. In Aristophanes this subjectivity is carried to an extreme; unrelated to the world, it reveals the abstract possibility of subjectivity in-itself to be not so much an incommensurability with actuality as an empty unconsciousness of it.

When subjectivity in-itself is viewed as actuality, however, the relation with externality is once again present. This moment appears when Socrates' individual position in the state is considered. By virtue of his daimon, which is external but speaks to him internally, Socrates can stand up to the awesome power and substance of the state. His subjectivity is still only in-itself, an abstract negative relation to the world, but in the daimon a for-itself or truly subjective element is intimated, for here subjectivity begins to relate itself to actuality.

The necessity of the concept of irony is the moment in which its in-itself (possibility) and for-itself (actuality) moments are united. The issue here is again that of how subjectivity is to be related to the external world. For the Sophists, it is an instrument for achieving advantage in the world, thereby reinstating the criterion of Xenophon in a subtle and negative form. For Socrates, subjectivity is freedom from the world, a pure negativity lacking any positive element. Thus Socrates' being in-and-for-itself is only for thought, and subjectivity in-itself is revealed as an abstract and inadequate inwardness.

Romanticism as a dialectical movement plays two roles. First, it negates Socrates' abstract subjectivity by setting out to destroy the external, actual world. This position is clearest in Schlegel, who initiates the attack, and Tieck, who withdraws from the attack into utter indifference. Second, this extreme negativity also leads to the intimation of a positive relation to actuality as that which is presupposed or implied by the notion of subjective negation. It is Solger who pushes negation to this infinity, where it in fact negates itself. This moment completes the development of subjectivity for-itself as a violent opposition between inwardness and externality.

"Irony as a mastered moment," then, is subjectivity in-and-for-itself. Throughout this dialectic, subjectivity has struggled to achieve a proper relation with actuality. Every claim that subjectivity is utterly incommensurable with actuality has collapsed from the weight of its own contradictions, whether it be the claim of Aristophanes, Socrates himself, or the Romantics. In other words, although irony is indeed the negativity that results in incommensurability, subjectivity is not and can never become mere negativity, for an utterly negative subject could never exist. Thus irony (negativity) is a mastered moment *within subjectivity*, which embraces it as one pole of its own internal differentiation, positivity being the other pole. This is not a return to the commensurability that lacks inwardness (Xenophon); it is the achievement of a totality that is adequate to the task of embracing all the formerly incommensurable elements. The truth of irony is that it is *only* the negative moment within true subjectivity, anthropologically considered. Conversely, the truth of subjectivity is that it embraces both the positive and the negative poles in relation to the external world and should never one-sidedly limit itself to one or the other.

For all the parodying and polemicizing, then, Kierkegaard's dialectic turns out to have a thoroughly Hegelian conclusion and a corresponding systematic structure,[25] as Chart 1 illustrates. This outcome may be his conscious intention in *The Concept of Irony*, since that structure correlates so well with the obvious organization of the book. In other texts, however, such correlation becomes much more difficult, and the resulting obscurity indicates that Kierkegaard himself thought in these dialectical patterns not so much by conscious decision as by training and unconscious habit.

CHART 1.

The Dialectical Structure of
The Concept of Irony

A. Subjectivity in-itself (Socratic irony) [Part One]
   1. Irony as possibility (in literature) [Chapter I]
      a. Xenophon—mere externality
      b. Plato—external dialectic of individual versus world
      c. Aristophanes—individual as useless, empty subjectivity
   2. Irony as actuality (in individual life) [Chapter II]
      Socrates' daimon (inner and outer) versus the state
   3. Irony as necessity (in world history) [Chapter III]
      Socrates' pure negativity versus Sophists' opportunism

   ABSTRACT SUBJECTIVITY:
   IRONY'S BEING-IN-AND-FOR-ITSELF ONLY FOR THOUGHT

B. Subjectivity for-itself (Romantic irony) [Part Two]
   1. Schlegel—attack upon actuality
   2. Tieck—indifference to actuality
   3. Solger—"Knight of the Negative" (negation of negation as glimpse of affirmation)

   CONCRETE SUBJECTIVITY:
   IRONY AS NEGATION OF ACTUALITY

C. Subjectivity in-and-for-itself (Hegel, Goethe)
   Irony as a mastered moment.

   ABSOLUTE SUBJECTIVITY:
   IRONY AS A NEGATIVE MOMENT WITHIN ACTUAL WHOLE

TWO

The Dialectic of Aesthetic Contradiction

KIERKEGAARD'S major writings on the aesthetic stage are volume I of *Either/Or* and "In Vino Veritas," which is the first section of *Stages on Life's Way*. It is striking that here contradiction is not only the mechanism of the dialectic, as in *The Concept of Irony*; it is also the subject matter of the entire discussion. Whereas a Hegelian dialectic always continues until all contradictions are overcome, aesthetic contradiction, as presented in these works, is itself the essential concept that develops through the complex unfolding of movements and moments.

EITHER/OR, I

That the principle of contradiction is central to *Either/Or* is clear from a remark made by Victor Eremita, the pseudonymous editor of the two volumes.[1] He opens his Preface with a discussion of the work in terms of the dialectical opposition between the internal and the external. Expressing doubt about the Hegelian maxim that the internal and the external are ultimately identical (in an absolute unity or reconciliation), Victor says that the writings he is presenting in *Either/Or* confirm his doubt:

> These papers have afforded me an insight into the lives of two men, which has confirmed my hunch that the external is not the internal. This was especially true about one of them. His external mode of life has been in complete contradiction to his inner life. The same was true to a certain extent with the other also, inasmuch as he

concealed a more significant inwardness under a somewhat commonplace exterior. (E/O,I, 4)

The two men mentioned by Victor are the pseudonymous authors of the papers in the two volumes of *Either/Or* respectively. In the first volume, which represents the aesthetic stage, Victor sees a "complete contradiction between the external and the internal."[2] He designates the unnamed author of this volume "A," in order to distinguish him from "B" (Judge William), the author of volume II. The Judge represents the ethical stage, and in him the contradiction between the internal and the external is present only "to a certain extent."

Prior to the commencement of the dialectic of contradiction as such, its centrality is reiterated in several ways. Victor relates that he found the papers that constitute *Either/Or* when he tried to force open a recently purchased secretary by striking it with a hatchet and thereby accidentally discovered a secret compartment. He then gloats that this incident provided not only the papers themselves but also an illustration of internal riches that were not communicated by external appearances (E/O,I, 6).

In the "Diapsalmata" (refrains), which function as an overture to volume I, A maintains that no amount of care with language or reason can adequately articulate his profound inner melancholy (E/O,I, 20, 23, 25). So great, for A, is the contradiction between inner feeling and external expression that Victor warns in his editor's Preface that, although "A's papers contain a number of attempts to formulate an aesthetic philosophy of life," in fact a "single, coherent, aesthetic view of life can scarcely be carried out" (E/O,I, 13). As shall become evident, coherence is given to volume I primarily by the development of a dialectic of contradiction, a structure of which both A and Victor seem completely unaware.[3]

A. Implicit Contradiction: Desire

The pseudonyms' lack of awareness does not extend to the first essay, where A's analysis of desire is explicitly presented in systematically dialectical terms. "The Immediate Stages of the Erotic or the Musical Erotic" opens, significantly, with the longest sustained discussion of language to come from Kierkegaard's pen (*E/O*,I, 49-73). A's intention is to explain why sensuous or erotic desire can be expressed in music but not in words. He begins by distinguishing artistic "realms" in which subject matter is irrelevant (music, sculpture, architecture) or incidental (painting) from those in which it is of central importance (poetry and "all artistic productions based upon language and historical consciousness"). Although this remark (*E/O*,I, 50) is immediately qualified in terms of its adequacy as a basis for classification, in fact A elaborates upon the schema just a few pages later, when he argues that the linguistic and historical arts are more concrete and susceptible to repetition than are "abstract" arts, which lack a comparable influx of new subject matter from the events of history (*E/O*,I, 53). This is why, he claims, there are so many more poems written than sculptures made: each new event elicits many responses in poem and story, but abstract media are not so responsive to such events.

Although the abstract arts are not appropriate for historical events, they are nonetheless far more adequate than language for expressing such abstract realities as desire. If the thought that desire is abstract seems incongruous, perhaps a clarification of terms is in order. A asserts that sensuousness[4] is "the most abstract idea conceivable," being "a sort of inner qualification of inwardness" that "moves always in an immediacy." In other words, abstraction and immediacy are correlative terms, just as the mediation of language correlates with the concreteness of historical events. Immediate experience is abstract for A because (as for Hegel) it is *only* immediate, it is not yet developed in terms of a concrete subject matter, in this case a particular object of desire. It is merely desire in itself, desire pure and simple, without the complications involved in desire for concrete objects. This is clearly a very abstract idea of desire. Indeed, it is desire in name only, for immediate desire as such eludes all efforts at analysis. A's discussion is really concerned only with the idea of desire and therefore presupposes that he already has some reflective distance on desire itself. Just as he somewhat ironically suggests that the discovery of the principle of sensuousness can be credited to the greatest opponent of sensuousness—Christianity—so also it is possible to analyze desire only if one has moved beyond the experience of desire.[5]

Desire, then, is an abstract immediacy that can be expressed only by music. No sooner is it made concrete in thought and language than it becomes "reflected in something other than itself," a mediated reality that is thereby "subject to ethical categories" (E/O,I, 63). Desire can no more be expressed in words than can thought be articulated in music.[6] But A also wants, in good Hegelian fashion, to show that music and language are not mutually exclusive realities, indeed, that music is itself in some sense a language. He lists several characteristics they share: language communicates best when its sensuous medium is of the least consequence, a mere instrument, and music likewise "constantly emancipates itself from the sensuous" (E/O,I, 66); both language and music address themselves to the ear; and both have time as their element, which is another way in which they both negate sensuous immediacy (E/O,I, 67). Despite these common features, music remains "an imperfect medium for expressing the spiritual" (E/O,I, 71), whereas "language is the one absolutely spiritually qualified medium" (E/O,I, 65). Ultimately, their relation is a negative one;[7] music is a limit to language, and language (at least by implication) is a limit to music, just as immediacy and mediation both define and limit one another: "Music always expresses the immediate in its immediacy; . . . Language involves reflection, and cannot, therefore, express the immediate. Reflection destroys the immediate, and hence it is impossible to express the musical in language; but this apparent poverty of language is precisely its wealth" (E/O,I, 68-69).

Since music is the medium of desire, A turns to Mozart for insight into the dialectic of desire, and there he finds that three of the composer's operatic characters correspond—to a greater or lesser extent—to the three moments of desire. The type of desire in-itself is the page from *Figaro*, who appears to A as a "mythical figure" in whom desire "is not yet awake" (*E/O*,I, 74). A admits that the type he sees in the page does not correspond in all respects to the actual page in *Figaro*. Whereas the page in the play may well love one woman more than another, the mythical page has "the eternal feminine" as his object (*E/O*,I, 76), and thus his desire has a dreamy, un-awakened quality, failing to focus on any one particular object. Indeed, desire in-itself is incapable of acquiring any object at all (*E/O*,I, 83); it remains simple, passive, undeveloped, and unable to relate its own inner energy to any particular "other."

When A turns to Papageno in *The Magic Flute*, he encounters a similar discrepancy between the demands of his dialectic of sensuous desire and the actual dramatic plot of the opera. Dialectically, Papageno is the type of desire for-itself, desire that has awakened from the dreamy consciousness of the page to pursue actively the objects of its longing. Musically, Papageno's theme expresses this mythical or typological role perfectly, for it is "cheerfully chirping, vigorous, bubbling with love" (*E/O*,I, 80). Dramatically, however, Papageno commits himself in marriage to Papagena, which distresses A deeply. Not only does it make his dialectical interpretation seem arbitrary; it also renders the opera itself unmusical (*E/O*,I, 77-78), for marriage is, in A's view, an "absolutely unmusical" relation (*E/O*,I, 82). Ideally, Papageno represents desire as it awakens to the "manifold" of objects that it might pursue and delights in pursuing them, but with no thought of actually catching any one of them, let alone being caught by one: "the objects [of desire] swiftly vanish and reappear; but still before every disappearance is a present enjoyment, a moment of contact, short but sweet, evanescent as the gleam of a glowworm, inconstant and fleeting as the touch of a butterfly, and as harmless" (*E/O*,I, 79).

The dialectical goal of this entire development is, of course, A's famous portrayal of sensuous desire in the figure of Don Juan. It is by appeal to Mozart's *Don Juan* that he will justify his apparently arbitrary treatment of the page and Papageno, for the partial representations of desire that they offer culminate or become absolute in him: "in the first stage [= "moment"], desire is defined as *dreaming*, in the second as *seeking*, in the third as *desiring*" (E/O,I, 79):

> The contradiction in the first stage lay in the fact that desire could acquire no object. . . . In the second stage, the object appears in its manifold. . . . In *Don Juan*, on the other hand, desire is absolutely determined as desire; it is, in an intensive and extensive sense, the immediate unity of the two preceding stages. The first stage desired the one ideally, the second stage desired the particular under the qualification of the manifold; the third stage is a unity of these two. Desire has its absolute object in the particular, it desires the particular absolutely.[8]

Although much of the interest of "The Immediate Stages of the Erotic" derives from the long discussion of Don Juan that follows, the essential elements of his dialectical role as the type of absolute desire are already present in this statement. Just as A's interpretations of the page and Papageno are justified in terms of their dialectical relation to Don Juan, so also Don Juan is understood primarily as an *Aufhebung* of what they represent. In the page, desire remains abstract, not limited to one object but also unable to break out of its own dreamy consciousness. In Papageno, this ideal desire for the eternal feminine gives way to an actual desire for every particular instantiation of the feminine, for every woman. Thus the page's subjective or passive fullness of desire is opposed by Papageno's desire, which actively dissipates itself among its objects. In themselves, these two stages of desire negate one another, but they are reconciled in Don Juan, who preserves the truth of them both. Like the page, Don Juan desires not just one woman but "the whole of womanhood" (E/O,I, 98). Like Papageno, he actively fulfills that desire by seducing a manifold of particular women, 1,003 at last count. In this way desire becomes absolute (in-and-for-itself). Don Juan sublates the universal and the particular dimensions of desire in his own musical individuality.

What, then, is the character of the contradiction between the internal and the external that determines this dialectic of desire? The common thread running through these three moments of inwardness as desire is the notion of an inwardness that remains utterly indifferent to everything that is external or other to it.[9] Just as language and music are portrayed as indifferent to the sensuous instruments by which they are expressed (*E/O*,I, 66), so Don Juan and his prototypes are indifferent to the women whom they appear to desire. The page is filled with desire and yet desires any and every woman indifferently and interchangeably, for his desire is only a dreaming. Papageno flits from one woman to another in an apparently passionate state of desire, but remains indifferent to the particular differences that might attract him to one woman rather than another. Likewise, Don Juan thinks of the women he has seduced not as individuals but as statistics; his delight is in seduction as an activity, not in those whom he seduces. Although the particular women constitute the external occasions so necessary for seduction to occur, Don Juan's desire for them remains unrelated to them as persons. He is unable to come out of his indifferent inwardness and establish an objective relation, one that could be expressed in language: "Thus he does not have a stable existence at all, but he hurries in a perpetual vanishing, precisely like music, about which it is true that it is over as soon as it has ceased to sound, and only comes into being again, when it again sounds" (*E/O*,I, 101).

Thus Don Juan and his prototypes together represent the first or in-itself movement in the dialectic of aesthetic contradiction between inner life and external appearance. Since Don Juan seems to lack any awareness of an inner life at all, it may be premature to refer to his indifference as an early form of aesthetic inwardness.[10] In this regard, he is as unawakened to inwardness as is the page to desire. Yet it is out of his erotic desire that the conditions for inwardness emerge; when desire is frustrated, it turns to grief, and grief begets inwardness in the form of reflection. It is as aesthetic grief that the contradiction between inner life and external mode of life enters into its second or for-itself movement.

B. Explicit Contradiction: Grief

The essays that constitute the movement of grief as the negation of desire are distinguished formally from the rest of the volume in that they are all presented as lectures that A has delivered to a society of which he is a member, the *symparanekromenoi* or "fellowship of buried lives."[11] There is indeed a ghostly quality to this negative movement: A describes the purpose of the fellowship as the "art of writing posthumous papers" (*E/O*,I, 150) and notes that the one passion uniting all members of the society is "a sympathetic interest in the secrets of sorrow," for "we love only grief, grief alone is the object of our search" (*E/O*,I, 172).

First comes grief in-itself. In an essay entitled "The Ancient Tragical Motif as Reflected in the Modern," A purports to explore the character of "the true tragedy" by means of comparing ancient with modern tragic themes (*E/O*,I, 138). In fact, however, his emphasis throughout the essay is upon the differences between ancient and modern tragedy. Whereas the ancients accented the action of the plot and subordinated character to it, for the modern mentality "situation and character are really predominant" (*E/O*,I, 141). Similarly, in "ancient tragedy the sorrow is deeper, the pain less; in modern, the pain is greater, the sorrow less" (*E/O*,I, 145). This distinction hinges on the fact that reflection is so much greater in modern than in ancient tragedy. The Greek tragic figure was the victim of conflict between irreconcilable obligations, a conflict that could be endured only in passive sorrow. For example, Antigone had to choose between her civic duty (as a subject of King Creon) not to violate his prohibition against burying his dead enemies, and her familial responsibility (as a sister to Polyneices) to see that his corpse be properly cremated or buried. In contrast,

the modern tragic heroine, whom A calls "our" Antigone
(*E/O*,I, 154), is imagined by him to have discovered the in-
cestuous relationship between her father (Oedipus) and her
mother/grandmother (Jocasta), and is then consumed by anxiety over the question of whether Oedipus himself had learned
of Jocasta's true identity before his death. Such anxiety is more
painful than sorrowful, for it involves a more personal, subjective identification with the tragic situation. Although the
Greek Antigone is certainly guilty, her sense of guilt is the
result of specific action and is muted by her belief that she is
a victim of fate; she is still carefree in her essential nature
(*E/O*,I, 153-154). In contrast, the modern Antigone has voluntarily internalized her father's guilt: "Her life does not unfold like that of the Greek Antigone; it is not turned outward
but inward, the scene is not external but internal; it is an
invisible scene" (*E/O*,I, 154-155). Here is the beginning of
reflection. The modern Antigone becomes a "bride of sorrow"
and therefore brings with her a "dowry" of pain to any possible
love relationship (*E/O*,I, 156, 160). She is doomed to a life of
secrecy, to an anxious reflection from which only death will
be able to release her (*E/O*,I, 152, 162).

A has cleverly distinguished between the substantiality[12] of
ancient tragedy and the reflective nature of its modern counterpart. In the process, however, he fails to carry out the task
he had set for himself: the identification of the true, enduring
character of tragedy. In the development from the ancient to
the modern Antigone, the tragic consciousness has become
reflective, which is indeed a crucial step in the dialectic of
inwardness. But what is the constant that unites them and
gives to tragic grief its special nature? Here we can only surmise
on the basis of the parallels that A has drawn between the two
Antigones: the one is dominated by external forces, yet remains
innocently carefree within; the other is not bound by any
external actions demanded of her, but she is utterly and painfully bound by inner anxiety. The common element is that
both are victims of the contradiction between externality and
inwardness, between the objective relations that constitute fate

for the Greek and the subjective uncertainty and guilt that are the modern's prison.

In terms of dialectical development, it is the modern Antigone who proves to be decisive. The Greek Antigone never attains reflection, but our Antigone conceals thoughtful anxiety beneath an outer calm. Thus she represents the positing of grief (grief in-itself) as a movement characterized by precisely this contradiction between inner suffering and an external appearance of serenity.

In "Shadowgraphs," which is the second lecture to the *symparanekromenoi*, this dialectic of grief is developed in a reflective (for-itself) moment. Whereas tragic grief (both ancient and modern) passively submits to the contradiction between the inner and the outer, here that passivity is sundered by the active effort of the grieving consciousness to reflect upon its own grief. By internalizing her father's guilt, the modern Antigone reflected herself into intense pain; but she did not reach the point of reflecting upon her grief as such. Such "reflective grief," writes A, "lacks inner repose" and therefore remains secretive, resisting and eluding every effort at artistic representation (*E/O*,I, 168). The very title "Shadowgraphs" alludes to the procedure necessary in order to investigate reflective grief. Because it is such an introverted or repressed state, it cannot be studied directly, but must be discerned indirectly by means of the shadow that it throws upon some external surface (*E/O*,I, 171). The irony here is clear: reflective grief is a refusal to communicate or externalize an inner suffering that can nevertheless be observed by the ways in which it unintentionally externalizes itself.

It is worth digressing a moment to mention the way in which A portrays drama as the medium or language in which inwardness as grief is expressed. Whereas ordinary dramatic action is understood precisely as the externalization of inner states, A claims that these subjects of suffering are unable to do that—thus the need for shadowgraphs. Grief's negative or indirect relation between inwardness and action bears the same ambiguous relation to drama that we found in the relation of desire to music, which is rarely understood as indifferent to its sensuous vehicles. Clearly, A is exploiting these artistic modes for the purposes of his dialectic and not presenting Kierkegaard's theory of the arts.[13] His point is that grief, like desire, is a form of aesthetic inwardness and therefore cannot be communicated directly by means of language, or even by ordinary dramatic means: "The face, which ordinarily is the mirror of the soul, here takes on . . . an ambiguity that resists artistic production. . . . This may then escape our attention for a long time, until by chance one day a look, a word, a sigh, a quaver in the voice . . . treacherously betrays the carefully guarded secret" (E/O,I, 173).

The dramatic "signs" that A explores in this essay are fascinating, but of more importance for understanding the dialectical development of reflective grief are his discussions of three seduced and abandoned women: Marie Beaumarchais in Goethe's *Clavigo*, Donna Elvira in Mozart's *Don Juan*, and Margaret in Goethe's *Faust*. All three exemplify the *symparanekromenoi* quest, for they are "human beings whose stony exterior conceals an eternal life of secret sorrow" (E/O,I, 174). In a sense, this is the heart of the aesthetic stage, the dialectical center where negativity reaches its most intense pitch—the moment of grief for-itself (reflective grief) within the movement of contradiction for-itself (grief). Therefore, it is hardly surprising that here alone (in Volume I of *Either/Or*) there is yet another level of dialectical development, namely, the three dialectical phases[14] represented by Marie, Elvira, and Margaret.

The type of reflective grief in-itself is Marie Beaumarchais. Deserted by Clavigo, she dwells incessantly upon the question of whether he did or did not deceive her. Her mind is preoccupied with an inquiry that is never finished. This inquiry, writes A, is a form of reflection that can never be conquered by mediation (E/O,I, 186). Because Marie cannot settle the issue of Clavigo's guilt, the "characteristic feature of her grief is . . . the restlessness which prevents her from finding the object of her grief" (E/O,I, 187). She cannot, like Antigone, simply sorrow over her loss, for it may be that Clavigo really has deceived her and is therefore not worthy of her love; but to withdraw from him completely would be to remove herself from the aesthetic sphere of interest in favor of an ethical stance. No, as the type of this phase in the dialectic, Marie must passively submit to a life of being defeated in her internal inquiry, while "reflection constantly remains victorious" (E/O,I, 186). Her explanations for Clavigo's behavior change continually, and each change brings a corresponding alteration in her feelings toward him. One moment she is revolted by his "cold craftiness," and the next she interprets the story "in a more beautiful manner. But as the explanation becomes different, the fact also becomes different. Reflection, therefore, has immediately enough to keep it busy, and the reflective grief is unavoidable" (E/O,I, 190-191).

Such immediacy of reflection is not the case with Donna Elvira. For her the facts are quite clear: "no doubt lures her grief into the discussion room of reflection; she is dumb in her despair" (E/O,I, 191). Yet she is not paralyzed. She pursues Don Juan relentlessly, for "she knows only one passion, hate, only one thought, revenge" (E/O,I, 195). At first glance, A seems to be moving from the positing of reflective grief in Marie to a dialectical negation of reflection in Elvira. His ironic boast that he has "gone through a whole course in dialectics" with a couple of women (E/O,I, 197) is preceded by this observation: "The fact that Marie had to go on was in itself so controversial that reflection with all its exigency could not help seizing it immediately. But with respect to Elvira, the factual proof for Don Juan's deception seems so evident that it is not easy to see how reflection can get hold of it" (E/O,I, 196). In fact, however, Elvira does not represent the end of reflection, merely a new motive for it. Marie was forced immediately or passively into reflection by her doubt about Clavigo, but Elvira freely chooses the path of reflection by virtue of her decision to go on loving Don Juan despite his deception: "For her own sake, consequently, she must love Don Juan; it is self-defense which bids her do it, and this is the spur of reflection which drives her to fix her eyes upon this paradox: can she love him although he has deceived her" (*E/O*,I, 197).

In Goethe's Margaret, A finds that the dialectical tension between Marie's passive reflection in-itself and Elvira's active reflection for-itself is overcome in a type of reflective grief that, by embracing them both, can be called absolute or in-and-for-itself. Much of his analysis of Margaret is elusive, for he is drawn into a discussion of the similarities and differences between Faust and Don Juan. Nevertheless, A states that the problem he faces is to establish that reflection is "set in motion in Margaret," a task made more difficult by her "feeling that she is absolutely nothing" (*E/O*,I, 210). Yet this sense of nothingness that Margaret has by virtue of her relation with Faust provides precisely the "dialectical elasticity" that A wants to find in her. As a result of her absolute love for Faust, her feeling of nothingness indicates that she has totally identified with him, thereby negating in her own mind the finite distinction between Faust as the object of her love and herself as its subject: "His conduct is then not merely a deception, but an absolute deception, because her love was absolute. And herein she will again be unable to find rest; for since he has been her all, she will not even be able to hold this thought fast except through him; but she cannot think it through him, because he was a deceiver" (*E/O*,I, 210). This tension between her absolute love and his absolute deception initiates in her an inner movement, a movement of absolute reflective grief in which Margaret cannot distinguish herself from Faust any more than she could in her absolute love. The resulting agony finds expression only in her lament that she cannot grieve over having lost him, even though she is enshrouded in grief: "Am I then absolutely nothing, unable even to weep without him?" (*E/O*,I, 212). Margaret is lost in a sea of reflection, unable to find any firm resting point, since her only point of reference has become her deceiver. So completely has her own identity merged with him that her consciousness is nothing less than absolute reflective grief.[15]

These "three brides of sorrow" (*E/O*,I, 213) together constitute the for-itself moment of grief, which stands in opposition to the in-itself moment (tragic grief). From Margaret it is a small step to the absolute, in-and-for-itself moment that overcomes that opposition within A's dialectic of grief. This absolute grief is portrayed by A in his last address to the *symparanekromenoi*, "The Unhappiest Man." The essay is explicitly based upon Hegel's famous discussion of the unhappy consciousness in the *Phenomenology of Spirit*. A expresses gratitude to Hegel for discerning that the unhappy person is "one who has his ideal . . . in some manner outside of himself" (*E/O*,I, 220), which A takes to mean either in the past or in the future. He adds, however, that those who live in the past *or* future may thereby be present rather than absent to themselves. Only one who is alienated from both past and future is completely alienated and unhappy. And the only way for this to happen is for the past and future to cancel one another out: "when it is memory which prevents the unhappy individual from finding himself in his hope, and hope which prevents him from finding himself in his memory" (*E/O*,I, 223).

The absolute nature of the grief of the unhappiest man can be understood only in its dialectical relation to the preceding stages of the developing contradiction between inwardness and externality. In contrast to the indifference of inwardness as desire to the external occasions for its erotic fulfillment, inwardness as grief is determined precisely by the fact that its desire is negated by the very objects of its desire. Don Juan recalls no names, only statistics, but Donna Elvira chooses to love only Don Juan, even though he has deceived her. The negative character of this contradiction between inwardness and externality in the stage of grief makes it considerably more complex than its counterpart in the movement of desire. It begins with a passive acceptance of grief as caused by the tragedy of life, but then it turns against its own passivity and actively, through reflection, attempts to master its grief. Initially, in Marie, this is simply an effort to understand it, but in Elvira reflection becomes a defiant negation of grief as mere grief, and Margaret so thoroughly reflects herself into Faust that she is rendered quite incapable of grieving over him. Yet none of the three really masters grief; they must submit to it—they have no choice—for they have been abandoned by those whom they love. Therefore, absolute grief must be the *Aufhebung* of tragic grief in-itself and reflective grief for-itself. The former passively laments the grief inflicted externally; the latter actively and internally struggles against grief; to become in-and-for-itself, grief must become both passive and active within internal reflection. This means: it must be *self-inflicted*.

This is precisely the astounding character of the unhappiest man. He is the ideal *symparanekromenos*, one who loves grief and actively pursues it (*E/O*,I, 172): "For there he stands, the ambassador from the kingdom of sighs, the chosen favorite of the realm of suffering, the apostle of grief, the silent friend of pain, the unhappy lover of memory, in his memories confounded by the light of hope, in his hope deceived by the shadows of memory" (*E/O*,I, 227). In the unhappiest man, the realm of the external is negated by being ignored. Unable to think grief away, reflection learns to create and to enjoy grief. It does not concentrate upon desire and its objects, for grief itself is its only object. It does not focus upon hope for this or memory of that, but upon hope and memory themselves as the immediate locus of its fulfillment. They succeed in this role only when they do not refer reflective grief back to anything external. The "apostle of grief" is an aesthetic Christ figure, dramatized simply by the title "The Unhappiest Man" inscribed over an empty grave somewhere in England (*E/O*,I, 217).[16] He has conquered grief by joining himself to it. Although the external world is the initial cause of all grief, the unhappiest man renders it superfluous by seeking grief within himself. Even happiness, the dialectical opposite of grief, is claimed for him by A in a frenzy of paradox:

> So live well, then, unhappiest of men! But what do I say: the unhappiest, the happiest, I ought to say, for this is indeed a gift of the gods which no one can give himself. Language fails, and thought is confounded; for who is the happiest, except the unhappiest, and who the un-

happiest, except the happiest, and what is life but madness, and faith but folly, and hope but the briefest respite, and love but vinegar in the wound. (*E/O*,I, 228)

On this ambiguous note, the lectures to the *symparanekromenoi* end. Contradiction for-itself culminates in an absolute grief that denies all externality and yet must be acknowledged as a gift of the gods. Even unhappiness cannot be accomplished by inwardness alone, and so the dialectic of contradiction between the internal and the external has by no means come to an end.

C. Absolute Contradiction: Deception

At first glance, the transition from "The Unhappiest Man" to "The First Love," a tongue-in-cheek review by A of Augustin Scribe's play of that name, seems far too abrupt to constitute a dialectical development. The gloom of an empty grave surrounded by melancholy *symparanekromenoi* is suddenly replaced by ironic musings on this French situation comedy and on the nature of humor in general. A closer look at the text, however, reveals that "The First Love" is indeed the first moment in the dialectic of contradiction as it appears in a third and final movement—a movement in which absolute contradiction is seen to be a dialectic of deception.

A discusses situation comedy and the concept of occasion on several levels in "The First Love." He opens with the theory that, in the case of literature, "it is a little accidental external circumstance which furnishes the *occasion* for the actual production" (*E/O*,I, 231). A observes that the unity of such occasions with the inspiration behind each creation is not always complete; rather, the "occasion quite often plays the master" (*E/O*,I, 232). Indeed, the concept of occasion is utterly paradoxical, for it is, in relation to events, both a mere circumstance and an essential element:

> The occasion is at one and the same time the most significant and the most insignificant, the most exalted and the most humble, the most important and the most

unimportant. Without the occasion, precisely nothing at all happens, and yet the occasion has no part at all in what does happen. The occasion is the last category, the essential transitional category, from the sphere of the idea to actuality. (*E/O*,I, 236)

The next level on which A discusses the nature of occasions consists of his remarks on the circumstances leading to the writing of the review. He describes the ways in which Scribe's play has affected his personal life (*E/O*,I, 238ff.) and the events that provided the actual occasions "for the present little critique" (*E/O*,I, 241-242, 245). They involve chance meetings, accidental encounters, and the like, culminating in the absurd picture of A spilling ink over an editor's manuscript and thereby obligating himself to replace it with (this) one of his own. (The final irony is that the review never was published, since the journal for which it was intended is supposed to have failed before its first issue!)

Finally, A turns to the play itself. In the course of discussing the concept of occasion, he distinguished between the aesthete as critic and the poet as producer (*E/O*,I, 234-235), and he now draws on that distinction to classify *The First Love* as a work of poetry. By poetry, however, he means not a particular way of using language but a specific relation between language and the external situations it expresses:

> If one would indicate briefly the merit of modern comedies, particularly those of Scribe, in comparison with the older, one might perhaps express it thus: The personal substance and value of the poetic figure is commensurable with the dialogue, the outpourings of the monologue are rendered superfluous; the substance and value of the dramatic action is commensurate with the situation, novelistic explanations are made superfluous; the dialogue finally becomes audible in the transparency of the situation. Hence, no explanations are necessary to orient the spectator, no retardation of the drama is necessary to give suggestions and statements. That is the way it is in life,

where we constantly need explanatory notes; but it ought not to be so in poetry. (*E/O*,I, 245)

In a "poetic" figure, the words spoken are adequate to the situation, so no explanatory notes are needed. Unlike communication in real life, poetic dialogue fully reveals a situation to the spectator; more precisely, that situation is already fully revealed by its own transparency, and this is what makes the dialogue intelligible. On this basis, A judges Scribe's play according to whether or not the "characters become revealed in speech and situation" (*E/O*,I, 246).

The plot of *The First Love* revolves around the "romantic orthodoxy" (*E/O*,I, 252) of Emmeline, who believes that her first love (Charles) must be her true love. Complexity and comedy enter through the occasion that Emmeline has not seen Charles since she was eight years old and can in fact identify him only by the ring that he once wore. Rinville, who shares in none of her romantic fantasy, wants to win her as his wife, and so he passes himself off as Charles; and, when he is wearing Charles's ring (but only then), she does love him. At this time Charles, now married and deeply in debt, returns home in order to clear his debts and resolve the situation with Emmeline. He does so incognito, and is immediately mistaken for Rinville by Emmeline's father, Dervière, who is aghast at the thought that his daughter is being courted by the dissolute "Charles" (Rinville):

> With his entrance the play comes completely to life, manifested by a wantonness, an almost insane crossing of the situations. Altogether four persons are mutually mystified. Emmeline wants Charles, Charles wants to be rid of her; Charles the mystifier does not know that Rinville is passing himself off as Charles and is trying in this way to captivate the girl. Rinville does not realize that Charles as Rinville is no recommendation for him; Dervière backs Rinville, but the Rinville he backs is Charles. Emmeline backs Charles, but the one she backs is Rinville. So the whole operation dissolves into nonsense. That

which the play turns on is nothing, that which comes out of the play is nothing. (*E/O*,I, 259-260)

To set "The First Love" in its dialectical context: A opened the essay by defining occasions both as "little accidental external circumstance[s]" and as "the essential transitional category from the sphere of the idea to actuality" (*E/O*,I, 231, 236). Occasions, then, are the means by which internal inspiration becomes actual, even though they bear no apparently necessary relation to the idea itself. For the unhappiest man, however, actuality is irrelevant; he lives within his own consciousness, concerned only that his hopes and memories mutually nullify one another. For such inwardness to be resurrected from its total disembodiment, it must return to the world of external actuality. This awkward effort is the dialectical moment of "The First Love": it is a review of a farce in which the characters attempt to impose their inner desires upon the realm of actuality. They cannot yet perceive externality for what it is, for they are still bound by their own inner wishes. Thus the "father finds nothing pleasing about the supposed Charles; on the contrary, he finds the supposed Rinville highly attractive, the daughter just the opposite; he finds it so because he wishes it so; she, likewise" (*E/O*,I, 254).

In psychological terms, the deceptions here are caused by the wishful thinking of the characters. From their points of view, however, it is the realm of external occasions that deceives them: they are but its passive victims. That it is just this passive deception that A wishes to present at this moment of the dialectic is clear from his final judgment on the play. Returning to his question about the extent to which the characters and their speech are rendered intelligible by the situations, A declares that Scribe has been successful, for the dialogue follows along as the situation becomes "more and more meaningless in spite of its reasonableness" (*E/O*,I, 275). Repeating his appreciation for the transparency of the situation, A assures his readers that they will never forget it, but the dialogue, however witty, will not long remain in their memories (*E/O*,I, 276).

"The First Love" is the last section of *Either/Or* that is presented as a discussion of characters found in operas, plays, and religious literature. For each development up to this point, A has provided a type as the ideal representation of that dialectical moment. This is the explicit role of Don Juan, Antigone, and the others; and it is implicitly true of the Christ figure who is the object of frequent allusions in "The Unhappiest Man." Only in "The Rotation Method" does A state his own point of view in a totally direct manner. Its subtitle, "An Essay in the Theory of Social Prudence," suggests that he intends it to be his conclusion to the dialectic of contradiction between inwardness and externality.

A opens the essay with a "principle" that he takes to be self-evident: "all men are bores" (*E/O*,I, 281). He muses ironically on the decisive role boredom has played throughout history, from moving the gods to create man (and woman for man) to developing the class structure of the world today, in which the mob consists of those who bore others, while the aristocrats are those who have the privilege of boring themselves. The root of all evil, asserts A, is not idleness but boredom (*E/O*,I, 285). There is even a dialectic of boredom, according to which natural or innate boredom must be distinguished from boredom as a learned response, which is an *"acquired immediacy."*[17]

Given the premise that boredom is the central social problem, it comes as no surprise to find that A's ethical theory addresses that problem directly: "we can only sublate boredom by enjoying ourselves—*ergo*, it is our duty to enjoy ourselves."[18] His strategy for enjoying a world that is intrinsically not at all enjoyable is to force his experience of the world to conform to his wishes. In contrast to Scribe's characters, whose wishes are thwarted by the deceptive intrusions of external reality, A proposes that it is possible to take control of the process of deception, to exploit it actively rather than remain its passive victim.

According to A, the method to be employed in this strategy is rotation. There are two types of rotation, one a "vulgar and inartistic" effort to overcome boredom by constantly seeking new stimulation in the external world (*E/O*,I, 287), the other an internal method. The external type of rotation method is self-defeating, for it can never find lasting satisfaction. The internal way, however, is recommended by A:

> My method does not consist in change of field, but resembles the true rotation method in changing the crop and the mode of cultivation. Here we have at once the principle of limitation, the only saving principle in the world. The more you limit yourself, the more fertile you become in invention. A prisoner in solitary confinement for life becomes very inventive, and a spider may furnish him with much entertainment. . . . How entertaining sometimes to listen to the monotonous drip of water from the roof! How close an observer one becomes under such circumstances, when not the least noise nor movement escapes one's attention! Here we have the extreme application of the method which seeks to achieve results intensively, not extensively. (*E/O*,I, 288)

It is striking that A's rotation method involves a change in the meaning of poetic language, a change that corresponds to the development from passive to active deception. In "The First Love," poetic dialogue is said to reveal transparently the external situation. Here, in contrast, the entire effort is to wrest from externality that priority. The weapons employed by A are selective remembering and forgetting. Though reminiscent of the unhappiest man, whose goal was to sever all relation to externality in order to to exist in an utterly inward world of mutually annulling memory and hope, the rotation method, in contrast, is a means for reshaping external reality according to one's internal demands. This is a creative or "poetic" task, yet it is an active poetizing of externality, in contrast to the passive poetic dialogue of Scribe's comedy: "The more poetically one remembers, the more easily one forgets;

for remembering poetically is really only another expression for forgetting. In a poetic memory the experience has undergone a transformation, by which it has lost all its painful aspects" (*E/O*,I, 289).

In the last few pages of "The Rotation Method," A discusses a number of ways in which the control it requires can be promoted. One is the careful avoidance of excessive enjoyment, for such intensity will make it more difficult to forget the experience later (*E/O*,I, 289). There are also several sorts of relationships that are inimical to control: friendship, marriage, any official position in the government, and, implicitly, all nonleisure activities. These must be eschewed, for all involve unpredictable elements that will render total control impossible (*E/O*,I, 291-294). Even when pursuing leisure activities exclusively, it is important to remain in control of one's own moods: "To control them in the sense of producing them at will is impossible, but prudence teaches how to utilize the moment" (*E/O*,I, 295). Using the moment, in turn, means cultivating a total arbitrariness in one's behavior, a task that A says is far more difficult than is usually appreciated. One attends only the middle act of a play or reads only the last section of a book. In every situation, the goal is to respond not as the author or some other external agent intends but arbitrarily, with a whimsey that is equal to the accidental nature of external occasions and in fact "corresponds" to it (*E/O*,I, 296). Arbitrariness, then, is the means by which A moves from passive deception in-itself to its negation in active deception for-itself.

"The Diary of the Seducer" is the dialectical as well as the literary culmination of volume I of *Either/Or*. By far the longest (one-third of the whole) and most famous of these essays, it presents a vision of absolute deception and frequently recapitulates themes from the earlier moments of inwardness as deception. For example, as Johannes (the seducer) is looking for a way to meet Cordelia (his prey), he finds himself relying upon situations and occasions, and at one point becomes so frustrated by them that he cries out, "Accursed Chance!"

(*E/O*,I, 322). After their engagement, Johannes complains that such a relation is boring ("tiresome"): "The curse of an engagement is always on its ethical side" (*E/O*,I, 363). Yet neither occasions nor boredom constitute more than moments in Johannes's patient effort so to manipulate Cordelia that she will voluntarily do as he wishes. Denying that he is a bungler or even a seducer, A insists that he is an aesthete and eroticist who knows "how to poetize himself in a girl's feelings so that it is from her that everything issues as he wishes it" (*E/O*,I, 363).

Johannes's plan is for Cordelia to reach a point where she herself will break their engagement "in order to raise herself to a higher sphere" (*E/O*,I, 432), all the while believing that her decision is completely her own. To this end, he gives her lessons in deception, beginning with a situation in which he induces her to smile ironically at his own solicitous behavior toward her suitor, Edward (*E/O*,I, 346). Throughout their developing relationship, his every action toward her is calculated both to deceive her and to make her perceive appearances as themselves deceptive in relation to reality. This full-scale use of deception is not, for Johannes, some sort of necessary evil: he believes that "perfect aesthetic conduct" will always result in one party deceiving the other (*E/O*,I, 375). When he asks himself if he loves Cordelia, he answers in the affirmative, on the grounds that faithful love "in an aesthetic sense" requires "something more than honesty," namely, duplicity (*E/O*,I, 380). In the end, Cordelia does break their engagement. The next night Johannes seduces her and immediately abandons her: having accomplished this final deception of her, he is no longer interested in her.

Dialectically, the role of Johannes is to portray absolute deception. Although this phrase was used by A in reference to Faust's deception of Margaret (*E/O*,I, 210), the absoluteness there was clearly dependent upon something external, namely, Faust, whom Margaret loved absolutely. Johannes's deception of Cordelia is not, in this sense, derived. It is, rather, a transformation of the passivity of deception in-itself and the activity of deception for-itself into deception in-and-for-itself. This transformation occurs in both Cordelia and Johannes. Although she is passively deceived by his calculated behavior, she experiences her own deception actively, for she believes that she has broken their engagement of her own free will. Likewise, he is totally committed to manipulating her and all the circumstances of their relationship as actively as A had advocated the poetic transformation of memories; and yet his ultimate goal is to receive her love passively, as a gift "freely given" (*E/O*,I, 363). Thus, in each of them, deception overcomes the opposition between the passive and the active, in which it is respectively determined either objectively or subjectively. The element of otherness or externality is utterly internalized by them both, which results in deception in-and-for-itself.

There remains, of course, the fact that Johannes and Cordelia must still be related to one another as deceiver and deceived. From the aesthetic point of view, this is not so much a problem as a dialectical presupposition: deception is a relation, and every relation must have at least two members. Yet A is not able to accept Johannes's deception so easily. In his introductory remarks to the diary (which A claims to have transcribed from Johannes's notebook), he calls Johannes a "depraved personality" with a "scheming mind" (*E/O*,I, 299). He also suggests that Johannes is too strong a personality for reality, that reality fails to give him "a sufficient stimulus" (*E/O*,I, 302). Yet the earlier denunciation is never retracted, and it remains the first real criticism of the aesthetic mode to be found in volume I. Indeed, Victor Eremita even suggests that A's denunciation of Johannes is really a self-criticism, that A himself is the author of "The Diary of the Seducer" but that he presents it pseudonymously because he is terrified by his own production (*E/O*,I, 9).[19]

The horror of Johannes is that he attempts to internalize everything external; he acknowledges nothing at all as legitimately beyond his powers of manipulation. For him, as eventually also for Cordelia, external reality is only an element of self-consciousness. For the first time, the contradiction between the internal and the external is appropriated within consciousness with no remainder of otherness. Even the ethical dimension in the engagement, which Johannes finds so tiresome and which would appear to restore an element of externality to their relationship, is aesthetically appropriated by Johannes in the claim that the engagement had preserved the interesting (which is the only goal of aesthetics) "by the fact of the outward appearance being in contradiction to the inner life" (E/O,I, 432).

So, although the otherness of an ethical judgment on aesthetic inwardness is beginning to emerge in A's criticism of Johannes, the otherness of the contradiction between external appearance and inwardness has been totally appropriated by Johannes. Inwardness is no longer indifferent to the external, as in desire; nor is it determined as estrangement from the external, as in grief. Inwardness is now in control of the external, by means of deception. Yet this very sense of control is itself an illusion. Because he cannot accept the otherness of external reality, Johannes falls victim to his own self-deception. He is both deceiver and deceived. He is absolute deception incarnate, and absolute deception is revealed in him as the truth of absolute aesthetic inwardness.

It is only with this moment of absolute deception that the poetic can be understood as, in aesthetic terms, a language of deception.[20] In "The First Love," the poetic first appears as a form of dialogue that is merely the passive expression of external deception. In "The Rotation Method," poetizing becomes memory's distortion of external reality. Finally, "The Diary of the Seducer" presents the poetic as the means by which Johannes alters external reality itself, both misleading Cordelia about the truth of their relationship and, in the process, distorting her so as to make her more interesting to himself. This twofold movement of poetizing is clearly described by A: "The poetical was the *more* he himself brought with him. The *more* was the poetical he enjoyed in the poetic situation of reality; he withdrew this again in the form of poetic reflection" (*E/O*,I, 301). By deceiving Cordelia, Johannes intrudes upon her consciousness and attempts to change or distort her. He actively poetizes her, just as A had argued that one must actively poetize one's own experiences. In so doing, he makes her more interesting to himself, for what he sees in her is now nothing less than his own creation, a work of poetic production that he can enjoy and upon which he can reflect. His poetizing has, therefore, both an active and a passive dimension, and the development of poetry as a language of aesthetic inwardness is seen to have its own dialectic. On this basis, it is possible to speak of the language or self-communication of Johannes as absolute poetry, for it is a production by the self and of the self, using the other only as material for its own internal creative activity.

This is why the diary form is so perfect an expression of Johannes's consciousness. A diary is the only literary medium in which one explicitly addresses no one other than oneself. A diary is reflection upon things and persons external to the writer, but it internalizes them all, submitting at no point to the dialogical constraints of social communication. There is no one in a position to correct or even respond to the writer of a diary. Its language, therefore, is virtually a private language—which is to say, no language at all.

In this respect, poetry is indeed a fitting culmination of the various so-called languages of aesthetic inwardness. In desire, music is that which best expresses inwardness; but it does so precisely because it remains indifferent to its own external expressions. Music can serve as the language of the erotic only so long as the erotic does not become self-conscious about itself and its appearance in the world. In grief, ordinary language is still inadequate to the inner life of the subjects; they reveal themselves only through a chance gesture or involuntary response. Thus their language is drama, but a dramatic action in which behavior is employed to conceal rather than to reveal inner truth. Finally, the resulting tension between a relation of indifference and one of negation is overcome only in poetry, for "poetry," as presented in the last three essays, appears as a more subtle form of indifference and a more successful negation of the otherness of the other. Rather than simply ignore the external or submit to a lifelong struggle with it, A's poet conquers "reality" by internalizing it and making it serve his own desires. Poetic language is thus an instrument of internalization that makes absolute aesthetic inwardness possible, an inwardness that attempts to transform the external world into its own creation.

The dialectic of music-drama-poetry is, however, only one expression of the fundamental structure of *Either/Or*, a structure in which each dialectical advance is accomplished by a development in the relation of inner states to outer appearances. This structure does not include "Diapsalmata," which functions as an overture in which the major themes of the entire volume are anticipated. It begins with "The Immediate Stages of the Erotic," and there alone is it an explicit dialectical structure, one that is clearly articulated by the pseudonym himself. That first essay portrays the three moments within desire as dreaming (the page), seeking (Papageno), and absolute desire (Don Juan). Together they constitute the in-itself movement of aesthetic contradiction. Each moment reveals a greater contradiction between inner desire and the putative external object of desire than its predecessor, although none of them becomes conscious of that contradiction.

It is only as grief, which is aesthetic contradiction for-itself, that the opposition between the desiring self and the external object of desire becomes conscious. This consciousness produces yet another contradiction, for the desiring self now attempts to conceal its grief beneath an outer calm. Here again a dialectic of moments occurs, in which several dramatic characters successively reveal more complex forms of grief: tragic grief is relatively passive; reflective grief actively seeks its object and has a further internal development of phases (Marie, Elvira, and Margaret); and absolute grief is the self-enclosed, passive activity of the unhappiest man. This dialectic can be recapitulated in terms of the relation between subject and object: in grief in-itself, the subject and object of grief are not yet distinguished, for the Antigones do not challenge the legitimacy of their grief; grief for-itself (the shadowgraph ladies) shows a separation and opposition between the subjects and the objects of their love; and, in the unhappiest man, subject and object are reunited in an orgy of grief in-and-for-itself.

Deception is the final aesthetic movement in which the opposition between desire and grief is sublated. This is accomplished in a very complex way: the lack of consciousness of the inner/outer contradiction (desire) and the hyper-consciousness of that same contradiction (grief) are united in Johannes and Cordelia, in the sense that their self-contradiction is mutual and their opposition is reciprocal. This *Aufhebung* is a unity in absolute contradiction, a relationship that is based upon deception of one another and even of oneself. In this sense, deception can be designated aesthetic contradiction in-and-for-itself.

Within deception, there are again three moments of development. "The First Love" portrays deception in-itself, in which the subjects unconsciously (yet willfully) misinterpret the occasions they encounter. "The Rotation Method" raises deception to a conscious principle for-itself. And "The Diary of the Seducer" glorifies deception in-and-for-itself as the most liberating way for two people to relate to one another, even though the end result is that each person is simultaneously both estranged from the other and dependent upon the other for self-realization. Deception also progresses from a confusion of subject and object in "The First Love" through their active opposition in "The Rotation Method" to the unity of subject and object as identical although opposite poles within the dialectic of deception in "The Diary of The Seducer."

The dialectic of aesthetic inwardness is thus propelled from start to finish by the idea of contradiction. It is inherently unstable and will accordingly be criticized from the ethical point of view. Before turning to Volume II of *Either/Or*, however, it is worth looking at another pseudonymous portrayal of the aesthetic stage, one where this dialectical structure of contradiction finds a remarkable confirmation.

"In Vino Veritas"

There are striking differences between the two presentations of the aesthetic stage, of which the most significiant is that "In Vino Veritas" appears to begin where volume I of *Either/Or* ends. The new pseudonymous author, William Afham, may in fact be A, for the ideas he expresses are quite similar to those encountered in "The Rotation Method" and "The Diary of the Seducer."[21] Afham plays a mysterious role at the banquet that is the main subject of the essay. He is present, but says nothing: he "participated without being a participator" (*SLW*, 32). His greatest enjoyment, he admits, comes from recollection, which he compares to wine, for it preserves "the bouquet of experience." Recollection is much more than mere memory; it is the consecration of those experiences which are recalled by memory. Thus children can remember prodigiously but are not yet able to recollect; on the other hand, old men, whose memories have begun to fail them, find that their "best faculty" is now their poetic ability to excel in recollection. Afham also describes farsight as poetic, emphasizing that recollection is "removing, putting at a distance." Memory is an indifferent act by which data are recalled; recollection is an ideality by which one can see the "eternal continuity in life" (*SLW*, 27-28).

As Afham develops this notion of recollection, it becomes clear that it is virtually identical with the concept of poetizing found in the last essays of *Either/Or*:

> Memory is immediacy and comes immediately to one's aid, whereas recollection comes only by reflection. Hence it is an art to recollect. Like Themistocles I wish to forget, as the opposite of remembering. But to recollect and to forget are not opposites. The art of recollecting is not an easy one, because at the instant recollection is taking shape it may assume a great variety of forms, whereas memory merely fluctuates between remembering right and remembering wrong. Take homesickness for example. What is it? It is due to recalling something which

is remembered. It is brought about most simply by being away. The art would be to be able to feel homesick notwithstanding one is at home. Expertness in the use of illusion is requisite for this. . . . To bring back to oneself the past by enchantment is not so difficult as to remove from oneself by enchantment the object nearest to one for the sake of recollecting it. This properly is the art of recollection, employing reflection raised to the second power. (*SLW*, 30-31)

This notion of recollection recalls the concept of poetizing in at least two ways. First, recollection can occur only by means of reflection, that is, by the negation of immediacy. Likewise, the third movement of the aesthetic dialectic (deception) emerges only after reflection, in the form of grief, has negated the immediacy of desire. More significantly, recollection involves the distortion of external reality according to inward demands. In the example of homesickness, Afham suggests that the real art is "to be able to feel homesick notwithstanding one is at home." This use of illusion, like poetic activity, assumes a contradiction between inwardness (one feels distanced from home) and externality (one is nevertheless at home) that can be overcome only by imaginative recollection. Such self-enchantment may bring back a distant past or remove the present in order to recall it later. In either case, external reality is subjected to the process of poetic internalization.

Appropriately, Afham's meditation on recollection leads to the admission that his account of the banquet is the product of his own recollection rather than mere memory: "How small a part my memory has in the matter I can perceive from the fact that I sometimes feel as though I had not experienced it, but had poetically invented it" (*SLW*, 32). When the time comes to commit his recollection to writing, he seeks out a solitary spot in the forest where immediate impressions will contrast sharply with the festive atmosphere of the banquet. His penchant for contradiction is manifest in his delight at finding a "quiet, remote and forgotten" place that is called the Nook of Eight Paths, as though it were actually a busy intersection (*SLW*, 33). Furthermore, Afham professes a profound suspicion of language. As he sinks into recollection, "the silence grows—what a formula of enchantment to conjure with! How inebriating is quietness" (*SLW*, 34). Here language is deception, everything external contradicts inwardness, and recollection is the art of poetic internalization. It appears from Afham's Prefatory Note that his presentation of the aesthetic stage will expand upon the themes in *Either/Or*, I, but not in any way confirm that the stage itself is structured by a progressive dialectic of contradiction between inwardness and externality.

Nor is there any hint of a dialectical structure in Afham's description of the origin of the banquet. At their favorite coffeehouse sometime before the July night on which the banquet takes place, the five principals discuss the idea of such a banquet and who might plan it. A young man, described by Afham as one who, being "coddled up—exclusively by thought, nourished by the content of his own soul, had had nothing to do with the world" (*SLW*, 37), likes the idea of a banquet but considers himself unqualified to arrange it. Another nameless participant, the ladies' tailor, seems to Afham both self-assured and self-ingratiating; he claims that he has no time for such an endeavor. Johannes the seducer, also one of the participants, objects to planning in general, insisting that any actual banquet "should be so arranged as to be accomplished all of a sudden," complete with an external setting created especially for that evening and ready to be destroyed immediately afterwards. The others seem to agree with Johannes that "nothing is more disgusting than to know that somewhere or other there is an external setting which directly and impertinently gives itself out to be a reality" (*SLW*, 38). A fourth principal is Victor Eremita, the pseudonymous editor of *Either/Or*, who expresses the view that it is enough to have imagined the banquet, and therefore no actual banquet is necessary. This suggestion is vigorously disputed by Constantin Constantius, the fifth participant and the pseudonymous editor of *Repetition*,[22] who objects to Victor's "highhandedness in thus transforming the projected banquet into a sheer illusion." Victor replies by asserting that a "banquet in and for itself" can be accomplished only by luck and "a happy concord of moods" (*SLW*, 39); it must be devoted exclusively to eating and drinking, with no diversions, such as the presence of women or discussions about politics. Undeterred, Constantin plans a banquet and sends invitations to the others. He gives it the motto, "In Vino Veritas," stipulating that speeches are to be made only under the influence of wine, since "wine vindicates the truth and the truth vindicates the wine" (*SLW*, 41).

What Afham presents, then, is a collection of personae who represent certain ideas already encountered in *Either/Or*: the young man typifies the inwardness of reflection; the ladies' tailor is the image of self-contradiction; Johannes continues to deny integrity to external reality; Victor extols the ideality of a banquet in-and-for-itself; and Constantin represents, here as in *Repetition*, the idea that the fulfillment of aesthetic imagination lies not in mere recollection but in the actual enactment of what has been imagined. Afham's perception of the five principals goes only this far, however. In order to discern their dialectical relations to one another, it is necessary to turn to the banquet itself and the speeches they deliver.

A. *Implicit Contradiction: The Concept of Love*

As host, Constantin determines how the banquet will proceed. No speeches are permitted until after the meal, when ample drinking will have loosened thoughts and tongues. Everyone is instructed that the speeches "should deal with love, or with the relationship between man and woman" (*SLW*, 45). Constantin cautions his speakers to remain on a general level, rather than indulging in descriptions of personal experiences with love. Nevertheless, no sooner does the young man begin to deliver the first speech, than Constantin interrupts to say that his lack of personal experience in love should disqualify him

as a speaker. Constantin's self-contradiction is a clever introduction to the obscure relation that exists between thought
and experience.

And obscurity is precisely the point of the young man's
speech, which opens with a discussion of the contradiction
between the ideal of love and its reality. The problem, he
argues, is that no one can ever define the actual object of love;
to say simply that one loves the lovable is a ridiculous tautology
(*SLW*, 48-50). Lovers are always unable to explain the reasons
for their love. Comically, they regard kissing as an adequate
(commensurable) expression of it, yet kissing is no more intelligible than love itself and certainly lacks its significance
(*SLW*, 53-54). Here again, the obscure or incommensurable
relation between real experience and the ideality of thought is
clear. Another illustration of the contradiction of love is the
phenomenon of two distinct individuals thinking of themselves
as halves of a single self, as a union in "one flesh." This, he
insists, is simply ludicrous: "The more one thinks of it, the
more laughable it becomes; for if the man actually is a whole,
he does not become a whole in love, but he and the woman
make one and a half" (*SLW*, 56).[23] Finally, the young man
also has a few thoughts (his is by far the longest of the speeches)
on parental love. Although he admits that it can be a source
of great joy, he sees a contradiction here, too, for that joy
results from bringing an eternal being into the world, but "an
eternal being cannot be born." The result is "a contradiction
. . . fit both to laugh and to weep over" (*SLW*, 58).[24]

The young man concludes by renouncing all love. That
renunciation should not, however, obscure the parallels between his speech and the structure of "The Immediate Stages
of the Erotic." He begins by criticizing love for having no
clearly defined object, an excellent characterization of the page.
He then turns his attention to the futile attempt to fulfill
oneself in union with another person, which captures nicely
the nature of Papageno's quest. Finally, the desire of parental
love to unite the eternal with time ironizes the dialectical
notion of "absolute," just as Don Juan represents the absolute

moment in the dialectic of desire. This dialectical structure is admittedly very obscure in the young man's speech and would not occur to a reader independently of the other essay. Less obscure is the fact that both the young man's speech and "The Immediate Stages of the Erotic" portray indifference toward women as the actual objects of love. It is this contradiction that is developed in the later speeches, where the parallels between the two works are substantially easier to demonstrate.

B. Explicit Contradiction: Woman

The significance of the young man's indifference to actual women is implicitly emphasized by Constantin, who immediately follows him and who says he would have forbidden such a speech on the contradictions of love if he had been able. Instead, he announces that he will simply go ahead and speak about woman. It soon becomes clear, however, that he intends to do so not in admiration of women but in a spirit of misogyny. For Constantin, man is absolute, but woman "has her being in relationships." This incongruity—between the self-sufficiency of man and the dependent nature of woman—makes reciprocity between them impossible. It also leads Constantin to the conclusion that woman can best be understood under the "category of jest," which he describes as "not an aesthetic but an imperfect ethical category." Man approaches woman seriously, that is, ethically, and must invariably realize that "all her ideality is illusion," so that his ethical experiment on her results only in jest (SLW, 61).

What disturbs Constantin Constantius about woman is that she lacks constancy: "she does not possess sufficient power of reflection to insure her against self-contradiction for any considerable time, say a week at the maximum, if the male does not help her regulatively by contradicting her" (SLW, 64). It is especially in relation to love that man cannot trust woman. She remains faithful only to a man she cannot have. She "dies" of love, but is just as easily reborn, and with astounding frequency. In short, she seeks emancipation from the aesthetic sphere, but she is not "man enough" to attain the ethical; thus, she is jest. Citing Plato and Aristotle, Constantin concludes that woman is "an incomplete form, that is, an irrational quantity, which perhaps some time in a better existence might be brought back to the male form" (*SLW*, 67).

His speech concluded, Constantin asks Victor Eremita to begin immediately. Victor seems to share Constantin's misogyny, for he opens by expressing his gratitude that he was born a man rather than a woman. Yet there is a significant shift in the thrust of his comments:

> To be a woman is something so strange, so mixed, so complex, that no predicate expresses it, and the many predicates one might use contradict one another so sharply that only a woman can endure it, and, still worse, can enjoy it. The fact that she actually has less significance than man is not what constitutes her misfortune, even if she were to come to know it, for after all this is something that can be endured. No, the misfortune is that, owing to the romantic way in which she is regarded, her life has become meaningless, so that one moment she has the utmost significance and the next moment none whatever, without ever coming to know what her significance really is. . . . (*SLW*, 68)

Here the self-contradictory nature of woman is not denied, but it is attributed to the way man sees her, that is, to the inconsistent "significance" that she has for him. If one must be a woman, Victor adds, it would be better to be a slave also (as in the orient), for that would give to a woman a definite, noncontradictory, identity (that is, insignificance). Victor's initial misogyny now appears to include a criticism of man.

Within Victor's analysis of female self-contradiction, three phases can be discerned. The first is gallantry, which is a tendency to idealize or view in "fantastic categories" another person. Gallantry toward a man is an insult, for it can avoid condescension only by being reciprocated. Woman would do well to avoid it also, and the confusion she experiences in response to it (*SLW*, 68-69). In the second phase, woman inspires man by awakening his genius. But she acomplishes this only "negatively," by dying or otherwise being lost to the man. Only then can his consciousness of immortality be born, a product of woman's "sorcery of illusion" (*SLW*, 70-73). Preferable to either the idealizing of woman in gallantry or the exploiting of woman in sorcery, Victor concludes, is a relationship based upon deception. For example, a husband should appear to be faithful, and be unfaithful; or appear to be unfaithful, yet really be faithful. In this way, immediate existence will be negated, which Victor considers a necessity for man but impossible for woman (*SLW*, 75). He labels this annihilation of immediacy "reduplication," which, in his usage, is not simply the dialectic between existence and thought: it is the exploitation of that dialectic in order to create woman in the image of self-contradiction.[25] Thus what had appeared to be a criticism of Constantin's misogyny in fact turns out to be far more insidious. Constantin merely attacked woman for inconsistency; Victor's exoneration of her actually presupposes that her entire value derives from her usefulness to man.

With Victor's speech, the parallel to *Either/Or*, I, begins to emerge more clearly. Both the characters from Mozart and the young man manifest an implicit contradiction between interest (sensuous or theoretical) in love and indifference toward the particular objects of love as individual persons. They are all representative of aspects of contradiction in-itself. In the movement of contradiction for-itself, the lectures to the *symparanekromenoi* are paralleled by a series of three speeches, all of which represent relationships as intense oppositions. At first this opposition is unconscious, merely implicit in the objective situation, whether that be a tragic conflict (the Antigones) or the inherently self-contradictory nature of woman (Constantin). But then the negative moment brings the opposition into the open in a very complex way. Just as the three shadowgraph ladies are consigned to grief by the cruelty of the men they love, Victor analyzes three ways in which man makes woman self-contradictory. Moreover, there is a parallel development of phases within these two moments. Gallantry is essentially condescension disguised as adoration and leaves the woman just as confused about whether she is or is not loved as was Marie Beaumarchais. Sorcery is man's imputing of powers to woman on the basis of the responses she elicits from him. Here she has a more active role than in gallantry, but the appearance of independence is illusory, for she remains totally dependent upon man for her identity. Likewise, Donna Elvira actively decides to go on loving Don Juan, even though he has determined that for her that act of loving will always be a source of grief. Finally, reduplication is Victor's term for the ideal effort of man to deceive woman at every opportunity. This strategy recalls the absolute deception of Faust toward Margaret, which also reduces the woman to a nothing, a mere immediacy that is annihilated by male reflection.

The dialectic then moves to the third moment within contradiction for-itself. The structural parallel to the unhappiest man is the ladies' tailor. In a speech that is short but trenchant, he accuses both Constantin and Victor Eremita of spinning theories about woman that are not based upon experience. As an authority on fashion, he constantly witnesses woman's weaker side, for fashion is "a contraband trade in indecency licensed as decorum" and an "idolatrous worship" (*SLW*, 76). From this privileged vantage point, he sees that woman lacks neither consistency nor reflection, as Constantin and Victor have argued. Rather, her weakness lies in the superficiality of her life, in the fact that her spirit is dedicated to the pursuit of being fashionable. Man as man can neither judge nor create her, for "she belongs to that phantom which is formed by the unnatural intercourse of feminine reflection with feminine reflection, i.e. fashion" (*SLW*, 79).

Here the dialectic of female self-contradiction reaches its *Aufhebung*. Constantin's focus upon woman as immediately self-contradictory is negated by Victor's claim that she is made so by the external influence of man. The ladies' tailor both affirms and denies Constantin's position by defining woman's immediacy as a consistent pursuit of change, that is, fashion.

He likewise takes up Victor's claim by internalizing feminine reflection as "unnatural intercourse." This internalization is parallel to that of the unhappiest man with regard to past and future: both have the illusion of autonomy from the external force that controls them. In the case of a woman, fashion is actually dictated by man—the ladies' tailor! Likewise, the unhappiest man cannot succeed in internalizing the objective power of time. Together they represent the in-and-for-itself moment within the dialectical movement of contradiction for-itself.

C. Absolute Contradiction: Deception

The final movement, contradiction in-and-for-itself, is represented here, as in *Either/Or*, by Johannes the seducer. After criticizing the other speakers and praising the "abundant intrinsic value" of woman (*SLW*, 81), he tells a little myth to illustrate her superiority over man. It seems that woman was created by the gods in order to captivate man within "all the prolixities of finiteness." The only ones who understand this ruse are "erotics" (mistakenly called seducers), men who know how to "dine constantly upon bait" without ever getting caught (*SLW*, 84). They are masters of the deception perpetrated upon them by the gods:

She is a deception, but that she is only in her second phase and for him who is deceived. She is finiteness, but in her first phase she is finiteness raised to the highest power in the delusive infinity of all divine and human illusions. Not yet is the deception—but one more instant and a man is deceived. She is finiteness, and so she is a collective term, to say one woman means many women. This the erotic alone understands, and hence he is so prompt to love many, never being deceived, but sucking up all the voluptuous delights the cunning gods were capable of preparing. Therefore woman cannot be exhaustively expressed by any formula but is an infinity of finitudes. (*SLW*, 85)

Two "phases" are mentioned in this passage, which correspond to two moments in the technical terms of this dialectical analysis. In the first, woman, who is finiteness, appears infinite to man and thereby attracts him to her. She is not just finiteness; she seems to be "an infinity of finitudes." In the second moment, man is actually deceived. His own infinity is negated, for he succumbs to temptation, with the result that "she is related to [him] as his mate" (*SLW*, 85). Marriage, argues Johannes, is the means by which the gods conquer and subdue man (*SLW*, 87).

These two moments correspond to *Either/Or*, I, as follows: deception in-itself is passive, in the sense that people are deceived by external appearances in "The First Love" and man is deceived by woman as the illusion of infinity. This moment is negated by deception for-itself, which reveals that the deception is really a voluntary or active self-deception, as illustrated by both "The Rotation Method" and the vows of marriage. Absolute deception unites the passivity of the first moment with the activity of the second. This *Aufhebung* is revealed in the complex self-contradictions portrayed in "The Diary of the Seducer," and here Johannes returns to the same theme: "for every woman there is a corresponding seducer. Her good fortune consists in encountering precisely him" (*SLW*, 87). Now deception (seduction) has become the goal, but it is a mutual deception between woman as the ruse of the gods and man as her so-called seducer. Seduction is an absolute deception in which subject and object become interchangeable, for each deceives and is deceived.

"In Vino Veritas" closes with a fanciful scene in which the the men leave the banquet table quickly, "breaking off" their evening much as Johannes says that man must break off a relation with a woman (*SLW*, 88). While the setting of their banquet is being destroyed, Constantin drives his guests to a nearby point where he has five carriages waiting for them (the fifth is presumably for Afham). They pause to take a brief stroll and happen to come upon a garden where Judge William is being served breakfast by his wife. She is overheard saying that he could have become a much greater person had he never married. He demurs. While they are thus acting out an ethical counterpoint to Victor's speech on gallantry, Victor himself is busy stealing a manuscript from the Judge, which is in turn immediately stolen from him by Afham. This is a whimsical transition to the ethical stage, represented (as in *Either/Or*) by Judge William, whose essay is entitled: "Various Observations about Marriage, in reply to objections."

ONE DIMENSION of the dialectic of aesthetic inwardness that appears in *Either/Or* but is missing from "In Vino Veritas" is the problem of a language in which inner states might be externalized. In its place another emphasis emerges: the dialectic of inner and outer is here shown to be more than simply a matter of the contradiction between inner states and external appearances or expression. The dialectic of inner and outer as it is developed in "In Vino Veritas" is, despite the extremely limited (not to say perverse) relationships used to illustrate it, nothing less than a dialectic of self and other. In the aesthetic sphere, love is understood as the contradiction between man and woman. Told from man's point of view, this casts woman in the role of "other" to man. Thus the entire dialectic of indifference, opposition, and internalization can be characterized as modes of self-other relations. The tension between inner and outer is but a logical way of formulating what Kierkegaard in fact presents as a profound social insight: that selfhood, however self-centered, develops only in relation to others.

The parallel structures of dialectical contradiction in *Either/Or*, I, and "In Vino Veritas" also offer a new way to understand the problematic relation between immediacy and reflection in Kierkegaard's concept of the aesthetic sphere. In the former work, the essays progressed from erotic immediacy through emerging reflection to the seducer's claim that reflection had become his immediacy and immediacy his reflection. That same point is reached in the latter piece by the opposite route, beginning with the young man's abstract reflections on love and moving through the discussion of woman as immediacy to an identical conclusion. In short, these two works taken together show that the aesthetic stage is to be understood not simply as a polarity in which immediacy yields to reflection,[26] but as a triadic development in which the opposition between immediacy and reflection (in whichever order) culminates in their mutual sublation within aesthetic inwardness, an inwardness that attempts to conquer every externality or otherness it encounters.

Finally, "In Vino Veritas" confirms that the dialectic of aesthetic inwardness is a systematic dialectic of contradiction (see Chart 2).[27] The in-itself movement posits a contradiction between inwardness and external appearance that remains implicit. Contradiction for-itself is fully conscious of both the contradiction between subject and object and the self-contradiction within either the subject (the *symparanekromenoi* lectures) or the object (speeches on "woman" in "In Vino Veritas'). The final movement, contradiction in-and-for-itself, restores the unity of the first movement yet preserves the opposition of the second. It accomplishes this in deception, understood as a mutual or absolute deception of self *and* other within a relationship. Here contradiction is internalized, with the result that the oppositions of inner/outer, self/other, and subject/object can all be declared *aufgehoben*, transcended in the higher unity of aesthetic selfhood.

CHART 2.
The Dialectic of Aesthetic Contradiction

Either/Or, I	"In Vino Veritas"
A. Desire ("The Immediate Stages of the Erotic")	A. Concept of love self-contradictory (the young man)
1. Dreaming desire (the page)	1. Object of love obscure
2. Seeking desire (Papageno)	2. Claim of union ludicrous
3. Absolute desire (Don Juan)	3. Parental love absurd

CONTRADICTION IN-ITSELF (IMPLICIT)

DESIRE FOR EXTERNAL OBJECT VERSUS INDIFFERENCE TO IT	THEORY VERSUS EXPERIENCE; NO AWARENESS OF OTHERS AS OTHER

B. Grief (lectures to the *symparanekromenoi*)
  1. Tragic grief: contradiction in objective situation ("Ancient Tragical Motif . . .")
  2. Reflective grief: subject's self-contradiction due to rejection by object of love ("Shadowgraphs")
     a. Subject uncertain about object of grief (Marie)
     b. Subject chooses grief but uncertain how to grieve (Donna Elvira)
     c. Subject totally dependent upon object for identity (Margaret)
  3. Absolute grief: contradiction internalized by subject ("The Unhappiest Man")

B. Object of love (woman) self-contradictory
  1. Woman as self-contradictory object (Constantine)
  2. Woman made self-contradictory by man (Victor Eremita)
     a. Woman confused by man (gallantry)
     b. Woman falsely portrayed as independent of man (sorcery)
     c. Woman created and confused by man (reduplication)
  3. Woman internalizes self-contradiction as fashion (ladies' tailor)

CONTRADICTION FOR-ITSELF (EXPLICIT)

INWARD DESIRE FOR EXTERNAL OBJECT VERSUS OUTWARD INDIFFERENCE; SUBJECT NEGATED BY OBJECT

OTHER ACKNOWLEDGED AS OTHER BUT REJECTED AS SELF-CONTRADICTORY

C. Deception
  1. Deception by occasions ("First Love")
  2. Intentional deception ("Rotation Method")
  3. Absolute deception ("Diary of the Seducer")

C. Deception (Johannes the seducer)
  1. Woman as means for deception of man by the gods
  2. Marriage as means for deception of man by the gods
  3. Man achieves infinity deceiving (finite) woman

CONTRADICTION IN-AND-FOR-ITSELF (ABSOLUTE)

SUBJECT AND OBJECT MUTUALLY SELF-CONTRADICTORY AND IN RECIPROCAL OPPOSITION

MUTUAL SELF-CONTRADICTION WITHIN RECIPROCAL DECEPTION

THREE

The Ethical as a Stage

ALTHOUGH Kierkegaard wrote many edifying discourses that treat one or another aspect of the ethical life, it is in the writings of the pseudonym Judge William that the notion of the ethical as a stage is developed. The Judge is credited with volume II of *Either/Or*,[1] comprising two long letters to A, "Aesthetic Validity of Marriage" and "Equilibrium Between the Aesthetical and the Ethical in the Composition of the Personality," and supplemented by "Ultimatum," which is purportedly a copy of a sermon written by a priest and friend of the Judge; and "Various Observations about Marriage, in Reply to Objections," which constitutes the second part of *Stages on Life's Way*. It is well known that a major thrust of these writings is the repudiation of the aesthetic philosophy and life style, but the precise character of that repudiation is somewhat obscure. By investigating the ways in which the Judge's writings are and are not dialectical with regard to both the question of structure and the inner/outer and self/other relations,[2] it will be possible to clarify the ethical attitude toward the aesthetic stage and the curious use of religious language in the ethical stage.

Some scholars have questioned the status of the ethical as a stage,[3] and for very good reason. In the first place, even a cursory reading of the Judge's letters in *Either/Or* will convince the interpreter that there is hardly any organization in them, to say nothing of possible dialectical structures. Without question, these are the most problematic among the pseudonymous writings for the method of analysis I am employing. It requires extraordinary patience and skill on the part of an interpreter just to work out a reasonable outline of the contents of "Validity" and "Equilibrium."[4]

This style makes it impossible to trace a *development* in the argument presented in volume II (as I did for volume I). A better approach to understanding the Judge's thought is to identify a number of questions that are relevant to this study and then to survey his letters with these in mind. Accordingly, I shall begin with a discussion of the ethical stage as both affirmation ("transfiguration") and negation ("ethical resolution") of the aesthetic; then explore the various types of dialectic in the Judge's thought and how his apparent inconsistencies have been interpreted; and conclude with an examination of the inner/outer relation in the letters to A and the light that it sheds on the issues previously discussed. Following this treatment of the letters to A, I shall turn to "Observations," which offers several intriguing answers to the questions raised by *Either/Or*.

Either/Or, II

Ethical Transfiguration and Negation of the Aesthetic

One major theme of the letters to A is that the ethical transfigures the aesthetic stage, in particular romantic love. In "Validity," the Judge argues that "romantic love can be united with and can persist in marriage, yea, that marriage is the true transfiguration of romantic love" (*E/O*,II, 31). The Judge assumes that the aesthetic idealization of first love is sincere (rather than a tactic in the pursuit of deception) and accordingly hopes to convince A that first love is "transfigured in a higher sphere" by marriage (*E/O*,II, 57). In "Equilibrium," the metaphor of transfiguration is used for the relation between the stages: the ethical, asserts the Judge, "will not annihilate the aesthetical but transfigures it" (*E/O*,II, 257-258). Moreover, this transfiguration is accomplished by the fact that the ethical "explains" the aesthetic, a pun on the dual meanings of *forklarer* (to transfigure or to explain). As examples, the Judge cites vocation as well as marriage (*E/O*,II, 298, 309).

Several aspects of this concept of transfiguration need to be brought into sharper focus. First, it expresses the Judge's belief that the various spheres of existence can be harmonized. This notion is especially clear in the first essay, where he proclaims "the harmonious accord of these different spheres," which all perceive love as "the same thing, except that it is expressed aesthetically, religiously, and ethically" (*E/O*,II, 60-61). Marriage is the ethical preservation of the aesthetic quality in first love, in particular its "infinity" or "apriority," and its ability to unify the contradictions of love: it is both sensuous and spiritual, both freedom and necessity, both a moment and eternity, and so on (*E/O*,II, 61). The goal, affirms the Judge, is to "reach the point of seeing the aesthetical, the ethical and the religious as three great allies" (*E/O*,II, 150).

Second, in saying that the path from the aesthetic to the ethical is one of transfiguration, the Judge implicitly qualifies the very harmony he posits. In relation to love, it is marriage that has the courage to resolve the paradoxes of aesthetic reflection (*E/O*, II, 113), that does not fear anything, not even infidelity in the spouse (*E/O*,II, 121), and that unites sameness and change like the happy sound of purling water (*E/O*,II, 146-147). In short the harmony of the aesthetic and ethical spheres is achieved only when the aesthetic submits to the demands of the ethical and is mastered by it (*E/O*,II, 243). Exults the Judge: "duty comes as an old friend, an intimate, a confidant, whom the lovers mutually recognize in the deepest secret of their love" (*E/O*,II, 149).

This explanation leads to a final and decisive characteristic of the ethical transfiguration of the aesthetic. One of the Judge's favorite expressions for the relation of marriage to first love is the obscure phrase, "higher concentricity."[5] The primary meaning of this image is that it defies all mediation, for "no reflection molests it" (*E/O*,II, 48). Even more explicitly: "We have seen, then, how first love could come into relation with the ethical and the religious without the intervention of a reflection which would alter its nature, since it was merely drawn up into a higher concentricity, always in the sphere of immediacy" (E/O,II, 58). Thus the ethical vow of marriage will not destroy the immediacy of first love, provided that aesthetic immediacy really does submit to the ethical. Indeed, from the Judge's ethical point of view, it is aesthetic reflection that is the real threat to the immediacy of love and ethical resolution that alone is capable of preserving it through time.

Ethical resolution accomplishes the transfiguration of the aesthetic into the ethical. In relation to first love and the vow of marriage, resolution has a double effect: it enhances the aesthetic beauty of the marriage, and it "makes the individual free" (E/O,II, 95). Yet this freedom involves a negative element in relation to the aesthetic.

As the Judge sees it, there is no freedom at all in the aesthetic way of life. Freedom can be won only by an act of choosing oneself. Although it could be argued that some of the characters in volume I have chosen themselves (for example, the "unhappiest man"), any choice that results in abstraction of the self from concrete life is false, even suicidal (E/O,II, 235-236). In order for the choice of self to be ethical, argues the Judge, all mystical efforts to transcend the individual, historical self must be rejected:

> He on the other hand who chooses himself ethically chooses himself concretely as this definite individual, and he attains this concretion by the fact that this act of choice is identical with this act of repentance which sanctions the choice. The individual thus becomes conscious of himself as this definite individual, with these talents, these dispositions, these instincts, these passions, influenced by these definite surroundings, as this definite product of a definite environment. But being conscious of himself in this way, he assumes responsibility for all this. (E/O,II, 255)

In the Judge's view, only such an ethical choice of oneself as a definite, clearly defined self can constitute genuine self-consciousness. To choose oneself is to know oneself (E/O,II,

263). The self chooses itself as a particular self and no other self. This choice can be accomplished only by an act of repentance: "He repents himself back into himself, back into the family, back into the race, until he finds himself in God. Only on these terms can he choose himself" (*E/O*,II, 220). Thus ethical self-choice is a conscious repudiation of the abstraction and autonomy of the aesthetic stage. The aesthetic individual pursues self-fulfillment without regard to the demands of other individuals, social institutions, or God. To advance beyond the aesthetic, the individual must repent it: "for only when I choose myself as guilty do I choose myself absolutely" (*E/O*,II, 221). Doubt and despair constitute the way of repentance from the aesthetic to the ethical—doubt not as the first moment in a philosophical system but as "a despair of thought" itself, just as "despair is a doubt of the personality" (*E/O*,II, 215).

These statements about the act of choosing oneself, which all happen to be located in the first half of "Equilibrium," demonstrate none of the unqualified optimism of "Validity." The Judge's concern here is with the challenge and suffering involved in the ethical stage, dimensions not mentioned in his earlier discussion of the transfiguration of aesthetic immediacy. The aesthetic is seen not merely as naive immediacy but also as an indifference to self and to God, and therefore as that which must be repented. The choice of self is an encounter with "the eternal power itself," in which the self actually "receives itself" (*E/O*,II, 181): "It is a serious and significant moment when for an eternity one attaches oneself to an eternal power, when one receives oneself as a person whose memory no lapse of time shall efface, when in an eternal and unfailing sense one becomes aware of oneself as the person one is. And yet one can leave it alone!" (*E/O*,II, 210). The seriousness of this "instant of choice"[6] is the note on which "Equilibrium" opens, and it introduces the reader for the first time to the ethical meaning of the title of the work: either/or.

The phrase "either/or" is not at this point entirely new. In volume I, one of A's diapsalmata is a short "ecstatic essay" with the title "Either/Or." The point of that cryptic essay is that the eternal lies before rather than behind us and that therefore all human endeavor is in vain: whatever we do, we will regret it.[7] Thus the "successive dialectic in either/or" is to be rejected in favor of "the eternal dialectic here set forth" (*E/O*,I, 38). This aesthetic "eternal dialectic" repudiates what the Judge calls the "disjunctive" (*E/O*,II, 163) or successive element in either/or in favor of a synchronic leveling of all options in the name of futility. Thus the Judge, who believes that the either/or has "absolute significance," denounces A's frequent use of the term as a motto that is reduced to "one word" (*E/O*,II, 163), that is, to ethical meaninglessness, and he insists upon an either/or choice between righteousness and lust (*E/O*,II, 161, 163). There can be no compromise: "one either has to live aesthetically or one has to live ethically" (*E/O*,II, 172). Good and evil, he argues, stand in total opposition to one another, an "absolute contradiction" that will remain incomprehensible to the philosophical thought that deals in "relative differences" (*E/O*,II, 228). Moreover, the Judge believes that anyone who is capable of choosing between good and evil will choose the good (*E/O*,II, 172). To choose the good is to accept the absolute significance of the either/or. To deny that significance is de facto to consign oneself to a life lacking in self-consciousness, to condemn oneself to the path of "lust and base propensities and obscure passions and perdition" (*E/O*,II, 161).

The Judge as Dialectician

The disjunctive logic of either/or would appear to commit the Judge to a dialectic of contradiction. In all his discussions of choosing oneself, the emphasis is upon the absolute nature of that choice—there is no way for the self to choose itself only in part or relative to other selves. The failure to take responsibility for any aspect of the self means that one has not yet really accepted the ethical challenge. On these grounds, the Judge criticizes the aesthetic stage as an attempt to annul the contradiction inherent in the ethical either/or. He sees a parallel between that attempt and the philosophical doctrine of mediation of all oppositions. Such a mediation is impossible, he argues, if the person who does the mediating stands (with that which is to be mediated) within the relativity of history. A mediating dialectic involves "necessity," and necessity is possible only in logic, nature, or, the Judge concedes, the "world-historical process." But no necessity can invade the inwardness of the individual; there freedom rules (E/O,II, 174-180).[8] It is to this inevitable opposition in every either/or that the Judge attributes A's equivocations: he demonstrates "one of the sorry consequences of the fact that a man's nature cannot harmoniously reveal itself" (E/O,II, 166).

Nevertheless, the Judge does not rest content with mere oppositions. One example of the complexity of his thought occurs in his discussion of self-choice, where he remarks that choice must involve "two dialectical movements: that which is chosen does not exist and comes into existence with the choice; that which is chosen exists, otherwise there would not be a choice" (E/O,II, 219). In other words, one cannot choose to be a self that does not already exist as a possibility, and yet only with the choice of that possibility does it come into existence. This is one example of a paradoxical dialectic. Another is the Judge's comment on despair as an act of will: "One cannot despair at all without willing it, but to despair truly one must truly will it, but when one truly wills it one is truly beyond despair; when one has truly willed despair one has truly chosen that which despair chooses, that is, oneself in one's eternal validity" (E/O,II, 217).

In addition to these dialectics of contradiction and paradox, the Judge also implicitly affirms a dialectic of mediation. This is often demonstrated in "Validity," where he discusses the ethical transfiguration of the aesthetic: "the immediacy of first love perishes, yet it is not lost but lifted up into the collective knowledge of conjugal life."[9] Other formulas that imply a mediating dialectic are not hard to find: love is described as the unity of universal and particular (E/O,II, 91), and conjugal love is declared "a unity of more opposites" than first love (*E/O*,II, 98). These are only a few examples of the Judge's tendency to engage in the very sort of mediating thought that seems to be repudiated by the dialectic of either/or.

Even more striking, the Judge's analysis of "stages" (movements) within the aesthetic displays, for all his digressions, a miniature dialectical structure of the sort analyzed in the previous chapter. The Judge identifies three such movements, in the first of which personality is determined in a physical rather than a spiritual (or mental) sense.[10] Here the immediacy in which the individual lives is bodily health or physical beauty, and both are immediately given to the particular individual. In the second movement, the conditions of enjoyment are wealth, glory, high station, and even romantic love (*E/O*,II, 187). The defining characteristic is that all these conditions come from outside the individual, from social relations, thereby determining the personality by an external immediacy that is, relative to the first movement, mediated.[11] The third and final movement is the sublation of the previous two. Here the Judge places talent, for talent is a phenomenon in which the condition of enjoyment is both immediately given to the individual and requires careful cultivation if it is to be realized (*E/O*,II, 187). This cultivation is a form of mediation, for the self submits to social discipline in order to develop its gift. Thus this third movement is, dialectically, a mediated immediacy.

With this, the Judge announces that he has completed his outline of "the territory of the aesthetical view of life" (*E/O*,II, 195). He does not connect his own analysis with the text of volume I, although the appropriateness of his designations for Don Juan (immediate physical), the characters in *symparanekromenoi* lectures (socially constituted), and Johannes the seducer (cultivated individuality), are evident. Neither does he seem to be aware of or to care about the dialectical logic of his threefold analysis. Indeed, no sooner does he complete it than he wanders off on a long digression about despair and decides somewhat after the fact that despair should really be designated the final stage of the aesthetic, beyond the other three (E/O,II, 198).[12] The impression is thereby given that the Judge is inclined to think about problems dialectically, but that he lacks the desire or the rigor to do so systematically.

Judge William's identification of movements within the ethical stage is, by comparison, very brief, but it follows the same pattern as those in the aesthetic:

> You now will have perceived that the ethical individual has gone through in the course of his life the stages which earlier we showed to be distinctive stages. In the course of his life he will develop the personal, the civic, the religious virtues, and his life and its progress consist in the fact that he constantly translates himself from one stage to another. So soon as a man thinks that one of these stages is sufficient and that a person may venture one-sidedly to concentrate upon it, that man has not chosen himself ethically but has overlooked the importance either of isolation or of continuity, and above all has not apprehended that the truth consists in the identity of the two. (E/O,II, 266)

This ethical progression from personal to civic to religious virtues recapitulates the logic by which the aesthetic stage was said to involve a development from particular (personal) to social (civic) to individual (religious). Thus the aesthetic and ethical stages share a formal dialectic of immediacy, mediation, and mediated immediacy.

This dialectical structure cannot, however, be correlated with the literary structure of volume II. No sooner does the Judge complete his comments on the movements within each stage than he shifts the focus and tone of "Equilibrium" altogether. Early on, he had remarked that its purpose was to examine the dynamics of choosing, in contrast to "Validity," which deals with the "harmony" in human nature (E/O,II, 181). Now, however, he returns to the theme of harmony (and, by so doing, finally justifies the title, "Equilibrium Between the Aesthetical and the Ethical in the Composition of the Personality"). It is to this question that the last major section of the letter is devoted (*E/O*,II, 270-334). Here the necessity for choosing either the aesthetic or the ethical is replaced by the question of how they are combined in several areas of life. But this combination is no dialectical *Aufhebung* of the movement of transfiguration in "Validity" and the movement of opposition in the early part of "Equilibrium." On the contrary, in this section the Judge simply explores a few practical applications of his theory about the ethical transfiguration of aesthetic immediacy (*E/O*,II, 281).

The three practical situations that the Judge discusses are vocation, marriage, and friendship. Vocation, he argues, is the ethical transfiguration of talent, which would otherwise amount to no more than egoism (*E/O*,II, 296-298). Similarly, the ethical state of marriage is said to "ennoble" the aesthetic immediacy of love (*E/O*,II, 307). After a digression on the differences between men and women, the Judge defines friendship in terms of the duty that friends have to reveal themselves to each other, to translate the particularity of their individual lives into the universal through the medium of communication (*E/O*,II, 327, 334). Indeed, all three of these concrete situations are presented as part of an argument for the ethical universalization of aesthetic particularity. However, a systematic dialectical development by which this transformation comes about is nowhere to be found. The Judge is clearly attracted to dialectical thought, and yet the precise dialectic that governs his thinking is very difficult to discern.

The problem here is that of consistency: one moment the Judge defends the dialectics of opposition and paradox, the next he seems somewhat arbitrarily to employ a dialectics of mediation. On the level of ethical rhetoric, he is an adamant critic of Hegel, yet his actual thought process frequently follows a pattern that appears to be an an almost absent-mindedly Hegelian logic.[13] Since structural analysis has failed to illuminate this inconsistency, it is worth asking if some other method of interpretation might not be more helpful at this point.

Interpreters have dealt with the inconsistency in the Judge's position in different ways. Perhaps the simplest path is to try to ignore it. Since his real contribution to Kierkegaard's theory of stages is the concept of choosing oneself, the problem of the Judge's interest in conventional morality and mediation might be left to the side without impairing one's understanding of the ethical stage as such. This approach to understanding the Judge is exemplified by Johannes Climacus, who dismisses the Judge's traditional side as "distractions of an abundant thought-content" (*CUP*, 227).[14]

Another path is *ad hominem* argumentation, much in the manner that the Judge argues against A. His reiterated charges of equivocation (*E/O*,II, 169), exploitation of others (*E/O*,II, 238), and antisocial reserve (*E/O*,II, 338) are too numerous to recount (one especially sustained barrage is *E/O*,II, 200-208), and their effect is to suggest that ideas can best be judged by the character of the people who espouse them. Following this line of reasoning, it is worth recalling the observation of Victor Eremita that the Judge "concealed a more significant inwardness under a somewhat commonplace exterior" (*E/O*,I, 4). Victor's comment suggests that the Judge's inconsistency can be attributed to a profound but unconscious tension within his personality. This strategy has attracted a fair number of interpreters. One scholar has branded the Judge's "touching picture" of happy marriage "false to the core," on the grounds that it does not reflect the reality of his own life.[15] To another, the Judge's marriage is "suspect," and he is personally a "simple-minded and soft-hearted" thinker who lacks that very seriousness which he so frequently demands of A.[16] Such judgments recall A's own caustic remark: "There was a man whose chatter certain circumstances made it necessary for me to listen to. At every opportunity he was ready with a little philosophical lecture, a very tiresome harangue" (*E/O*,I, 295).[17] Even a scholar who resists such *ad hominem* criticisms of the Judge likens his literary style, in relation to A's, to the style of Polonius in relation to that of Hamlet.[18]

Of greater relevance to this study are those interpretations that seek a more systematic or theoretical explanation for the Judge's inconsistency. On the relation of the ethical stage to the aesthetic, one scholar has pointed out that the Judge fails to understand the necessary "collapse of immediacy presupposed by all irony" and that his claims for the ethical transfiguration of immediacy therefore remain abstract and artificial.[19] Another argues that his ethical program reveals a self-contradiction between his call for radical self-choice and the utter conventionality of the traditional moral values he espouses.[20]

One popular way to explain the Judge's inconsistencies is in terms of his obviously problematical attitude toward the religious stage.[21] In spite of his demand for repentance before God (*E/O*,II, 220), the Judge treats the religious as an element *within* the ethical. In a word, he domesticates it, cuts it down from an infinite and inward movement to one that is finite and almost external. Although this attitude surfaces in many passages, several examples will suffice. In speaking of providence, the Judge maintains that "one believes also in the existence of a providence, and the soul reposes securely in this assurance, and yet it would not occur to one to try to permeate every accidental circumstance with this thought or to become convinced of this faith every minute" (*E/O*,II, 262). In contrast with the actual religious point of view (to be discussed in later chapters), this statement is striking for its *lack* of passion. One reason the Judge can be so sanguine about the religious demand is that he believes that a major religious problem is actually resolved within the ethical stage. That problem, in a word, is sin; and, despite his Lutheran education, the Judge affirms that sin and frailty are "regarded as overcome" by ethical resolution,[22] a view that also conflicts with the religious perspective presented in other works (especially *The Sickness unto Death*). Finally, the Judge concludes *Either/Or* with a short sermon that, he says, was written by a friend of his. Although he insists that "Ultimatum" confirms his own views, its central theme is that the only choice we have is "the choice of being nothing before God, or the eternal torture of beginning over again every instant, but without being able to begin" (*E/O*,II, 348). It is hard to imagine a sentiment less like the Judge's own appeals to God as the ground and guarantor of ethical self-choice and stable, traditional, moral relationships.

The Ethical Dialectic of Inwardness

As in the previous chapter, the theme of the inner/outer relation provides a means for grasping the logic that underlies the Judge's apparent inconsistencies. It is a theme that is central to his own concerns and one that has been somewhat obscured by a misleading line of interpretation originally suggested by Johannes Climacus.

To begin with the most obvious and constant refrain: the Judge frequently states that the aesthetic is a mode of externality and that the ethical alone qualifies as inwardness. The eternity claimed by romantic love, he argues, "was built upon the temporal . . . in a medium which was entirely external" (*E/O*,II, 28). In contrast, the ethical ideal of conjugal love really does have "the characteristic of eternity" (*E/O*,II, 33), an eternity gained through the movement of faith: "Conjugal love possesses this movement, for in the resolution the movement is turned inward" (*E/O*,II, 98). The Judge believes that "the main point in marriage is inwardness, which can neither be seen nor pointed out—but of this the precise expression is love" (*E/O,*II, 155). This conviction undergirds his argument against trying to justify marriage rationally. It is not that he opposes the use of reason; rather, he views appeals to the objective benefits of marriage (it fosters maturity, promotes child-bearing, and establishes stable homes) as an implicit denial of the claim that "marriage has, of course, its teleology in itself" (*E/O*,II, 63ff.). In discussing the difficulties that must be faced in marriage, the Judge distinguishes between those that are internal and those that are external. Significantly, the internal challenges arise in the actual relationship, whereas those that are merely external are encountered in drama or some other form of art (*E/O*,II, 124-129). Even more to the point, in marriage an "individual is not fighting with external foes but fights with himself, fights out love from within him. . . . Conjugal love does not come with any outward sign" *E/O*,II, 142). In "Equilibrium," there is a much-quoted passage in which the Judge comments that "he who lives aesthetically sees only possibilities everywhere . . . whereas he who lives ethically sees tasks everywhere" (*E/O*,II, 256). His subsequent discussion makes clear that aesthetic involvement in possibilities is a matter of being oriented toward externalities, which constantly change, while the ethical orientation toward actual tasks results from a primary commitment to holding fast to the inward and constant self: "for in the ethical realm there is never any question about the external but only about the internal" (*E/O*,II, 269).

The impression that the inner and outer are opposed to each other, and that the inner alone has ethical validity, is strengthened by the Judge's comments on history. The "historical factor" in conjugal love, he maintains, is due to the necessity for persevering in the face of conflict, in the knowledge that "every little act of self-control is very much more commensurable with the infinity of love" than is the mere wishing of first love.[23] In another passage, however, the Judge remarks that each individual has an "inward work," and "neither history nor world history can take that from him" (*E/O*,II, 179). Is history, then, a matter of internality or externality? Ultimately, it is both: "As it is related to the individual life, history is of two kinds: external and internal. They are currents of two sorts with opposite movements" (*E/O*,II, 136).

The Judge appeals to this distinction in order to explain the difference between aesthetic conquest, which is the self-forgetfulness of external history, and ethical possession, which is internal, self-conscious stewardship. Likewise: "Internal history is the only true history; but true history contends with that which is the life principle of history, that is, with time. . . . Whenever the internal process of blossoming in the individual has not yet begun and the individual is shut, there can only be external history" (*E/O*,II, 137). Furthermore, it is in external history that romantic love has its only hope, for without an external opportunity, it could never conquer the beloved. In contrast, conjugal love "begins with possession and acquires inward history" (*E/O*,II, 140), for it begins with the wedding vows and then develops through time. It seems evident that the aesthetic is the external, whereas the ethical constitutes inwardness.

In other passages, however, aesthetic concealment is praised as a vital ingredient of marriage: "If conjugal love is a genuine first love, it has something hidden about it, it does not wish to display itself, does not devote its life to the ostentation of family visits" (*E/O*,II, 105). Here it would appear to be the romantic-aesthetic element that gives depth and inwardness to the conjugal-ethical relation. Conversely, the Judge also argues that significance is often revealed through insignificant externals. He extols marriage as a "lowly incognito" that, while seeming utterly prosaic, really "concealed a poet" (*E/O*,II, 311). He admits that the universal does not actually exist anywhere "as such" but that consciousness must energetically seek it in the particular (*E/O*,II, 334). Here the ethical task appears to be turned toward externality rather than inwardness, or toward an inwardness that can be identified only in externals. This is most evident in the Judge's demands for self-revelation and candor in marriage (*E/O*,II, 100, 114-119, 164). This tension between the ethical as inwardness and the ethical as meaning-in-externals is particularly striking when the Judge affirms that conjugal love has "movements [that] are not outward but inward" just over a page after remarking that "he who loves has lost himself and forgotten himself in the other" (*E/O*,II, 112-113).

The ambiguity of the relation between inner and outer in the ethical stage appears again in relation to the question of artistic expression, a subject already familiar from volume I. On the one hand, the languages of art (for example, drama) express themselves in external symbols, and for this reason they deal with external rather than internal history, since only external history can be externally represented (*E/O*,II, 137).

On the other hand, even these representations are not adequate to the aesthetic. Since all forms of artistic expression are subject to the destructive effects of time, the only way to represent the aesthetic truly is "by living it" (*E/O*,II, 139). Conversely, no sooner has the Judge denied that conjugal love can have "any outward sign" than he claims that it is "capable of rejuvenating itself by means of these outward signs" (*E/O*,II, 142, 144). It is this sort of affirmation of the external that renders questionable Climacus's claim that the external is merely "neutral" for the ethical point of view.[24]

It is unlikely that all of these apparent inconsistencies can be explained as either paradox or irony. There is, however, a way out of the dilemma, a way that attempts not to explain it away but to illuminate it by reference to the Judge's philosophy of transformation. Throughout his rambling discourses, a constant if merely implicit theme is change: the aesthetic is transfigured by the ethical; the self is transformed by choosing to be a particular self in its particular situation. Thus the Judge's talk about inwardness and externality can be interpreted in terms that are less static than his own analyses often seem. In short, what I have discussed as an inconsistency between the emphasis on inwardness and that on externality can be seen in terms of two distinct processes.

Corresponding to the notion of transfiguration, the ethical can be related to the aesthetic as a process of internalization. The Judge sometimes comments that the task of marriage is to internalize the external, whether external obstacles to marriage or external duty (*E/O*,II, 126, 151). At one point in "Validity," he offers this theoretical formulation: "In the resolution is posited another thing, but at the same time this other is posited as overcome; in the resolution this other is posited as an inward other, inasmuch as even the outward is visible by means of the reflection in the inward experience" (*E/O*,II, 100).[25] This "other" is not joined in a dialectical *Aufhebung*; it is conquered, the passive object of a process of internalization. At the same time, however, it is precisely this internalization that renders the external visible. Without the "reflection in the inward experience," the other would never enter into meaningful relationship with the inward self.

Conversely, the "prime requisite" for the aesthetic validity of marriage is the preservation of mystery through externalization: "Inwardly this prime requisite may be expressed by its polar opposite: open-heartedness, candor, publicity on the largest conceivable scale; for this is the life-principle of love, and here in the intimate life secretiveness is its death" (*E/O*,II, 106). Here the very survival of the ethical relationship of marriage depends upon its ability to externalize itself, to reveal the love that is its inward foundation "on the largest conceivable scale." This idea recalls the Judge's much-repeated claim that the key to marriage is self-revelation (although, in this context, that revelation extends beyond the conjugal pair to the entire society). Thus the inconsistency about whether the inner or the outer is to have hegemony in the ethical stage can be seen as the tension between two processes—internalization and externalization.

The way in which those two processes are related can be further illuminated by a passage in "Validity":

> First love is strong, stronger than the whole world, but the instant doubt occurs to it it is annihilated. . . . Marital love is armed; for by the resolution the attention is not directed merely towards the environment, but the will is directed towards itself, towards the inward man. And now I invert everything and say: the aesthetic does not lie in the immediate but in the acquired—but marriage is precisely the immediacy which has mediacy in itself, the infinity which has finiteness in itself, the eternal which has the temporal in itself. (*E/O*,II, 96)

It is this inversion that provides the key to the Judge's dialectical thinking.[26] Marital love has the strength to internalize first love, but that very internalization also results in the aesthetic externalization of love. When marriage conquers the immediacy of first love by internalizing it, it also submits itself to the transfigured aesthetic and thus to the process of externalization. This is what the Judge means by such Hegelian formulations as "the immediacy which has mediacy in itself, the infinity which has finiteness in itself, the eternal which has the temporal in itself." The internal bears the external within itself, and the external cannot survive without the internal. The relation between them is less one of struggle than one of reciprocity, a dialectical reciprocity in which inner and outer are neither a dichotomy nor a unity but can be understood rather in terms of mutual interdependence.

The concept of reciprocity provides the necessary context for understanding the Judge's apparent inconsistencies. It makes intelligible his desire to see the aesthetic transfigured in the ethical. At the same time, it illuminates his rejection of the aesthetic as a mode of contradiction, for contradiction and reciprocity are antithetical to one another. The commitment to reciprocity can also account for his use of a dialectic of mediation one moment and one of opposition the next, as well as the thinness of his occasional attempts at paradox. As Kierkegaard observes in *The Concept of Irony*, in a dialectic of reciprocity there is "no moment of unity" and "the true moment of duality is essentially lacking, since the relationship exhausts itself in mere reciprocity" (*CI*, 73). It is this sort of reciprocity that characterizes the ethical affirmation/negation of the aesthetic, and also renders the ethical position of Judge William incapable of the intensity of religious passion and paradox.

"VARIOUS OBSERVATIONS ABOUT MARRIAGE"

Perhaps because it is, by comparison with volume II of *Either/Or*, such a brief text, "Various Observations about Marriage" offers a means for further clarification of the ethical stage. This is particularly true for the question of a possible structure, the dialectical nature of the Judge's thinking, and the issue of the ethical use of religious language.

The Ethical as Negation

The text of "Various Observations" opens with a brief introduction in which the Judge announces that marriage is his primary concern. A long (over half the essay) section follows, in which the Judge offers his rebuttals to putative objections to marriage. Whereas he responds to and criticizes A directly in volume II of *Either/Or*, here he expresses himself in essay form; presumably he was not present at the banquet described in "In Vino Veritas."[27]

The Judge directs his first rebuttal to the objection to love as such (*SLW*, 123): "If the objection is to be fundamental, it ought in aiming against marriage to aim first against love." In his opinion, a depraved man's objection would elicit less pity from an audience than that of a youth who had skipped over the stage of erotic experience to that of reflection. Such a young man would, of course, be very unhappy, for he would be committed to the impossible task of thinking the erotic. More precisely, rather than receiving love as the miracle it is, he would understand it as the choice of a particular object as lovable. This, says the Judge, is not possible. It is best just to let "the deity" select one's beloved and then be grateful, avoiding all "senseless critical discourse" on the reasons for choosing one rather than another (*SLW*, 124). Love is a miracle that is present "as soon as God exists for consciousness," but it is paralyzed by any attempt of reflection to explain it in terms of its consequences (*SLW*, 125-126).

The Judge then goes on to what he calls another aspect of the matter. Commenting that love is "commonly only too much extolled," he turns his attention to how "the gallant's flattering adoration of the sex ends with insult" (*SLW*, 126). Far more Christian, the Judge counters, is to affirm simply that woman is just as good as man. The Judge is not given to criticism—after eight years of marriage, he still has no definite idea, "in the aesthetic sense," what his wife looks like (*SLW*, 127-128). Neither is he inclined to glamorize woman, unless in jest, for marriage indeed makes men into humorists.

Nevertheless, the Judge's prolix defense of woman often seems to indulge in the very sort of gallantry that he criticizes. The Judge asserts that his wife's "tender glance" would recall him to life even if God did not (*SLW*, 132)! He praises woman for having a beauty that grows with the years, for manifesting in maternal love genuine self-sacrifice, for being even more beautiful in sorrow than in happiness, and for providing husbands with earthly happiness (*SLW*, 142). Such judgments reveal a touch of condescension not unlike that found in Victor's defense of gallantry.

The Judge admits that woman is the weaker sex and can appear queer or even comic. But he mounts several arguments aimed at diffusing the force of these criticisms. First, such a fate befalls only a single woman. When she takes her proper place at a man's side, a woman will stand as firm as he; indeed, they will both stand more firmly together than could either of them alone. Second, woman appears weak, queer, or comic only when viewed aesthetically, not as wife and mother. Her capacity for endurance is actually greater than that of man, but a wife will often appear weaker than her husband because she uses her strength to support him (*SLW*, 143). Finally, the Judge concludes this discussion of the objections raised against woman with further reflections on gallantry, which he calls the mother tongue of irony, and with the observation that all such objections fail as explanations of human existence, for they ultimately deny any positive being to woman and treat her negatively as "an occasion for awakening the unhappy lover's ideality" (*SLW*, 146).

This last passage makes obvious the extent to which the Judge's argument follows the sequence of objections to love and marriage at the banquet in "In Vino Veritas." He begins by rebutting objections to love as such, assuming that such a position would be expressed by a young man. However, the Judge's defense consists in an *ad hominem* argument against the young man; at no point does he deal with the substance of the young man's claim that love is a self-contradictory concept. Next the Judge addresses criticisms of woman, and here again his understanding of the objection seems fuzzy. He thinks that her detractors consider her failing to be weakness, whereas in fact they are critical of her self-contradictory nature. Of Victor's main point—that man is responsible for woman's foibles—the Judge has no inkling. He does, however, focus his rebuttal on the concept of gallantry, which he says "ends in insult," and which he conflates with the attempt to see woman's significance as a negative occasion for man's self-realization (which corresponds to the phase of sorcery in "In Vino Veritas"). In short, however "beautiful" the Judge's defense of woman may appear to some interpreters,[28] it stands in the text as a rebuttal to several of the speeches at the banquet by one who has not really understood them. In structure, his ethical reply follows the pattern of the aesthetic argument in form but not in substance.

This impression is confirmed when the Judge turns from his defense of woman to a long discussion of the relation between love and the resolution of marriage: "Love penetrates the whole of life, and it does this in marriage" (*SLW*, 146). At the opposite end of the Judge's spectrum is the seducer, who realizes that love is "a thing he cannot bestow upon himself . . . but the demoniacal spirit within him causes him with demoniacal resolution to resolve to make the enjoyment as short, and in this way, so he thinks, as intense as possible."[29] The Judge is speaking here of what he calls love's "critical moment," which he had earlier described as that moment when love's immediacy falters and it "cannot therefore come to its own aid" (*SLW*, 108). At this moment two possibilities exist: either the resolution of marriage is present, and it takes over when immediacy fails; or it is not, and the lover refuses to let go of immediacy, thereby resolving not upon marriage but upon seduction. Now, as the Judge returns to this theme, he stipulates that one must actually make the demoniacal resolution to qualify as a seducer; without it, one simply "insults love; he is not evil enough to form a demoniacal resolution, but neither is he good enough to form the good resolution" (*SLW*, 147).

Rather than examine the seducer's objections to marriage directly, the Judge next appears to digress with a discussion of the type of aesthete who fails to make any resolution whatever, using Goethe's self-portrayal in *Aus meinem Leben* as his example. This digression, however, does in fact deal with the essence of the defense of deception put forward by Johannes. The Judge criticizes Goethe for his rejection of resolution in favor of reflection: he is a "poetic figure" who "is not a seducer, he does not become a married man, he becomes . . . a connoisseur" (*SLW*, 149-150). With woman, as with religion, Goethe avoids all contact, and his negative attitude is amply reflected in his artistic creations, in which femininity is dishonored. But this self-distancing, the Judge argues, is a poetizing and therefore a deception:

> So then whenever a life-relationship is about to overwhelm him he must remove it to a distance by poetizing it. . . . What does it mean to poetize a life-relationship? . . . To poetize an actual life-relationship by the aid of distance . . . is neither more nor less than to falsify the ethical element in it and to stamp upon it the counterfeit impression of a casual happening and a mere problem for thought. . . . Among criminals one often finds this talent for poetizing, i.e. for viewing at a distance in poetic outline the actual life-relationship. (*SLW*, 152-153)

The Judge's attack on the poetizing of the seducer concludes his defense of woman and confirms that the only structure to be found in his thought process is a vicarious one. Just as the text of *Either/Or*, II, takes up issues raised by A but has no clear structure of its own, here also the Judge replies in turn to the positions of the young man, Victor Eremita, and Johannes the seducer. To the charge that love is self-contradictory, he answers obliquely that it is better understood as a miracle. To the criticism of woman as self-contradictory, whether in the sense of gallantry or that of sorcery, he defends her integrity, although again in an almost self-defeating way, for his argument is that she has integrity only at the side of a man. (This requirement can be distinguished from Victor's claim—that woman is made self-contradictory by man—by the Judge's insistence that woman's need for man is reciprocated by man's need for woman.) Omitting the positions of Constantin and the ladies' tailor, the Judge concludes by attacking poetic deception as criminal, which is a direct reference to the view defended by Johannes the seducer. Thus the Judge illustrates in this essay that the ethical stage is a reaction against the aesthetic, a negative position that can be grasped only in relation to that which it repudiates.

The Ethical Dialectic of Reciprocity

As in *Either/Or*, it is within the context of a dialectic of reciprocity that the negative position of the ethical can most adequately be understood. In "Various Observations," that dialectic is illustrated by the Judge's analysis of ethical resolution. In the defense of marriage and woman, the notion of resolution appears as that which must be united with love in a "synthesis" in order to result in a marriage (*SLW*, 114). Yet resolution is not without its logical difficulties:

> The difficulty is this: love or falling in love is utterly immediate, marriage is a resolution; yet at the same time falling in love must be taken up into marriage or into the resolution, the will to marry. That is to say, the most immediate of all things shall also be the freest resolution, that which because of its immediacy is so inexplicable that it must be ascribed to a god, shall also take place by the power of reflection, and therefore result in a resolution. Moreover, the one must not follow after the other, the resolution must not come sneaking along behind, but it must take place at once, both must be together in the moment of decision. If reflection has not exhausted thought, then I form no resolution, I act either by the inspiration of genius or by force of a whim.[30]

The dilemma of resolution is that is must occur both simultaneously with and after reflection. It must, in dialectical terms, be both immediate (like falling in love) and mediated (reflection is "exhausted"). Resolution, then, is like a mediated immediacy, a moment of decision that takes up into itself the opposing poles in the contradiction between love and thought. Yet the Judge does not underestimate the difficulty of this concept: "the decisive battle," he writes, "is to be fought over the question of "how this immediacy (love) can find a corresponding expression in an immediacy which is reached through reflection," or, as he puts it later, "how the reflection which is presupposed in the resolution can reach the point where it coincides with the immediacy of love."[31]

Nowhere, however, does the Judge actually fight that decisive battle and explain how such a dialectical union of immediacy and reflection might occur. Although he can list a number of advantages to the positive resolution to marry over the negative resolution not to marry (*SLW*, 113-114), he has no explanation for why some choose one and not the other. The Judge always seems to beg the hard questions. In the end, all he can say about the preservation of the immediacy of love in the resolution to marry is that it is a miracle (*SLW*, 155). This *deus ex machina* type of explanation is expanded a few pages later, when he adds that "reflection is brought to a conclusion in faith, which is precisely anticipation of the ideal infinity in the form of resolution." Thus the immediacy of resolution is "a religious life-view constructed upon ethical postulates." Only religion, argues the Judge, is recognized by love as having its own immediacy "of equally noble birth" (*SLW*, 159). On this view, however, religion is reduced to the role of "a supersensible guarantor of the validity of this moral position."[32]

Actually, then, two difficulties cloud the Judge's concept of ethical resolution. One is that it claims to unite immediacy and reflection, but there is insufficient dialectical development to affirm that this union is really, as the Judge implies, a mediated immediacy. On the contrary, the relation between immediacy and resolution within resolution, like the Judge's other dialectical efforts, at worst remains a contradiction and at best achieves some sort of reciprocity. The second difficulty is that the Judge attempts to escape from the first difficulty by appealing to such religious categories as miracle, faith, and a religious life-view. There is nothing in his view of religion, however, that helps to clear up the dialectical confusion in his analysis of resolution.

The ambivalence that the Judge feels toward the religious manifests itself in yet another apparent inconsistency. Resolution needs the religious in order to triumph over temptation: one must "either let go of love . . . or believe in God. Thus the miracle of love is elevated to the purely religious miracle, the absurdity of love to a divine understanding with the absurdity of religion" (*SLW*, 160). Here the primary relationship is between the individual and God, for it is the religious resolution that preserves the ethical resolution to marry. But the Judge is not willing to grant to the religious the sort of hegemony over the ethical that is implied by such primacy. If he were, then he would not condemn one who is a religious exception to the ethical as an instance of pride and abstraction from humanity (*SLW*, 169). Whether the so-called exception presumptuously disdains the universal or humbly confesses an inability to realize it, in either case there is a paucity of experience and a failure to comprehend real life and people, and so justification of any such position is impossible. Indeed, only after having fulfilled the ethical, after having married and loved life and enjoyed marriage, could a person become a religious exception (*SLW*, 172-173). Such a change would involve the most intense misery, for language, the universal, could never express it, and therefore all justification would remain a private affair between the individual and God (*SLW*, 175). Since the religious exception would stand above the universal, language could not even offer to such a person a private certainty that he is, in fact, a *religious* exception to the ethical (*SLW*, 177).

Once again, the alternative to accusing the Judge of mere inconsistency on the relation of the ethical to the religious is here, as for the relation of the ethical to the aesthetic, a dialectic of reciprocity. According to that dialectic, the religious preserves (and thus validates) the ethical, but at the same time it is suspect to the Judge on the grounds that it also negates or at least qualifies the ethical. This positive/negative relation is never understood in terms of either a clear duality or a higher unity.

The claim that the Judge thinks according to a pattern of dialectical reciprocity receives some support from his comments on the relationship he enjoys with his wife. Just as "In Vino Veritas" transposes the inner/outer dialectic of *Either/Or*, I, into a dialectic of self and other, "Various Observations" ignores the question of inner and outer in favor of the themes of love and marriage as relationships. The Judge has more to say about his wife in this essay than in the two long letters, perhaps because one purpose of the essay is to communicate what he "cannot say to her directly" (*SLW*, 103). Such a confession is striking from a man who believes that marriage must be built upon self-revelation and who sentimentally applauds his wife as co-author of the essay. Perhaps the Judge limits his self-revelations to telling his wife how pretty the young mothers in church appear to him (*SLW*, 139-140). This, from a husband who admits that he never thinks about his wife's own aesthetic appeal (*SLW*, 127-128), would hardly seem to be a formula for a happy marriage! What all these comments reveal is that the Judge has very little sensitivity to his wife as an individual, a person who is distinct from him and who has her own views and values and independent worth. She exists for him only in terms of their reciprocal relationship, a relationship in which he depends upon her in order to be a "genuine man," that is, a man who is married, who is a father, who is the head and defender of the home, and so on (*SLW*, 101). Their relationship is not only reciprocal; it is, from his ethical point of view, completely instrumental. It is only the context of reciprocity that saves this instrumental view of relationships from degenerating into a solipsism not unlike the aesthetic mentality.

The Structure of the Ethical Stage

It is easy to see why so many interpreters treat *Either/Or* and *Stages on Life's Way* singly or separately, without trying to relate them systematically to one another. Yet that procedure cannot be justified on the grounds that the first two parts of *Stages on Life's Way* ("In Vino Veritas" and "Various Observations") are "essentially a repetition of *Either/Or*."[33] On the contrary, although the later work can clarify a number of important issues raised by the earlier, it does so only within the context of stating their differences, which, Johannes Climacus notwithstanding, are far from obvious (*CUP*, 253).

One difference is that the dialectic in *Either/Or* is primarily a dialectic of inner and outer, whereas both "In Vino Veritas" and "Various Observations" are more concerned with the relation between self and other. This difference is a question of degree rather than kind, since each theme appears as a minor theme within the other. The two works do reveal parallel dialectical structures in the aesthetic stage and similar characteristics in the ethical, so it seems reasonable to conclude that the inner/outer and self/other categories are *formally* interchangeable in the aesthetic and ethical stages. Thus the aesthete seeks contradiction between inner and outer and opposition between self and other. In contrast, Judge William is committed to reconciliation of inner and outer and reciprocity between self and other.

A second difference involves the attitude toward religion. In *Either/Or*, II, the Judge remains quite sanguine about religious categories. They bolster his ethical position comfortably, and the only discordant note is the radical claim in "Ultimatum" that humans are nothing before God, a claim that the Judge presumably does not understand. In "Various Observations," however, the Judge is aware of the tension between the ethical and the religious. In his discussion of the religious exception, a defensiveness toward the religious emerges that shows greater self-consciousness about the limitations of his own position than do the naive statements in *Either/Or*, II. This discussion helps to clarify the dialectical relation between those two stages, which, like that between the aesthetic and the ethical, comprises both positive and negative elements.

The extent to which the ethical must be understood as a response to aesthetic contradiction is also clarified in "Various Observations," and in such a way as to illustrate a third difference between the two texts. In *Either/Or*, II, the Judge addresses A directly, and his argument for the ethical style of life is cast in part as a critique of aesthetic values and of the aesthete's character. On this point, "Various Observations" shows less self-consciousness rather than more, for the Judge unwittingly responds to speeches (that he has not heard) in the order in which they were delivered. The irony is that his defense of marriage somewhat undermines the integrity of his own position, for it is loosely structured according to the dialectic of aesthetic contradiction—the very dialectic that he is trying to repudiate—and he is totally unaware of that fact.

By far the most significant and problematic difference, at least for a structural analysis, is the change in the role of resolution. In *Either/Or*, II, the ethical affirmation of the aesthetic is portrayed as a transfiguration, while the negative relation is argued in terms of ethical resolution and the either/or choice that it requires. Here resolution represents the negative moment within the dialectic of reciprocity. In "Various Observations," the rebuttal of the aesthetic position consists in the Judge's defense of marriage and woman, and resolution plays a different role, for it is defined as the unity of immediacy and reflection. In terms of formal structure alone, this means that resolution now affirms or transfigures the elements of aesthetic contradiction, whereas previously it had negated them.

The result of all this confusion is a fitting irony: although Judge William's jargon and efforts at systematic analysis give the appearance of a Hegelian thinker at work, in fact his essays resist systematic analysis. More than any of the other pseudonyms, Judge William seems to be Kierkegaard's parody of Hegelian system building, for he is forever starting dialectical analyses and then leaving them in an incomplete or superficial form.

The simplest procedure, therefore, is to treat the ethical as a transition between the aesthetic and the religious rather than as a stage in its own right.[34] Nevertheless, I would like to suggest a possible systematic interpretation of the ethical stage as a dialectic of reciprocity. Such an interpretation helps to emphasize certain key elements in the Judge's position, elements that draw attention to the complex relation of ethical reciprocity to both aesthetic contradiction and religious paradox. It also helps to account for both the traditional and the existential dimensions in the Judge's thought. Thus the ethical can receive—in this systematic form—a more articulated representation within an analysis of the entire theory of stages (see the Conclusion). Although the dialectic I am proposing for the ethical is clearly *not* discernible in the texts in the way that it is in works dealing with the aesthetic (Chapter Two), it is, I believe, in accord with the spirit and substance of the Judge's point of view.

The rough schematization I wish to suggest is confined to the level of dialectical movements (see Chart 3). In the in-itself movement, there is a unity that is relatively undisturbed by the negative power of reflection. This is represented in *Either/Or*, II, by the Judge's naive proposal that the ethical can simply transfigure the aesthetic contradictions into higher forms in which the inner and outer become commensurable with one another. There is a corresponding element in "Various Observations," for there the Judge frequently makes equally naive statements about marriage (especially about his own marriage). These statements serve to posit a dialectic of aesthetic-ethical reciprocity, even while they implicitly negate aesthetic contradiction and deception. Together they constitute the in-itself movement within the for-itself stage (the ethical).

The for-itself movement of reciprocity explicitly negates that initial harmony. Here the opposition between the aesthetic and the ethical comes out into the open, especially in the demand that every self must choose to be itself in its concrete relationships. This theme pervades all of the Judge's writing and is rightly considered the key element in the ethical stage. It is both a negative element within the ethical—it stands in

CHART 3.

The Ethical as a Stage

EITHER/OR, II	"VARIOUS OBSERVATIONS"
A. Incommensurability (aesthetic contradiction) transfigured into commensurability	A. Interdependent selves and communication in marriage simply presupposed

RECIPROCITY IN-ITSELF:
SIMPLE HARMONY OF THE AESTHETIC
AND THE ETHICAL POSITED

B. Incommensurability (aesthetic deception) opposed by ethical resolution	B. Self must resolve to be related to the other

RECIPROCITY FOR-ITSELF:
HARMONY WITH AESTHETIC
CONTRADICTION NEGATED

C. Self-revelation: self must strive to make the incommensurable commensurable	C. Self chooses itself as distinct from and dependent upon the other

RECIPROCITY IN-AND-FOR-ITSELF:
AESTHETIC CONTRADICTION INTERNALIZED
AS MOMENT IN ETHICAL SELF-REVELATION

opposition to the naive harmony posited in reciprocity in-itself—and it also develops the ethical in its role as the negation of the aesthetic, a role that is expressed by the ethical "either/or" and that gives to the ethical stage its character as a dialectical transition from the aesthetic to the religious.

The opposition between these two movements is overcome in self-revelation. This concept preserves the initial affirmation of aesthetic incommensurability because it implies that there is something hidden that can be known only if revealed.[35] But, in accord with the ethical demand that the self strive to reveal itself, the concept also preserves the negation of aesthetic deception. As the *Aufhebung* of ethical reciprocity, self-revelation transcends the naive simplicity of the first movement and the merely negative opposition of the second. Moreover, as its hyphenated form expresses, self-revelation combines the interdependence of revelation (to reveal oneself, there must be another self to receive the revelation) with the demand for self-choice (to reveal oneself, one must have a self to reveal). It is therefore a fitting term for the final and fullest expression of the ethical stage, just as deception sums up the meaning of the aesthetic. In dialectical terms, the ethical consciousness opposes a logic of reciprocity to the aesthetic logic of contradiction. It is the tension in this opposition that propels the self forward and lays the foundation for the dialectic of inwardness in the religious stage.

FOUR

Approaches to the Religious Stage

WHEREAS Judge William domesticates religious language in an effort to make it serve his own ethical point of view, a number of the pseudonyms created by Kierkegaard present the religious as a sphere that is distinctly different from that which they themselves occupy. In this chapter, I examine those works in which the religious is portrayed primarily in terms of how it appears to those in lower stages: to an aesthete in *Repetition*, to an ethicist in *Fear and Trembling*, and to a speculative thinker who relates the religious to both the aesthetic and the ethical in " 'Guilty?'/'Not Guilty?'," the last and longest section of *Stages on Life's Way*. In addition to these structural relationships, a thematic continuity is also apparent among these three works, for all three deal to a greater or lesser extent with the concept of a religious exception to the universal demands of the ethical.[1]

REPETITION:
A VENTURE IN EXPERIMENTING PSYCHOLOGY

The pseudonymous author of *Repetition* is Constantin Constantius, a character already familiar from "In Vino Veritas" (which was actually published about eighteen months after *Repetition*). Constantin is concerned with the problem of whether a genuine repetition might be possible. In a much-quoted passage, he offers this definition of repetition:

> The dialectic of repetition is easy, for that which is repeated has been—otherwise it could not be repeated—but the very fact that it has been makes the repetition into something new. When the Greeks said that all know-

ing is recollecting, they said that all existence, which is, has been; when one says that life is a repetition, one says: actuality, which has been, now comes into existence. . . . Recollection is the ethnical [*ethniske*] view of life, repetition is the modern. (*R*, 149)

Although this paradoxical concept of repetition as the becoming of what has already been is hardly easy, it does clearly state a fundamental distinction: recollection presupposes being and is Greek or pagan ("ethnical"), whereas repetition involves becoming and is modern (that is, Christian). Recollection locates all knowledge and significance in the realm of the unchanging, while repetition looks for meaning in change, in the transformation of the old (which has been) into the new.

Just how this change occurs, Constantin does not say. At the beginning of the essay, however, he describes repetition as "an indestructible garment" that fits well, in contrast to recollection, which is "a discarded garment" that does not fit (*R*, 132). At the end of the first part he exclaims: "Move on, you drama of existence, where life is not given again any more than money is! Why has no one returned from the dead?" (*R*, 176). These statements point to the Christian doctrine of resurrection from the dead, according to which that which has been mortal *becomes* imperishable, as the religious idea to which repetition probably alludes.[2]

The plot of *Repetition* is the developing relationship between Constantin, the narrator, and a melancholy young man whom he befriends. The young man has recently fallen in love, and Constantin is pleased to see that he is able almost immediately to recollect his experience of love. This capacity, he declares, is "the sign of genuine erotic love" (*R*, 137), by which he means that the lover's primary relationship is with "the idea" that is stirring within him rather than with the person he supposedly loves (*R*, 140). The young man, however, lacks the "ironic resiliency" to see it that way (*R*, 137). He is so distressed by the realization that what really concerns him is not the girl but his own inner life that he decides to break off the relationship. He cannot appreciate Constantin's aesthetic ideal of love, namely, that it "may be true that a person's life is over and done with in the first moment, but there must also be the vital force to slay this death and transform it to life" (R, 137). Therefore, the young man rejects Constantin's advice—that he free himself from the girl by feigning a relationship with another woman—and simply disappears.

The rest of the first part is a long, ironical account by Constantin of his experiment with the possibility of repetition. The story revolves around a trip to Berlin, in which he attempts to repeat the external details of an earlier visit to the same city, and theoretical discussions about the nature of farce (theatergoing was a large part of both trips) highlight the frivolous nature of the entire experiment. Constantin concludes that repetition is impossible (R, 152, 169), that the "only repetition was the impossibility of a repetition" (R, 170). He soon becomes bored with the entire project and returns to Copenhagen.

The second part of *Repetition* develops both the plot and the central concept. Constantin begins to receive monthly letters from the young man, who recounts in them his own development in a religious direction. Constantin's response to that development demonstrates the limits of a purely aesthetic understanding of the religious stage.

In his first letter, the young man defends his decision to abandon the girl rather than follow Constantin's advice to deceive her. He accuses Constantin of possessing "a demonic power" that fascinates and tempts others (R, 189). The depth of the difference between them is evident in the following admission: "thus do I admire you, and yet at times I believe that you are mentally disordered. Is it not, in fact, a kind of mental disorder to have subjugated to such a degree every passion, every emotion, every mood under the cold regimentation of reflection!" (R, 189). Whereas Constantin denies the possibility of repetition and pursues the reflective activity of recollection, the young man rejects the rule of reflection and avoids "every external reminder of it all" in order to pursue the inwardness of repetition (R, 194).

In the next five letters the young man actually comes, by means of his meditations upon Job, to the conclusion that repetition really is possible. The second letter proposes Job as a model, for he is "a man who knows how to complain so loudly that he is heard in heaven" by the God who plots with Satan against him (*R*, 198). The young man's fear, the third letter makes clear, is that he has in fact become guilty by virtue of deserting the girl. He bases his claim to innocence upon the belief that to have married her would have crushed her, and yet he finds himself condemned as guilty by "language" (that is, the universal) (*R*, 200-201). In the fourth letter, the Book of Job is praised as his only nourishment, although the young man does admit his "nameless anxiety" that Job's terror will become his own, "just as one becomes ill with the sickness one reads about" (*R*, 205-206).

The young man's understanding of the religious challenge reaches its climax in his fifth letter to Constantin. There he concludes that Job's secret was that he maintained his innocence before God even when all of existence seemed to contradict him: "Job's greatness is that freedom's passion in him is not smothered or quieted down by a wrong expression" (*R*, 207). In terms of the dialectic of inner and outer, Job's inwardness stands firmly against the pressures of his external situation. That situation is not a demonstration of his guilt, it is a trial: "This category, ordeal, is not esthetic, ethical, or dogmatic—it is altogether transcendent."[3] In Job we see for the first time that the relation between inwardness and externality in the religious stage is one of contradiction. As in the aesthetic stage, here also there is rejection or at least criticism of the ethical point of view. Job declares that it is meaningless to place God under "ethical determinants" and shows that "he knows how to avoid all cunning ethical evasions and wily devices" (*R*, 207, 210).

These meditations upon Job are concluded in the sixth letter (*R*, 212-213), where the young man affirms that, since Job "received everything *double*," repetition must exist after all. But such repetition can occur only after "everything is lost," only when "every *thinkable* human certainty and probability were impossible." He is, therefore, glad that he did not follow Constantin's advice but fled in cowardice and impotence and was thus open to receive the aid of "Governance" in the task of resignation. Now he is waiting, he writes in the seventh letter, for a thunderstorm (the allusion is to the whirlwind in Job 38:1, 40:6) to usher in his own repetition, for a total change in his personality that will, he believes, "make me fit to be a husband" (*R*, 214).

It is important to appreciate, as Constantin does not, that the young man, for all his praise of Job's rejection of ethical evasions, has in fact committed himself to the ethical negation of aesthetic contradictions: "I am doing my best to make myself into a husband. I sit and clip myself, taking away everything that is incommensurable in order to become commensurable. Every morning I discard all the impatience and infinite striving of my soul—but it does not help, for the next moment it is there again" (*R*, 214). The young man is passing through "the sphere of ethical humanism,"[4] and it is this which prepares him for the actual experience of repetition reported in his final letter, which Constantin receives after a silence of several months. The occasion for this experience is the news that the girl has married someone else. This news, writes the young man, has hit him like a thunderstorm and served to give him back his own self. The repetition he has experienced is spiritual or inward, a rebirth to himself rather than a merely temporal reunion with the girl. At last, he exclaims, he can belong fully to the idea (*R*, 220-221).[5]

For a moment, this sort of language seems to jolt Constantin out of his condescending attitude toward the young man. That attitude is manifest in his introductory remarks to the letters, where he chides his young friend for wanting a one-way relationship with him and for being filled with self-contradiction (*R*, 179-180). Although it is already clear to Constantin that "there is nothing left for him except to make a religious movement" (*R*, 183), he ironically describes that movement in terms that are self-contradictory: repetition is beyond "the border of the marvelous," something that can occur only "by virtue of the absurd" (*R*, 185). It requires that a self be able to stand outside of itself: "repetition is too transcendent for me. I can circumnavigate myself, but I cannot rise above myself. I cannot find the Archimedean point" (*R*, 186). This irony, however, turns to impatience when Constantin receives word that the young man is awaiting a thunderstorm and his own experience of repetition: "He is suffering from a misapplied melancholy high-mindedness that belongs nowhere except in a poet's brain. He is waiting for a thunderstorm that is supposed to make him into a husband, a nervous breakdown perhaps" (*R*, 216). It would be far better, Constantin insists, simply to get rid of the girl.

Because the bitterness of this section is so pronounced, interpreters often content themselves with the observation that it was written in the first heat of anger and disappointment at the news that Regina, whom Kierkegaard had abandoned, had become engaged to her former suitor.[6] Yet there is a substantive point here of considerable importance. Constantin represents the aesthetic type, a person who tries to live entirely within the closed circle of the self. Aesthetic inwardness, however, arrives at its own self-understanding only in relation to someone or something external. This self-contradiction (which was discussed in Chapter Two) appears in the fact that Constantin both denies his own capacity for self-transcendence and believes that the young man should simply get rid of the girl. He understands selfhood in merely self-referential terms, and yet his solution to the self's problems is not internal but external. The bitterness of this section may well have an autobiographical source, but it also expresses nicely the frustration experienced by an aesthetic character caught in its own self-contradiction. Constantin cannot make the ethical movement of acknowledging interdependence with others, and yet his way of dealing with practical situations makes that interdependence all too obvious. This self-contradiction constitutes another source of his bitterness.

Constantin's tone changes considerably, however, in his conclusion. This section was written several months after receiving the young man's final letter, in which the inward repetition is claimed. This news seems to deliver Constantin from his anger. No longer is the young man hoping for the girl or for fulfillment through any external relationship. On the contrary, now he rejoices in the thunderstorm that has brought his new freedom and the sense that he is, once again, really himself (R, 220).

Constantin responds to this news by reflecting upon "the dialectical battle in which the exception arises in the midst of the universal . . . and affirms himself as justified, for the unjustified exception is recognized precisely by his wanting to bypass the universal" (R, 226). The justified exception, he implies, is like Jacob wrestling with the angel: "The whole thing is a wrestling match in which the universal breaks with the exception, breaks with him in conflict, and strengthens him through this wrestling. If the exception cannot endure the distress, the universal does not help him, any more than heaven helps a sinner who cannot endure the pain of repentance" (R, 227). This use of religious language does not mean that Constantin has finally granted that the young man really is a religious exception. On the contrary, he understands his new inwardness as that of a poet, one who lives in a "dialectical resiliency" that enables him actually to believe in a repetition even though he understands it as his "own consciousness raised to the second power" (R{L}, 156; cf. R, 229). Thus a poetic exception is subject to a great deal of ambivalence, not knowing whether he wishes to see an external expression of that repetition or not. An authentic religious exception experiences none of this ambivalence. Constantin writes of "the truly aristocratic exceptions" who respond to thunderstorms only if they come "from higher levels rather than from other people" (R, 228-229). Whereas a poet is not certain about whether he wants to see his creations "in the external and visible," a "religious individual . . . is composed within himself and rejects all the childish pranks of actuality" (R, 230).

There is a difficulty with this characterization of the religious, one that illuminates how the religious stage appears to an aesthete such as Constantin. The religious, in his view, is an intensification of inwardness, an inwardness that may even be a response to transcendent levels. But the claim that the religious involves a rejection of actuality indicates the extent to which Constantin sees it as an intensification of aesthetic inwardness. The poet remains ambivalent, attracted to externality yet disdainful of it. The religious individual, aesthetically conceived, disdains everything external. Unlike the young man, with his soft soul, the genuinely religious individual is able to die immediately to every new immediacy, "but there must also be the vital force to slay this death and transform it into life."[7]

The difficulty with this understanding of the religious is that it totally overlooks the ethical stage and the effect that passing through the ethical has had on the religious individual. The young man has experienced repetition *after* a profound ethical resolution, by which he becomes willing to be made commensurable to the universal (and external) demands of marriage. Constantin is angered by that willingness. Equally significant, Constantin remains silent about the young man's prolonged struggles with the possibility of guilt and the idea of a spiritual trial. Whereas Constantin advocates indifference and even cruelty toward the girl, the young man strives to resign his poetic, aesthetic self sufficiently to qualify as a husband.[8] It is this ethical dimension, one that is taken up into the religious no less than is the aesthetic, that Constantin cannot appreciate. To correct this imbalance, it is necessary to turn to *Repetition*'s companion volume, *Fear and Trembling*.[9]

FEAR AND TREMBLING: DIALECTICAL LYRIC

Kierkegaard believed that *Fear and Trembling* alone would make him immortal as an author.[10] But, as one interpreter observes, it "a little book which is as deeply misunderstood as it is widely read."[11] One example of the obscurity of some interpretations is the suggestion that Isaac is the real hero of the book, even though the pseudonymous author, Johannes de Silentio, concentrates almost exclusively upon Abraham. It is the paradox of Abraham's situation—commanded by God to sacrifice his only (legitimate) son—that fascinates Johannes, and the claim that the book's "hidden meaning" centers on Isaac is plausible only when *Fear and Trembling* is read primarily as a personal confession by Kierkegaard rather than as an investigation of the problem of understanding faith.[12]

Another recent challenge to the traditional view—that *Fear and Trembling* is primarily about the relation betweeen ethics and religion—proposes that the real message of the book deals with the conflict between despair and faith.[13] Although I shall defend the traditional view, this suggestion is helpful for interpreting the first three sections of the text.

The subtitle of *Fear and Trembling* is "dialectical lyric," and these three introductory sections are very lyrical indeed. In the Preface, Johannes contrasts the modern fad of "doubting everything" with the position of Descartes, who originated the method of doubt for philosophical work but "did not doubt with respect to faith" (*FT*, 5). The problem of the present age, writes Johannes, is that "everyone is unwilling to stop with faith but goes further" (*FT*, 7).[14]

The Exordium (*Stemning* really means "atmosphere") is lyrical to the point of being cryptic. First Johannes cites the text of Genesis 22:2, which relates that God instructed Abraham to offer his only son, Isaac, as a burnt offering. He then offers four quite different elaborations of the story. In the first, Abraham pretends that he really wants to kill Isaac in order to protect the boy from losing faith in God. The second follows the Genesis story in that Abraham obeys God and then at the last minute God provides a ram as a substitute for Isaac, but with this difference: forever after, Abraham resents God for having put him through this experience. The spiritual issue of pride emerges in the third elaboration of the story. There Abraham carries in his heart a sense of guilt over having been willing to kill his son and yet also a perplexity over whether the willingness to make such a sacrifice to God is in fact a sin. In short, he proudly seeks his own justification. The fourth portrays Abraham as obedient to God, but in despair as he pulls the knife to slay Isaac.

Although these four vignettes are far richer than such synopses convey, it is clear that they collectively continue and develop the theme of faith versus doubt. In all four Abraham obeys God, but in none of them is that obedience faithful. Deception, resentment, pride, and despair are four forms that doubt can take when it is an existential crisis, a loss of faith as a way of life rather than faith as mere mental assent.[15]

In his "Eulogy on Abraham," the third of the lyrical sections, Johannes explores in some depth the question of why Abraham is called "the father of faith" (*FT*, 18). Here an important point is made that is easily lost upon a secular age: the faith of Abraham is not simply his willingness to obey God even when God's command seems irrational or immoral. That sort of interpretation betrays the influence of modern, humanistic values, whether one applauds or decries such an Abraham.[16] No, the faith of Abraham is that he trusts God to keep his divine promise to make him the father of nations *through Isaac*. Thus the "absurdity" of God's command in Abraham's eyes has to do with God's self-consistency. The issue is: Does God keep his promises? Is he good to his word? Johannes marvels that Abraham believes and trusts in God's promise to him even at the moment when Isaac's death seems certain. Abraham never doubts, never seeks an understanding beyond faith (*FT*, 20). He is content to believe in a God beyond his understanding, beyond all intelligibility and communicability.[17]

The theme of these first three sections, then, is the conflict between faith and doubt. Despair as such is mentioned only occasionally, for example, in the fourth vignette on Abraham and the opening of the "Eulogy," where Johannes affirms that life would be despair if not for the fact of an eternal consciousness (*FT*, 15). It is evident, however, that doubt, as it is presented here, is considerably more intense than merely intellectual misgivings. In Danish, the word for despair (*Fort-*

vivlelse) is in fact an intensification of the word for doubt (*Tvivl*),[18] just as *Verzweiflung* intensifies *Zweifel* in German. This relationship is confirmed in a comment by Judge William: "Doubt is a despair of thought, despair is a doubt of the personality" (*E/O*,II, 215). In other words, although the text of *Fear and Trembling* does not demand the focus upon despair, the context and terms employed certainly legitimate it. Indeed, it could be plausibly argued that Johannes's intention here is precisely to draw the reader's attention to a common confusion of categories, namely, the conception of faith as an intellectual position rather than an existential relationship of trust in God. Doubt is an appropriate category for philosophy but not for religion, where the correct antithesis is faith versus despair.

But then comes the section entitled "Problemata," which constitutes the other six-sevenths of *Fear and Trembling*. Here Johannes shows very little concern with despair, whether directly or indirectly. Rather, his interest is in the conflict between faith and that sort of dialectical reason that would reduce faith to a stage or moment in reason's own development. As he puts it, he intends to explore the "dialectical aspects" of the Abraham story, in order "to perceive the prodigious paradox of faith," since "faith begins precisely where thought stops" (*FT*, 53). This is an explicit and consistent critique of Hegelian dialectics, one of the most carefully framed and developed of all such criticisms that Kierkegaard wrote (another is *Philosophical Fragments*). I shall first examine the three problems that constitute the bulk of this section and then return to the "Preliminary Expectoration," which serves as an introduction to them.

The first problem raises the question, "Is there a Teleological Suspension of the Ethical?" On the face of it, such a proposition would appear to be nonsense. The ethical consists of universal standards of right and wrong; it applies by definition to every person and every situation. In other words, the ethical is a matter of categorical imperatives, duties that are obligatory without regard to particular circumstances.[19] When an individual refuses to submit to the ethical, it is because that individual cannot measure up to it.

Abraham, however, was commanded by God to violate God's own ethical code and kill Isaac. Does his willingness to obey make him a murderer, a person who stands beneath the ethical code and is condemned by it? Johannes argues that faith is a special case: "Faith is namely this paradox that the single individual is higher than the universal—yet, please note, in such a way that the movement repeats itself, so that after having been in the universal he as the single individual isolates himself as higher than the universal" (*FT*, 55). Yet—and this is the tricky point—the special place of faith as "higher" than the universal does not justify Abraham ethically. As a murderer, Abraham violates the ethical; as a man of faith, he suspends it. In neither case can we breathe a sigh of relief and conclude that Abraham was (ethically) justified after all. There can be no *ethical* exceptions to ethical. The very effort to find an ethical rationale for Abraham's behavior reduces him from a man of faith to a tragic hero (*FT*, 57).

To restate the question in dialectical terms: Is it possible to think the reality of faith? According to Johannes, that's the rub: "This position cannot be mediated, for all mediation takes place only by virtue of the universal; it is and remains for all eternity a paradox, impervious to thought" (*FT*, 56).[20]

In problem II, Johannes takes up the question: "Is there an Absolute Duty to God?" This question is related, in his view, to the dialectic of inner and outer. Chastising Hegel for elevating externality above inwardness, Johannes insists that faith is "the paradox that inwardness is higher than outwardness." This does not mean that the inwardness of the aesthetic individual is higher than ethical commensurability but that there is a "new inwardness" that is just as "incommensurable" with the external as it is different from the first or merely immediate inwardness (*FT{L}*, 79; cf. *FT*, 69). On the level of this religious inwardness, Johannes can affirm that there is an absolute duty toward God in a sense that recalls the first problem: "for in this relationship of duty the individual relates himself as the single individual absolutely to the absolute," and the ethical, as the universal, is "reduced to the relative." Thus "love to God may bring the knight of faith to give his love to his neighbor—an expression opposite to that which, ethically speaking, is duty" (*FT*, 70).

Problem II is, therefore, not a second problem but a different perspective on the same question that was addressed in problem I. That question is the possibility of standing existentially beyond or above the ethical, by virtue of a particular relationship with God, the absolute. Such a proposition taxes the imagination and remains beyond the grasp of human intelligence. At all costs, a knight of faith must resist the ethical temptation "to become intelligible to oneself in the universal," for that would be, once again, the reduction of the religious to the tragic: "The tragic hero renounces himself in order to express the universal, the knight of faith renounces the universal in order to become the individual" (*FT{L}*, 86; cf. *FT*, 75-76).

In problem III, the unintelligibility of faith is addressed directly: "Was It Ethically Defensible for Abraham to Conceal His Undertaking from Sarah, from Eleazar, and from Isaac?" Johannes argues that he had no other choice, given the incommensurability of faith. If the dilemma had been an ethical one, he would have been both obligated and able to reveal himself to the others. But his situation was religious, and therefore any speech about it would have been that very self-translation into the universal which restores the individual to the ethical domain (*FT*, 113). If Abraham speaks at all as the father of faith, "he speaks in a divine language, he speaks in tongues" (*FT*, 114).

Johannes returns to a more lyrical style in problem III and devotes a long section to four poetic figures who struggled with similar problems. This aesthetic interlude must be addressed, especially because one of the four stories discussed contains some potentially misleading religious language.

The first poetic character is a bridegroom mentioned in Aristotle's *Poetics*, a man who learns on the eve of his marriage that misfortune will be its result. Since the news comes from the Delphic oracle, a public deity, the message is presumably intelligible to all. But, Johannes wonders, what if he has a "private relation to the divine" (*FT*, 93)? Should he not then refrain from explaining to his betrothed why he cannot go through with the wedding?

The second aesthetic sketch introduces a religious vocabulary that has been overemphasized by some interpreters.[21] Here Johannes relates the legend of Agnes, an innocent young girl, and a merman who sets out to seduce her. When she instead conquers him by her total and trusting surrender, the merman faces a dilemma. He repents of his sin toward the girl but does not know whether he should reveal his sin and repentance to her. If he does not, his concealed repentance is demonic, for it involves an absolute relation: "The demonic has the same quality as the divine, namely, that the single individual is able to enter into an absolute relation to it" (*FT*, 97). This is the familiar problem of the individual who has a direct or private relationship, one that cannot be mediated by speech. (If the merman were to talk about this paradox, adds Johannes, it would cease to be a paradox and he would become a tragic hero.) There is, however, the other possibility. The merman can reveal himself and then marry Agnes. Yet even this path will not deliver him totally to the universal: "He must, however, take refuge in the paradox. In other words, when the single individual by his guilt has come outside the universal, he can return only by virtue of having come as the single individual into an absolute relation to the absolute" (*FT*, 98). In thus becoming conscious of his sin, the merman arrives at "a later immediacy" beyond the universal, namely, the religious immediacy. This position distinguishes him sharply from Abraham, Johannes adds in a footnote, who transcends the ethical not by his consciousness of sin but by the fact that he is God's elect (*FT*, 98n).

The Book of Tobit provides the third personage. After each of Sarah's first seven husbands had died on his wedding night, Tobias had the courage to marry her anyway. Johannes's fascination is not with him, however; it is with Sarah's ability to receive such love and mercy (*FT*, 104). She, too, could withdraw into a demonic self-concealment. Alternatively, she can be "saved in the divine paradox" (*FT*, 106), which means that she receives deliverance from her dilemma by virtue of her absolute relation to God.

Finally, Johannes suggests that Faust might have chosen to conceal his doubt and thereby offer himself "as a sacrifice for the universal" (*FT*, 109). The point is that Faust would thereby become a paradox, a man who in some sense stands as an individual above the universal. Citing the teaching of Jesus that a person who is fasting should conceal that fact (Matt. 6:17), Johannes concludes that the deception involved in concealing something good is religiously mandated, for "subjectivity is incommensurable with actuality" (*FT*, 111-112).

My purpose in summarizing these four stories is to underscore the point I wish to make about the three problemata: all are primarily about the dialectics of paradox. The first problem argues for the category of the individual as a particular that is higher than the universal, using Abraham as the example of a man who is righteous (he fulfills the universal) yet is also willing to suspend the ethical in order to obey God's command. Thus Abraham embraces within himself the contradiction between the particular and the universal without in any way mediating or reconciling that tension. The second problem makes the same point with reference to the incommensurability of inner truth and external, intelligible expression. Here the term that corresponds to the category of the individual is "new inwardness." That this new inwardness is incommunicable is spelled out in problem III, both in direct statements and in the four poetic stories (including Agnes and the merman), all of which illustrate the paradoxical nature of a private or absolute relation to the absolute. Once the ethical has been transcended, speech fails, for language (as A explains in *Either/Or*, I) mediates every immediacy. The religious, when viewed from the perspective of the ethical, appears as a later immediacy, a new inwardness that intensifies rather than overcomes the contradiction between immediacy and mediation, as also that between aesthetic inner/outer incommensurability and ethical inner/outer commensurability.

Nothing could demonstrate more clearly than Johannes's portrayal of Abraham the radical difference between the dialectics of paradox and the dialectics of mediation. Both involve a third step beyond the basic opposition, but they take that step in mutually exclusive ways. Whereas mediation speaks of it as a "mediated immediacy," paradox insists that it is a "later immediacy." Where mediation internalizes the external or externalizes the internal, paradox speaks only of a "new inwardness" that transcends the externality through which it has passed. Thus the "third category"[22] of paradoxical dialectics is not to be identified with the third moment of systematic dialectics. On the contrary, the language of paradox intensifies that very contradiction which the language of *Aufhebung* reduces to an internal tension within a new totality.

In light of this radical distinction between paradox and mediation, it is possible to clarify Johannes's confusing use of terms for "spiritual trial" and "temptation."[23] The confusion arises from the fact that in every experience of testing the emphasis can be upon the glory of success or the humiliation of failure. Ideally, the words used for temptation would reflect that distinction and refer either to the righteous resolution or the lower attraction, as each case might require, but not interchangeably to either one. It is this ideal view of language that is presumed by Johannes Climacus in his discussion of the differences between spiritual trial (*Anfægtelse*, cf. the German *Anfechtung*) and a lower form of temptation (*Fristelse*, cf. the German *Versuchung*) in his analysis of religiousness A. Some such distinction has been made by many interpreters of *Fear and Trembling* since Climacus,[24] even though Johannes de Silentio's usage resists such precise definition of these terms.[25]

The most serious problem is that "spiritual trial" (*Anfægtelse*) is by no means always spiritual. It does, to be sure, refer primarily to the teleological suspension of the ethical and to Abraham's corresponding inability to express his situation in language (*FT*, 60). However, it is also used by Johannes for situations that resemble ordinary moral temptations. One example is the following: "But if he did not love as Abraham loved, then any thought of sacrificing Isaac would surely be a spiritual trial."[26] Here the putative temptation seems to be to kill an unloved son. Whatever the motive, such an act could never be construed as a sacrifice, still less as a spiritual trial, which is no doubt why Lowrie translates *Anfægtelse* in this one instance as "base temptation" (*FT{L}*, 42). Another example of Johannes's inconsistency is his remark that, if there is no absolute duty toward God, "then faith has no place in existence, then faith is a spiritual trial and Abraham is lost, as he gave in to it" (*FT*, 70). Here, again, the Danish is *Anfægtelse*,[27] but it refers to a temptation to obey a lower "faith" rather than the higher ethical alternative, a usage that reverses the normal relation of faith to ethics in *Fear and Trembling*.

The correlative terms involve similar difficulties. Abraham's situation, complains Johannes, has been domesticated as "only an ordeal," yet the word for ordeal (*Prøvelse*) is also used, along with "temptation," to describe Abraham as a knight of faith, which is hardly consistent with domestication (*FT*, 60, 71). As a helpful note to the Hongs' translation observes, all these terms "have essentially the same meaning" (*FT*, 341). But their use by Johannes is inconsistent and ambiguous, with the result that little progress can be made by mere definition of terms.

It is more helpful to recall precisely what constitutes temptation for the knight of faith. In all three problemata it is the same: to escape from the tension of the paradox through the power of mediation, a mediation that would employ language and thereby return Abraham to the realm of the universal (ethical). This dilemma is explicit in problem III, where Johannes writes that Abraham is "an emigrant from the sphere of the universal" who can at any moment "repent of the whole thing as a spiritual trial" but who cannot, if he would remain faithful, explain himself in words. He can never say what Johannes says, that for him "the ethical is the temptation"

(*FT*, 115). To repeat: the painful and paradoxical fact is that the only thing Abraham *can say* to Isaac is that his situation is a spiritual trial or *Anfægtelse* (*FT*, 118), but if he *does say* that, then it is no longer the case, for he has thereby submitted himself to the universal of language, and his willingness to kill Isaac is accordingly transformed from faithful sacrifice into (at best) a tragic murder.

This paradox brings me, at last, to a central concept in *Fear and Trembling* that can be understood only with the foregoing in mind—infinite resignation. I have reserved this part of my analysis for last because so many scholars interpret Johannes's notion of resignation in a way that inadvertently blurs an important distinction between the ethical and the religious. I hope the radical opposition between them is now clear: the ethical involves mediations of language that inevitably undermine religious contradiction and paradox.

The phrase that Johannes uses to describe the relation of the ethical to the religious in Abraham is "double-movement" (*FT*, 119; cf. 115). The knight of resignation makes only one movement, the renunciation of his claim to Isaac. But the knight of faith simultaneously makes a second, opposite movement, for he expects God to fulfill his promise to make him the father of nations through Isaac. A large part of the Preliminary Expectoration is devoted to this paradoxical double-movement of infinite resignation and absolute faith (*FT*, 36ff.). Johannes confesses that he can imagine making the movement of resignation but that the double-movement of faith is beyond him (*FT*, 34-35). Yet the distinction is crucial: "for he who loves God without faith reflects upon himself; he who loves God in faith reflects upon God" (*FT*, 37). Corresponding to this distinction, resignation lies within human capability, whereas the ability to receive something back again in faith is entirely a gift from God (*FT*, 49).

The best way to indicate the decisive character of Johannes's ethical concept of infinite resignation is to return to the dialectic of inner and outer. This theme is mentioned in problem II and is the point with which Johannes opens the Preliminary

Expectoration: the external world is one in which indifference and imperfection reign, whereas in "the world of the spirit . . . an eternal divine order prevails," for only the one who works, who is willing and able to live the contradiction and faithfully draw the knife on Isaac, is rewarded (*FT*, 27). But a few pages later, after he has introduced the concept of a double-movement, Johannes shows how crucial the inner/outer dialectic is for understanding the relation of resignation to faith:

> The knights of the infinite resignation are easily recognizable—their walk is light and bold. But they who carry the treasure of faith are likely to disappoint, for externally they have a striking resemblance to bourgeois philistinism, which infinite resignation, like faith, deeply disdains.
>
> I honestly confess that in my experience I have not found a single authentic instance, although I do not therefore deny that every second person may be such an instance. . . . The instant I first lay eyes on him, I set him apart at once; I jump back, clap my hands, and say half aloud, "Good Lord, is this the man, is this really the one—he looks just like a tax collector!" But this is indeed the one. I move a little closer to him, watch his least movement to see if it reveals a bit of heterogeneous optical telegraphy from the infinite, a glance, a facial expression, a gesture, a sadness, a smile that would betray the infinite in its heterogeneity with the finite. No! . . . Nothing is detectable of that distant and aristocratic nature by which the knight of the infinite is recognized. He finds pleasure in everything, takes part in everything, and every time one sees him participating in something particular, he does it with an assiduousness that marks the worldly man who is attached to such things. (*FT*, 38-39)

In addition to its literary virtues, this passage demonstrates an absolutely crucial point that is often overlooked by those Kierkegaard scholars—and they include some of the best—

who identify Johannes de Silentio's concept of resignation with that of Johannes Climacus in *Concluding Unscientific Postscript*.[28] The result of this identification is that the infinite resignation in *Fear and Trembling* is assumed to be an expression of religiousness A. This taxonomy would place Johannes de Silentio tentatively in the religious stage, for he can at least imagine taking such a step. But nothing could be further from the truth. As is well known, the mark of religiousness A is that the negative is the sign of the positive, for the external sign is incommensurable with the inner meaning.[29] But the ethical is a striving after precisely that commensurability. Given the unambiguous way in which Johannes understands the movement of infinite resignation as easily recognizable, it is clear that it, and his entire point of view, must be classified as ethical. Unlike Judge William, he appreciates the difference between the ethical and the religious, and that difference constitutes the main point of the book. But he has not himself entered into the religious stage. Accordingly, *Fear and Trembling* can be characterized as an ethical interpretation of how the religious stage differs from the ethical.[30]

As was evident in *Repetition*, the religious outlook shares with the aesthetic a conviction that inner reality and outer appearance are incommensurable with one another. But that incommensurability raises problems for an ethicist such as Johannes de Silentio that are never dreamed of by Constantin Constantius. The ethicist is committed to understanding, intelligibility, self-revelation, and to the reconciliation of inner meaning and outer expression that is necessary for the choice between good and evil to be articulated without confusion. Johannes understands infinite resignation as just such a movement, a trial that leaves a visible mark of aloofness or distance from the mundane world. But the religious viewpoint denies that very commensurability of inner and outer upon which all communication, self-revelation, and intelligibility depend. In his meditation upon the father of faith, Johannes realizes that Abraham's act, which is simultaneously murder and sacrifice (depending upon whether it is viewed ethically or religiously), must have filled him with anxiety (*FT*, 30). Yet he also admits that he cannot really look inside Abraham at all, for the inwardness of faith in God remains hidden from his ethical perspective: "He is continually making the movement of infinity, but he does it with such precision and assurance that he continually gets finitude out of it, and no one ever suspects anything else" (*FT*, 40-41).

" 'GUILTY?'/'NOT GUILTY?'—A PASSION NARRATIVE"

The third part of *Stages on Life's Way* is really a book in itself.[31] " 'Guilty?'/'Not Guilty?' " includes a long diary by Quidam (Latin for "a certain one"), followed by an "Epistle to the Reader," which is a commentary on the diary by a speculative writer named Frater Taciturnus. Although passages of genuine literary and philosophical interest appear throughout, it must be admitted that the style is often tediously repetitious.[32] Johannes Climacus comments that it is "an amiable hodge-podge of a little aestheticism, a little of the ethical, a little of the religious."[33] In this hodge-podge, however, it is possible to find confirmation and development of the themes already explored in earlier works. Accordingly, I shall examine the relation of inner and outer as portrayed in Quidam's representation of the religious stage, and then turn to Frater Taciturnus for his insights into the similarities and differences among the three stages. From these discussions it will become clear that Quidam can be taken as a religious type only in a carefully qualified sense.

Inner and Outer in Quidam's Diary

Taciturnus introduces Quidam's diary with an "Advertise-ment" in which he tells a story that anticipates beautifully the central theme of the diary. It seems that Taciturnus had taken a boat trip on Søeborg Lake with a friend who is a naturalist. Although not interested in marine plants, Taciturnus cast his friend's retrieval apparatus into the water. When he pulled it up, he found a locked rosewood box. Taciturnus pried the box open, only to find the key inside. His comment sounds a central theme: "thus is withdrawnness always introspective."[34] Like a wooden box, the withdrawn personality does not reveal externally what is inside. Moreover, the "key" to such withdrawnness is none other than the melancholy that withdrawnness conceals within itself (*SLW*, 188-190). The diary tells the story of Quidam's engagement and his gradual realization that withdrawnness does not provide the melancholy person with a satisfactory way to fulfill the demands of marriage; rather, it renders a person incapable of marriage (*SLW*, 326).

Withdrawnness, then, is deceptive external behavior intended to conceal the fact of inner melancholy. It is not itself the internal state of melancholy but the external appearance contrived to contradict and conceal that internal state. Indeed, at one point Quidam asserts that the very absence of external events or outward actions indicates that he is not suffering at that point from morbid reflection (*SLW*, 238).[35] In contrast to the ethical efforts of Judge William to reveal all, the religious type, Quidam, begins with the assumption that his inward state cannot be externalized or communicated to other people.[36]

The centrality of this theme is confirmed by its appearance in all of the six parables that appear as entries on the fifth of each month. These parables have been subjected to great hermeneutical gymnastics by interpreters, most often in efforts to show that they are cryptic autobiographical statements by Kierkegaard. Whatever the reliability of such interpretations, it is clear that the role of these parables in the diary is to illustrate in narrative form several varieties of the contradiction within withdrawnness between inwardness and external appearances or behavior.[37] "The Quiet Despair" (Jan. 5) portrays a father and son who are mirrors to one another in mutual melancholy, despite all their "gay and lively conversation." After the father's death, the son goes on to experience the quiet despair his father had prophesied for him and realizes that only his melancholy father had really understood him

(*SLW*, 191-192). The profound but hidden suffering of this pair is matched by that of Simon the leper (Feb. 5), who longs to be inwardly detached from his "disgusting figure" but who instead discovers an ointment to make the leprosy become internal and invisible, yet not a bit less real or contagious (*SLW*, 220-221). In "Solomon's Dream" (Mar. 5), David is punished for his sin by having to live in the contradiction of appearing outwardly royal but inwardly having his heart crushed by his own guilt (*SLW*, 236-237). "A Possibility" (April 5) is a parable about a man driven mad by the possibility that he had produced a child without knowing it; yet, as a result, he treats the poor children of his neighborhood with a charity that is anything but insane (*SLW*, 259-268). The subject of "A School Exercise" (May 5) is Periander, the tyrant of Corinth, who is said to have talked like a wise man and acted like a maniac (*SLW*, 298-302). The last parable, "Nebuchadnezzar" (June 5), is a loose adaptation of Daniel 4, in which the King of Babylon is transformed into a beast for seven years. In the parable he is described as terrified by his own thoughts, yet totally unable to communicate, since his every effort to speak results only in the sound of a beast (*SLW*, 330-333). Thus inner states of melancholy, sickness, guilt, madness, wisdom, and terror are hidden by, respectively, external liveliness, health, royalty, charity, madness, and frightening behavior. The common thread that connects the six parables is the incommensurability of inner and outer.

What the parables do not reveal, however, is the value that Quidam attaches to inner and outer respectively. The inner characteristics might seem negative, especially given the deceit employed by withdrawnness to hide them.[38] Wisdom is the only overtly desirable quality among the inner realities of the six parables. Yet Quidam does not employ withdrawnness to hide shameful inner states: its purpose is to protect his inwardness from bondage to *anything* external. At the beginning of the affair, he says he would rather love the girl in secret than in actuality (*SLW*, 196-197), and after the break he strives to go on loving her even while employing every device to get her to stop loving him. The Romantic's calling, as he sees it, is to be "just as cold externally as one is inwardly hot" (*SLW*, 216). Many other remarks (*SLW*, 274, 278, 311-312) bear out the priority that Quidam accords to inwardness over externality, even if that inwardness is one of melancholy suffering: his task is to be an "experimental man"[39] who must produce his own inwardness by being "wholly reflective" (*SLW*, 334-335).

Quidam, then, has significant points of agreement with both the aesthetic and the ethical positions. His life is a contradiction between inwardness and external appearance, a contradiction that he justifies and for which he employs deception. Yet he also implicitly admits the validity of the ethical demand for self-revelation in intimate relationships, a demand that is based upon the axiom that the inner and the outer must be identical (*SLW*, 343). Quidam believes that he could, with his "sense for insignificant things," become a good husband but that his withdrawnness stands in the way (*SLW*, 228). The problem is the incommensurability between inner suffering and the external insignificance of the cause ("object") of suffering (*SLW*, 277). Thus his story is one of "passion," a narrative of inward suffering.[40]

Quidam's attitude toward language also manifests common elements with both positions. Like the aesthete, he does not believe that language can overcome the contradictions within or between persons (*SLW*, 290, 296). He feels himself alienated and judged by the universal norms that language embodies, as when it latches onto his external behavior (desertion) and therefore denies the authenticity of his inner love for the girl (*SLW*, 219). But the problems that Quidam has with language are as much ethical as aesthetic. One such problem provides " 'Guilty?'/'Not Guilty?' " with its title. After he breaks the engagement, the girl leaves a note for him in which she claims that she will die without him. Quidam interprets this language literally and therefore agonizes over whether he might be guilty of murder. Likewise, since the girl implores him "for God's sake" in her note, Quidam considers himself to be bound to her by an oath (*SLW*, 190, 304-305). Thus Quidam shares the aesthetic alienation from language, but not its corollary— the belief that the purpose of language is to conceal thought. Conversely, he shares the ethical commitment to fulfilling obligations and vows expressed in language, but not the ethical belief that language exists for—and is adequate to—the task of communication. The formula Quidam himself invents to express his dual view of language reflects the perspective of one who is struggling with a religious challenge: the purpose of language, he suggests, is "to assist and confirm people in refraining from action" (*SLW*, 312).

The action that Quidam has in mind is repentance, and this is the central problematic of his diary. Again and again Quidam attempts to justify his situation by appeal to religious categories. He defends withdrawnness on the grounds that God's speech defies external expression (*SLW*, 292) and also that God employs deceptive tactics in many Old Testament stories (*SLW*, 218). God penetrates to the innermost depths of a person, so that even this diary was written in his view, although its external words still do not convey Quidam's real meaning (*SLW*, 183, 352). The utter inwardness of the God-relationship is reflected in prayer, which some may try to rationalize and justify but which is really "a favor graciously granted to every man," one that is nullified the moment any "extraneous reflection" is suggested in its support (*SLW*, 320).

In the end, Quidam realizes that his efforts to justify his cold behavior toward the girl in terms of her own well-being have been false: "I have been taken prisoner by the appearance I sought to conjure up. I have in fact treated a person shabbily" (*SLW*, 322). Rather than an inward love for the girl, all he has left is the realization that his motive has always been pride. He is no longer able to communicate with others. Isolated with God, Quidam can only endure the "peculiar pain" of his prison, reluctantly accepting the fact that he has, as it were, been forced into the religious mode against his will: "My idea was to construct my life ethically in my inmost being, and to conceal this inwardness under the form of deceit. Now I have been forced farther back within myself, my life is constructed *for me* religiously, and so much farther back in inwardness that with difficulty I reach actuality" (*SLW*, 323).[41]

Quidam finds that direct experience of the religious stage is a very different matter from his earlier childlike veneration for the religious "paradigm" (*SLW*, 242). Indeed, the fact that pride is his primary motivation raises the question of the difference between Quidam's religious dialectic of inner/outer contradiction and the dialectic of aesthetic inwardness. This is a question that Frater Taciturnus addresses in articles 1, 2, and 5 of his "Epistle to the Reader."

The Theory of Stages According to Frater Taciturnus

That Frater Taciturnus is preoccupied with the relation between the aesthetic and the religious is clear from his opening remark, where he criticizes Constantin Constantius for failing to take his hero in *Repetition* beyond the aesthetic to the religious (*SLW*, 367). The young man's contradiction, as Taciturnus sees it, is merely between the erotic and the poetic poles within the aesthetic stage; both remain as competing objects of his enthusiasm. In contrast, Quidam hides his enthusiasm for the girl "by an exterior the very opposite to it" (*SLW*, 368), thereby establishing that the contradiction is between the visible exterior and an invisible interior.

The varieties of unhappy love illuminate this difference (article 1). In erotic love, unhappiness is the result of some sort of opposition that the "aesthetic hero"—Abelard, Romeo, and Hamlet are mentioned as possible examples—encounters "outside himself" (*SLW*, 370). The religious contradiction, on the other hand, arises due to an "infinite reflection" that is alien to both the erotic and the poetic poles of the aesthetic:

> Immediacy is not entirely devoid of reflection; as poetry conceives it, it has a relative reflection by having its opposition outside itself. But only then is immediacy

really at an end when the immediate infinity shall be grasped by an equally infinite reflection. That very instant all tasks are transformed and made dialectic in themselves; no immediacy is permitted to stand by itself or exposed merely to strife with another power, but must strive with itself. (*SLW*, 375)

Like Johannes de Silentio, Taciturnus realizes that the religious individual affirms the very immediacy that he transcends. Although the phrase "infinite reflection" betrays his preference for speculative jargon (over such ethical terms as "infinite resignation") for the negation of immediacy, in both cases the religious idea is that of a paradoxical "double-movement" in which the immediacy of love is simultaneously surrendered and embraced. Furthermore, Taciturnus insists that this negative movement is in no way motivated by anything external: "the infinite reflection is not something heterogeneous to him but is the transparency of immediacy to itself" (*SLW*, 376).

In article 2, Taciturnus employs this distinction to develop his theory of comedy and tragedy. Both are aesthetic ways of representing the unhappy love between Quidam and the girl, since both would blame their unhappiness upon external events (fate). In comedy, an unhappy love is unavoidable, whereas tragedy portrays a happy love as impossible. The girl is comic, since she continues to love Quidam unhappily without understanding him; for him, their love is happy but cannot be fulfilled, so he is tragic, and becomes all the more so by virtue of his awareness of the comic aspect of their situation (*SLW*, 394). Nevertheless, the deeper difference between them is that her understanding is aesthetic, whereas he no longer really looks for external causes, having grasped their predicament dialectically, that is, as a contradiction that has been generated inwardly. This contrast corresponds to her aesthetic tendency to avoid actuality in favor of illusion, while he seeks something "higher than actuality after actuality, that is, by virtue of a God-relationship" (*SLW*, 383). That this is an inner actuality is clear in their encounters after the engagement is broken, for Quidam remains "preoccupied with himself, and not with her as an actuality outside himself" (*SLW*, 385).

Taciturnus discusses five ways in which Quidam and the girl differ, and in the process recalls a number of familiar themes. Quidam's withdrawnness has "language only in silence," in contrast to the language of immediacy, which is "easily pronounced" (*SLW*, 387). He is melancholy, she lighthearted. He is a thinker, she is not, which means that he strives passionately "to have the idea on his side in order to exist," while she is indifferent to the idea (*SLW*, 391). For him, suffering is an inner sense of responsibility and guilt, while she experiences it in response to an external loss (*SLW*, 392). Finally, comments Taciturnus ironically, Quidam appears to be guilty for breaking the relationship, but his only guilt is that he started it; and she appears to be innocent, but is really guilty "for taking advantage of the ethical side of their relationship so as to bind him to herself" (*SLW*, 392-393). The results of these differences are misunderstanding and a failure to love: "He fails to love because he lacks immediacy, in which love first has its place. . . . She does not love; . . . She has the impulses of immediacy . . . but in order to love she must also have resignation" (*SLW*, 395). It is a clear case of a contradiction between his religious inwardness and her externally determined immediacy.

Taciturnus's development of the different views of suffering in article 5 illustrates nicely how the religious can preserve an aesthetic insight even while rejecting the essential aesthetic orientation: "The aesthetic hero is great for the fact that he *conquers*, the religious hero is great for the fact that he *suffers*" (*SLW*, 411). When the aesthetic hero suffers, he is primarily tragic; the suffering is incidental. If a religious hero conquers, he is demonic, for he has turned away from inwardness and toward the world.[42] The religious hero's inward suffering is voluntary, whereas the aesthetic hero has no interest in suffering unless it is "related to the idea" (which he reduces to the notion of fate), for he assumes that "suffering must come from without, be visible, not having its origin and expression in the individual himself" (*SLW*, 413). While rejecting this externality, the religious hero still affirms the aesthetic connection of suffering with the idea: "When I now take leave of aesthetics I do away with its externality but retain the just principle, that only such suffering has interest as stands in relation to the idea. This remains true to all eternity. When a relationship to the idea is not visible in suffering, it must be rejected in the aesthetic field and condemned in the religious" (*SLW*, 414).

What corresponds to the aesthetic catharsis, in which the spectator experiences pity and fear and is inspired by the helplessness of the tragic hero who is undone by fate, is, in the religious realm, the realization of guilt. Here, again, the aesthetic turns outward, the religious inward (*SLW*, 417-418). Quidam's status as a religious hero depends upon his preoccupation with his own guilt. If he is concerned about any external forces or causes, he ceases to be religious, just as a religious orator is more interested in being "seriously moved" himself than he is in the reaction of others to what he says (*SLW*, 420).

Taciturnus discusses religious language in a supplement to article 5. Predictably, he is very critical of those who salt their language with frequent references to God, "as though the religious consisted in certain words and phrases." This use of so-called religious terms is, he maintains, "half aesthetic. Although the saying sounds religious, the individual is viewed only in an external relationship to God, not in an inward relationship to himself. . . . This is aesthetics with a spurious religious gilding" (*SLW*, 423).

The religious, then, can be both compared and contrasted with the aesthetic. They are alike in their commitment to the contradiction between inner truth and external appearance. In this, the religious is at odds with the ethical, as understood by Judge William. But the religious sides with the ethical against the aesthetic on another crucial question: both perceive the aesthetic as a mode of externality, lacking inner sources for consciousness and action. This distinction raises the question of the difference between ethical and religious inwardness, a question that Frater Taciturnus addresses in his third, fourth, and sixth articles.

Article 3 is a continuation of the discussion about tragedy and comedy begun in article 2, now in relation to the "need of historical reality." Here the ethical dimension of tragedy emerges. Taciturnus argues that comedy is interested only in unmasking contradictions and therefore seeks no support in history; in contrast, tragic poets, in their pursuit of ideality, always try to locate their heroes in history, with the result that tragedy "remains mired in the ethical difficulty that though the idea triumphs the hero is destroyed" (*SLW*, 396). The contradiction that Taciturnus sees in this ethical difficulty is that it really betrays the ideality for which tragedy strives. To need a historical witness to the ideal is like laughing at a joke because someone else says that it is funny. Ideality is a matter of possibility, not actuality; it "does not come conveniently bottled in history" (*SLW*, 398). Indeed, when faith is confronted with actuality, it immediately "resolves" it into an impossibility and believes by an act of will rather than on the basis of historical evidence.[43]

The real problem with historical argument is that its evidence is external. Like poetry, history "depends upon the commensurability of the outward and the inward, and therefore it shows the result in the realm of the visible" (*SLW*, 399). This trait reveals that the ethical is not yet completely inward: "The ethical result is already less visible, or rather it is demanded with such swiftness that one has not time to look around before it is there" (*SLW*, 399). The impatience of the ethical is that it demands that justice be made visible as world-order, divine governance, and providence; it does not wish to be "slowed down" by such aesthetic categories as fate and chance. In short, the ethical is a decision to reject the aesthetic and seek the religious: it "desires to be separated from the aesthetic and from the outwardness which is its imperfection, it desires to enter into a glorious alliance, and that is with the religious" (*SLW*, 400).

The paradox of the ethical is that it wants visible justice without aesthetic externality. It is sufficiently inward to reject mere aesthetics, but not enough to overcome its own impatience for results. Thus it finds itself seeking the religious and yet very much in tension with it:

> The religious then plays, though in a higher sphere, the same rôle as the aesthetic; it spaces out the infinite swiftness of the ethical, and development can take place; but the scene is laid in the interior, in mental thoughts which one cannot see, not even by the aid of a telescope. The principle of the spirit is that the outward and visible (the glory of the world or its wretchedness for the one who exists; an outward result or the lack of it for the agent) exist in order to test faith, and hence not to deceive, rather in order that a test can be made of the spirit's ability to be indifferent to all this and return into itself. The outward course counts neither one way nor the other—and for one thing the result remains in the inward sphere, and, secondly, it is constantly deferred.[44]

The inability of the ethical to become fully indifferent to externality is demonstrated by Quidam's equivocal repentance (article 4). According to Taciturnus, repentance is purely inward, and Quidam's difficulty with it is that "he remains stuck in a dialectic relationship to reality" (*SLW*, 404). This refers to Quidam's enquiry about his guilt and his pondering of that question in terms of the external results of his actions. For the religious individual, guilt is a presupposition rather than a problem, and one that is known inwardly rather than on the basis of external evidence.

Yet there is a sense in which Quidam's question does show a religious approach to the problem. After the engagement is broken and he has overcome the challenge to give up his inwardness in marriage, he does not simply forget about the whole affair. The diary entries that begin six months later attest to the fact that Quidam really is determined in the direction of religious inwardness: "he survives the crisis of reality and then falls into conflict with himself" (*SLW*, 406). Until he divorces the question of his guilt from the girl, however, his repentance remains merely ethical, partially external and partially internal, a "dialectic" in which he never becomes free of reality. The freedom of religious repentance, on the other hand, is that, once completed, the individual "lets the act of repentance go" (*SLW*, 408).

Article 6 returns to the question of repentance in a way that casts more light upon the relations among the three stages. To repent nothing is denounced as an aesthetic principle in ethical guise (*SLW*, 428). Repentance as a purely negative movement is ethical. And to repent as the negative aspect of a double-movement, in which joy is the positive aspect, is to arrive at the religious:

> There are three existence-spheres: the aesthetic, the ethical, the religious. The metaphysical is abstraction, there is no man who exists metaphysically. . . . The ethical sphere is only a transitional sphere, and hence its highest expression is repentance as a negative action. The aesthetic sphere is that of immediacy, the ethical is that of requirement (and this requirement is so infinite that the individual always goes bankrupt), the religious sphere is that of fulfilment, but note, not such a fulfilment as when one fills a cane or a bag with gold, for repentance has made infinite room, and hence the religious contradiction: at the same time to lie upon seventy thousand fathoms of water and yet be joyful.
>
> Inasmuch as the ethical sphere is a transitional sphere (which however one does not pass through once for all), and as repentance is its highest expression, repentance is also the most dialectic thing. So no wonder one fears it, for give it a finger and it takes the whole hand. As Jehovah in the Old Testament visits the iniquities of the fathers upon the children in subsequent generations, so does

repentance go constantly further back surmising objects for its investigation. In repentance is the jerk of this movement, and everything turns back for it. The jerk signifies precisely that the difference between the aesthetic and the religious is that between the outward and the inward.[45]

The negativity of the ethical is emphasized here in several ways. First, it is only a transition, a means by which an individual rejects the aesthetic in order to attain the religious. The ethical, according to this picture, has no positive content of its own. The conventional duties with which Judge William is preoccupied, and even his commitment to reconciling inner and outer in the demand for self-revelation, recede in this view of the ethical as the negation of aesthetic immediacy. Second, the ethical requirement is never satisfied, for each immediacy that is overcome is immediately followed by another. An individual who is trying to fulfill the ethical, as one might try to observe laws and duties, will never reach that goal. Even in the religious stage, the infinity of ethical resignation and repentance continues: one can never pass through it once and for all. Finally, repentance is like a jerk. It is not a smooth motion in which one is pulled steadily forward. Rather, the pull forward is experienced as an abrupt jerk in which forward pull and backward resistance are combined. Repentance causes that negative resistance because it never exhausts the "objects for its investigation." The fact that this jerk can be felt inwardly but never seen externally is a reminder that the religious, which always presupposes ethical repentance, is an inward rather than an external (aesthetic) movement.

But the religious does not stop with the negativity of the ethical. In addition to the external insecurity of resting upon seventy thousand fathoms of water, the religious individual finds in this experience a genuine joy. The ethical repudiates immediacy, and the religious arrives at a second immediacy (the forgiveness of sins), which in turn raises a final question (*SLW*, 436): if Taciturnus, by his own admission, cannot understand this new immediacy of the religious, and if Quidam, as portrayed by Taciturnus, "is no more than a demoniac figure in the direction of the religious," then how is it possible to claim that " 'Guilty?'/'Not Guilty?' " is about the religious stage at all?

The problem of Quidam's status as a type of the religious stage is expressed by the conflict between Taciturnus's (admittedly ambivalent) presentation of him in that capacity and the obvious fact that Quidam does not, in fact, fully achieve the religious, not even as it is defined by Taciturnus himself. His withdrawnness, inwardness, and willingness to suffer all appear to be religious characteristics; his equivocation over his own guilt is not.

Although it is not possible to resolve this ambiguity decisively one way or the other, it does help to understand it as, at least in part, a result of the obscure relationship between Frater Taciturnus and Quidam. On the one hand, Taciturnus frequently gives the impression that Quidam is his own literary creation (*SLW*, 363-367). He calls him a "conjured up" figure and adds that he created the girl only to shed more light on Quidam (*SLW*, 363). He asserts that Quidam "does not exist outside of my thought-experiment" (*SLW*, 367). And he implies that he, not Quidam, really wrote the six parables and the entire "story of suffering" (*SLW*, 389, 398). Thus Quidam's inability to attain the religious could be explained as the natural result of having been created by an author who, by his own admission, neither lives in nor understands religious mysteries (*SLW*, 394, 399, 402, 418, 436). On the other hand, Taciturnus frequently expresses frustration as he attempts to comprehend Quidam, which would be curious if he had in fact created him. The story of finding the diary in a box at the bottom of the lake gives an impression of distance between them. At one point, Taciturnus acknowledges Quidam's dialectical abilities: "It is by no means my purpose . . . to convince him, but to remark upon something true in him and . . . let him pass for what he is" (*SLW*, 367). Even more striking are two mistakes that Taciturnus seems to make. One is his description of the two sets of entries in the diary (retrospective daytime entries interspersed with midnight entries about Quidam's present development in inwardness) as treating "the same story" (*SLW*, 383), when in fact the two accounts overlap but are really quite distinct. The other is his comment in a footnote that he does not understand how Quidam had direct knowledge about the physician's report on the girl's health, when the diary clearly states that Quidam had heard the physician talking (*SLW*, 228, 386n).

Although Taciturnus's credibility as Quidam's creator is thereby undermined, it is not totally destroyed. For the good Frater is, in his own terms, a Sophist, a person who puts "the religious on all sides" but is not existentially religious. Thus the religious remains external to him, whether his enthusiasm for it be poetic, ethical, or dogmatic (*SLW*, 437-438). Taciturnus insists that "the religious consists precisely in being religiously concerned about oneself infinitely" and not in slipping into his sort of "equilibrium of spirit," which is "an offense against the holy passion of the religious" (*SLW*, 438). But it is this very infinite concern about oneself that does characterize Quidam. Preoccupation with Quidam is, as it were, the imaginative device by which Taciturnus places the religious on all sides. Quidam is the "certain one" that he might like to become, if only he could make the ethical movement of infinite repentance. It is Taciturnus who is withdrawn, as his name implies; Taciturnus who is preoccupied with inwardness, as the entire work testifies; and Taciturnus who is willing to suffer—if only he can understand why. And there's the rub. Taciturnus, and Quidam with him, can never fully enter into the religious, the joy of resting over deep waters, so long as they insist upon understanding *why* they must tread a path of guilt and repentance.

THAT THE religious stage is paradoxical is not difficult to grasp. Even Constantin, limited as he is to an aesthetic perspective, can grasp that the concept of repetition is paradoxical. From the ethical standpoint of Johannes de Silentio, the problem is that of accepting the incomprehensibility of the paradox, a paradox that cannot be named or classified without destroying its meaning. Taciturnus also understands that he cannot understand the mysteries of the religious sphere. All three comprehend the incomprehensibility of the religious, but none of them is able to let go of comprehension as his avenue of approach to it. Such intellectual approaches to the religious are apparently doomed to failure. As an inwardness that is incommensurable with its own outer expression, the religious cannot be captured in language or thought. Nevertheless, where abstract definitions fail to illuminate the concrete phenomena of existence, the path is sometimes revealed by the dialectical development of the whole, the skeletal system[46] that can occasionally be discerned by looking beneath all the covering matter. That can be accomplished by turning now to two experiments in religious dialectics.

FIVE

Varieties of Religious Dialectic

IN THE PRECEDING chapters, several types of dialectical reason have been found in the pseudonymous works examined. In volume I of *Either/Or*, the dialectical structure of aesthetic inwardness is systematic and progressive in character, much in the manner of a Hegelian phenomenological development. Volume II manifests only abortive efforts to create dialectical structures: the Judge's ethical views display a dialectic of reciprocity, a term Kierkegaard uses for dialectical reason that fails to establish either clear dualities or genuine unities. These two examples of dialectical thought, representing respectively the aesthetic and ethical stages, are each confirmed by the relevant sections of *Stages on Life's Way*. Finally, *Repetition*, *Fear Trembling*, and " 'Guilty'/'Not Guilty?' " are concerned with aesthetic and ethical approaches to the religious stage. The dialectic they portray in the religious is one of paradox—a unity of two contraries such that the opposition between the contraries is accentuated rather than overcome. In all of these texts, the dialectical structures both illuminate and are illuminated by the changing relation of inwardness to externality, a relation that corresponds in several of the texts to the dialectic of self and other.

It is in the religious stage that these themes find their culmination. Inwardness remains a central concept, providing the key to many aspects of the religious stage also. Moreover, the works dealing directly with the religious demonstrate that systematic dialectics are not limited to the aesthetic in Kierkegaard's works. Indeed, several of the most striking examples of this sort of structure are to be found in works that focus on aspects of the religious stage.

This chapter presents the contrast between two types of dialectic within the religious stage. On the one hand, *The Concept of Anxiety*, like *The Concept of Irony* and volume I of *Either/Or*, has manifestly Hegelian elements,[1] and close study reveals that it, too, conceals a clear and comprehensive systematic structure. On the other hand, *Philosophical Fragments* joins *Fear and Trembling* as an argument for and an example of the dialectics of paradox. According to one scholar, these two works "supplement each other in a very splendid and dialectically deliberate way,"[2] by which he means that *The Concept of Anxiety* moves anthropologically from below upwards, whereas *Philosophical Fragments* deals with revelation and therefore stresses the movement from above to below. In this chapter, I shall develop that contrast in detail and show that the different directions correspond to the radical disparity between systematic and paradoxical patterns of dialectical thought.

THE CONCEPT OF ANXIETY

The most recent translator of *The Concept of Anxiety* has described it as "possibly the most difficult of Kierkegaard's works."[3] Part of that difficulty is due to the fact that, as its subtitle reflects (*A Simple Psychologically Orienting Deliberation on the Dogmatic Issue of Hereditary Sin*), it is stylistically a work of extraordinary density, complex in thought and abundant in the use of abstract terms. Space does not permit anything like an adequate interpretation of the entire work—that would require a book in itself. Rather, I shall devote my investigation primarily to an analysis of the structure of the work, a structure that is one of Kierkegaard's most systematic but is by no means obvious, and to the themes of inwardness/externality and self/other.[4]

In the course of this discussion, I shall also dispute the common opinion that *The Concept of Anxiety* deals with the eternal in an external manner only.[5] Indeed, one of the major benefits of systematic, structural analysis is that it reveals the extent to which this text is about the internalization of the eternal and the crucial points in this process. The result of this transition is a new relationship between the inner/outer and self/other dialectics. Whereas in prior texts and stages it has often been possible to identify externality with otherness, in the religious stage otherness is encountered inwardly, in the relation to both God and self.

A third way in which I depart from some other interpretations is in treating *The Concept of Anxiety* as a text about the religious stage. Although it does bear many similarities to the aesthetic and ethical stages, I find the emphasis on the problem of original sin to be the compelling factor, for Kierkegaard frequently insists that sin-consciousness arises only in the religious stage.[6] The following analysis will show that *The Concept of Anxiety* has a complex and systematic structure, which in turn shows that the development of anxiety is the anthropological condition for religious inwardness.

The pseudonymous author of *The Concept of Anxiety* is Virgilius Haufniensis, which means "watchman of Copenhagen." He introduces himself in the Preface as a "layman who indeed speculates but is still far removed from speculation," presumably because speculation requires a rejection of all positive authorities, and Haufniensis has no desire to do that (*CA*, 8). Indeed, the purpose of the Introduction, which is a very involved discussion of the relation of psychology to ethics and dogmatics, is really to locate those disciplines and their various understandings of sin in relation to the question of authority. After criticizing Hegel for attempting to synthesize the realms of possibility (abstract thought) and actuality (existence) by means of mediation, Haufniensis characterizes the differences among the various approaches to sin. It is worth summarizing what he says about each discipline in turn (*CA*, 20-24). The "first ethics" is a pagan science that ignores sin and is "shipwrecked on the sinfulness of the single individual." This pagan ethics assumes the goodness of human nature and then cannot account for the actual sin that characterizes human behavior in history. Psychology[7] explores the real possibility of sin but ignores sin's actuality; it comes no closer than the "restless repose" out of which "sin constantly arises." It is in dogmatics that hereditary sin as sin's "ideal possibility" is explained, thus providing the foundation for "the second ethics," which Haufniensis calls the "new science." This is clearly Christian ethics, which is interested not in the possibility of sin or even in hereditary sin but only in the actuality of sin—the fact that human life is under the sway of sin. *The Concept of Anxiety* is presented as a psychological treatment of the dogmatic problem of hereditary sin, although it also deals in later chapters with "the second ethics," or the consciousness of sin as an actuality.

A. Anxiety Projected onto an External Other

The first two chapters are psychological in the sense stated above: they attempt to explain the real possibility of hereditary sin by appeal to the concept of anxiety.[8] Anxiety is said to explain hereditary sin "retrogressively in terms of its origin" in chapter I; in chapter II, it does so "progressively" in terms of its consequences. In both of these chapters, then, anxiety is posited abstractly as the possibility of sin. Sin and anxiety are posited in general, not in relation to the experience of individuals. Without ever claiming that his analysis is systematically dialectical, Haufniensis is opening his essay with the notion of abstract anxiety "in-itself."

Chapter I deals with the question: How could sin have entered the world? One traditional method is to pin the blame on Adam, to interpret the Genesis story as the passing from innocence to guilt by Adam and Eve, and then to attribute the sin and guilt of all subsequent generations to their first sin. This will not do, argues Haufniensis in article 1, for it places Adam "fantastically" outside of history and thus begs the question. If Adam is as different from historical human beings as this interpretation implies, then his first sin is not really a human event; by implication, it is almost shoved back into the creation event itself, which renders it fantastic or mythical. No, Adam's sin must be essentially *human* sin, so that whatever explains the sin of one explains the sin of all.

Article 2 develops the relation between Adam, the first sinner, and other sinners by means of a distinction between sin and sinfulness. Whereas sin enters the world identically in each individual, so that Adam is not to be blamed for any other person's sin, sinfulness entered the world with Adam's sin, and therefore cannot be said to have "entered" again. Sin is a *qualitative* leap from innocence to guilt that can occur only by an actual sin. Sinfulness is a *quantitative* designation of the disposition to sin. Sin is a dialectical contradiction, in that it presupposes itself. Sinfulness is the psychological/ethical characteristic that results from sin.

The third and fourth articles elaborate upon what has already been established. Because sin entered the world by a leap, a dialectical contradiction, it is wrong to say that innocence is "annulled," as Hegel does when he identifies innocence with immediacy. Haufniensis accuses Hegel of a category error, for immediacy, as a category of logic, has nothing to do with existence. Innocence is ignorance, an ethical state of existence that is "annulled only by guilt."[9] And the leap into guilt defies explanation; psychology can at best explain the conditions for the fall, not the fall itself.

This conclusion brings Haufniensis to the concept of anxiety (article 5). Interpreters often seize upon his paradoxical formulation of anxiety as "*a sympathetic antipathy* and *an antipathetic sympathy*" (CA, 42) as the essence of anxiety, but that phrase is intelligible only in terms of the discussion of otherness that constitutes its context. Haufniensis informs us that innocence is a striving against nothing and that this nothing "begets anxiety." Furthermore, "innocence always sees this nothing outside itself." That thought is developed in the following paragraph, in which innocent anxiety is defined as "a determination of dreaming spirit,"[10] and dreaming is compared with other states of consciousness in terms of how they perceive the other: awake, one is conscious of the other as other; asleep, the difference between self and other is suspended; and when dreaming, the other is "an intimated nothing." In short, if innocence is the spirit while dreaming, and dreaming consciousness perceives the other as nothing, then we can conclude that the nothing that begets anxiety is in fact the dreaming consciousness of an *undetermined other*. This identification is confirmed later in the article when Haufniensis asks: "How does spirit relate itself to itself and to its conditionality? It relates itself as anxiety. Do away with itself, the spirit cannot; lay hold of itself, it cannot, as long as it has itself outside of itself' (*CA*, 44).

From these passages, it is reasonable to conclude that the key to the anxiety of innocence is that the self is looking for itself in others, in externals, outside of itself, but without any focus upon specific others. Thus its other is a nothing, which in turn helps to explain the paradox of sympathetic antipathy and antipathetic sympathy. This other that is nothing both attracts and repels the innocent spirit, which both hopes and fears that it might lay hold of itself in the other, thereby finding and losing itself simultaneously. This paradox illuminates several other formulations for the anxiety of innocence: it is "pleasing anxiety"; it is "freedom's actuality as the possibility of possibility," that is, the actuality at this point is an other that is also a nothing and thus only the possibility of possibility; and "the less spirit, the less anxiety" (*CA*, 42), for spirit is the quest for selfhood, a quest that begets anxiety with its initial insight that the self is—a nothing.

In the course of the fifth article, Haufniensis defines man as a synthesis in the spirit of the psychical and the physical. He uses this definition in the sixth and final article to distinguish between sin and sexuality. The fall into sin occurs in the spirit. Thus it affects both the soul and the body, for they are united in the spirit. By virtue of sin, bodily sensuousness becomes sexuality, for "without sin there is no sexuality" (*CA*, 49). Simultaneously, with sin the soul becomes sinful. Thus sinfulness is not to be equated with sensuousness or even with sexuality, although psychical sinfulness and physical sexuality are the sibling offspring of sin.

With sexuality, history begins, and here again the question of freedom arises. Haufniensis denies the necessity of the fall (for that would be a contradiction and would eliminate anxiety) and also the notion of a voluntary fall by a totally free will, which he dismisses as "a nuisance for thought." Instead, he suggests that anxiety is "entangled freedom, where freedom is not free in itself but entangled, not by necessity, but in itself" (*CA*, 49). Once again, the implication is that of a leap: sin comes into the world by a sin, and there is no one else to blame for one's guilt but oneself. Sin is not mediated to the sinner by any means whatsoever: it is "that transcendence, that *descrimen rerum* [crisis] in which sin enters into the single individual as the single individual" (*CA*, 50).

But it is not yet time to consider sin and anxiety in relation to the individual. Haufniensis has offered his interpretation of anxiety as the presupposition or origin of hereditary sin, and these deliberations have led him to consider the problems of sensuousness and of history. In chapter II, he deals with these together under the rubric of generation. Generation embraces the double meaning of sexual reproduction and development through time, and so it focuses very nicely the issue that Haufniensis wishes to explore, namely, anxiety as the consequence of hereditary sin, as that which explains hereditary sin progressively. It is his belief that, although a more primitive person has more profound anxiety, in fact "hereditary sin is growing" (*CA*, 52).

The two areas in which sin and sinfulness produce anxiety give the chapter its structure. One is the natural world, the "eager longing" of creation mentioned in Rom. 8:19, which Haufniensis calls objective anxiety. The other is the self's subjective anxiety prior to positing itself as guilty of sin.

Objective anxiety is the "effect of sin in nonhuman existence [*Tilværelse*]" (*CA*, 57). It is not that inanimate objects are to be regarded as sinful, but that "creation is placed in an entirely different light because of Adam's sin," for now "sensuousness is constantly degraded to mean sinfulness" (*CA*, 58). What is really at stake here is the perception of creation by sinful

humans.[11] Because of the fact of sin, the distinction between
sensuousness (sinless bodily existence) and sinfulness (the
psychical result of sin) is blurred. This is tantamount to saying
that sinfulness is projected onto sensuousness. In the same
way, the external created world seems to manifest an objective
anxiety. This anxiety is, by virtue of its innocence or lack of
self-consciousness, analogous to (although less than) that of
Adam (*CA*, 60).

Subjective anxiety is also analogous to that of Adam, although it is quantitatively greater by virtue of generation.
Haufniensis is saying that the relationship of generation is "the
something that the nothing of anxiety may signify in the
subsequent individual" (*CA*, 62). That is, generation refers to
the subsequent individual's search for self in the other, in that
which is external. This observation explains why the bulk of
this section on subjective anxiety is devoted to what at first
appear to be two digressions, one on the relationship between
generation and woman (*CA*, 63-67) and the other on sexuality
(*CA*, 67-72). When Haufniensis announces, "We shall now
return to the subject with which we were dealing, namely,
the consequence of the relationship of generation in the individual" (*CA*, 72), one is tempted to ask what the preceding
ten pages have accomplished. The main point with regard to
generation was adequately made when he emphasized that
"anxiety about sin produces sin" (*CA*, 73). Born into a sinful
world, the individual becomes anxious about the possibility
of sin, and this anxiety, rather than any innate concupiscence,
is what results in sin; even anxiety about being thought guilty
can lead to guilt (*CA*, 75).

Once again, it is the dialectic of self and other that can
provide a fuller grasp of Haufniensis's argument, and for that
it is necessary to return to those apparent digressions on generation in relation to woman and sexuality. The first recalls
the synthesis of the psychical and the physical, for Haufniensis
claims that there will be more anxiety whenever that synthesis
is "cleft" by an imbalance in the two parts. Because woman
is more sensuous than man, he reasons, she must also have

more anxiety (*CA*, 64). The consideration of woman leads to a discussion of the medium of the male-female relationship (namely, sexuality), which confirms that the origin of anxiety is the search for self in another self.

Haufniensis's analysis of the erotic has a dialectical structure of its own. First he discusses the "sexual as such," which he says is not sinful. Since only beasts are genuinely ignorant of sexuality, human innocence must be understood as "a knowledge . . . that has ignorance as its first determination."[12] He suggests calling this state modesty, for it manifests the anxiety of shame if not yet the anxiety of lust. In other words, the awareness of the other as other is just beginning to appear in sexuality as such: "In modesty, the generic difference is posited, but not in relation to its other. That takes place in the sexual drive" (*CA*, 69), which is not only instinct but also propagation. Propagation is not yet love; indeed, from the point of view of paganism, it appears comic, which leads Haufniensis to comment: "The anxiety in modesty arose from the spirit's feeling that it was a foreigner; now spirit has conquered completely and perceives the sexual as the foreign and as the comic" (*CA*, 69). Thus the erotic is conquered by propagation, by means of its relationship to its other, whereas modesty remains afraid of the erotic and sexually inhibited by its lack of such a relationship. In Christianity, the self discovers that "the religious has suspended the erotic . . . because in spirit there is no difference between man and woman" (*CA*, 70). In other words, the distinction between self and other that sexuality has brought about is also sublated in the spirit— but at the price of the erotic. Because the erotic is suspended and spirit is excluded from it, there is still anxiety, for anxiety occurs whenever the spirit "feels itself a stranger" (*CA*, 71). Even if the sexual is brought fully "under the determination of the spirit," the result is "the victory of love" in which "the sexual is forgotten, and recollected only in forgetfulness. When this has come about, sensuousness is transfigured in spirit and anxiety is driven out."[13]

This analysis of the first two chapters of *The Concept of Anxiety* yields two significant results. First, anxiety is a matter of the dialectic of self and other. It originates when the self seeks itself in an other, and it can be characterized as the state of a self that is other ("a stranger") to itself. Anxiety is the root and result of alienation, understood as a distorted relationship to oneself *and* to others. Second, this concept of anxiety is susceptible to a systematic, structural analysis. As a mere concept, it is the movement of anxiety in-itself. This first movement simply posits anxiety as the theoretical origin and result of hereditary sin. Actual sin is not yet distinguished from the hereditary condition of sinfulness; nor is there as yet any consciousness of sin. Within this movement, three moments can be discerned. In the first, the self seeks itself in an indeterminate other. This is dreaming anxiety, the in-itself moment in which self and other have not yet been distinguished at all. It is followed by objective anxiety, a for-itself moment in which the self projects its anxiety onto creation, which is the nonhuman other.[14] Here self and other are distinguished, but in a very unsatisfactory way, for the self remains unaware of its own anxiety. That consciousness appears only in the in-and-for-itself moment, which Haufniensis labels subjective anxiety. Here the self finds itself in a human other, which is a good deal closer to its actual self than either the indeterminate or the nonhuman other.

Within subjective anxiety, the self finds itself by means of a dialectic of erotic relations. Modesty is the in-itself phase, in which the self is aware of sexual difference but not yet in relation to a particular other. That relationship first appears as propagation, a for-itself phase in which the opposition between spirit and sexuality becomes explicit. Whereas spirit feels alienated in modesty, now it is sexuality that is alienated from the self by virtue of being harnessed and subjected to the goal of propagation. This dialectical struggle between modesty and propagation illustrates that the erotic is not yet spirit, for both are phases in which the self is still seeking itself in an other. The theoretical resolution of this contradiction is posited by Christianity, which asserts the self's identity with its other.

With this new consciousness, the movement of abstract anxiety—that is, anxiety projected onto something or someone other—is complete. The self understands that its anxiety is about itself, and the for-itself movement of anxiety can begin.

B. Anxiety over External Determination

Chapter III presents anxiety as a consciousness of the eternal that is not yet conscious of hereditary sin, in short, a consciousness that is religious without being Christian. It is here that Haufniensis dialectically situates Christian paganism, paganism, and Judaism in relation to each other and to Christianity.[15] The fundamental dialectic here is no longer that of psyche and body; it is the eternal and the temporal. "In the individual life," he begins, "anxiety is the Moment" (*CA*, 81).[16] This Moment is neither a dialectical moment nor a temporal instant. On the contrary, the intention of this discussion is to refute the Hegelian theory that eternity is the totality and infinite succession of temporal moments.

The Moment occurs, writes Haufniensis, when "time and eternity touch each other . . . in time." He praises the Danish word *Øiblikket* (which, like the German *Augenblick*, means "blink of the eye") as a "beautiful word" (*CA*, 87). This touching-in-time of eternity and time is not in any sense a mediation of equal poles: "the Moment is not properly an atom of time but an atom of eternity. It is the first reflection of eternity in time, its first attempt, as it were, at stopping time" (*CA*, 88). Eternity, then, is that which attempts to stop time. Rather than an infinite extension of time, it breaks into time from the outside and limits it. This limitation, this instant in which the limit of time is revealed, is the Moment.

On the basis of this understanding of the Moment, it is possible to grasp Haufniensis's concept of temporality. Temporality is posited on the basis of the Moment, and history begins with it. In short, although the Moment occurs in the blink of an eye, it brings about a qualitative change within the temporal sequence. In the ordinary view, the past, present, and future spill into one another, for future time becomes present and then past in turn. The distinctions between them are merely relative to the particular point of view, which in itself is without absolute significance. But if the Moment is the limitation of time by eternity, then temporality is seen as a relation to that time-stopping eternity and not simply to infinite succession. Furthermore, the Moment when eternity breaks into time is not relative to the totality of time; on the contrary, the eternal relativizes time itself and thereby determines the condition of temporality. The distinction of past, present, and future now takes on real significance, for each is understood in relation to the eternal-in-time, the Moment, rather than in a "simple continuity." This is what is meant by the Christian concept of the "fullness of time" (*CA*, 90). However, it is true that temporality suffers the same consequence of the positing of sin that sensuousness does: it comes to signify sinfulness (*CA*, 93).

The dialectic of anxiety in the individual life is structured according to the distinction made by the Moment between present, future, and past. There are three moments, each reflecting a new consciousness of the Moment. The first such moment is Christian paganism, which "really knows no distinction between the present, the past, the future, and the eternal" (*CA*, 94). Haufniensis labels this "the anxiety of spiritlessness" (article 1). The dilemma of spiritlessness is that, on the one hand, it shares in the Christian relation to spirit, and, on the other, it represses its consciousness of this relation by affecting a pagan indifference to the eternal in time. However, paganism should not be confused with spiritlessness: "the former is qualified *toward* spirit and the latter *away from* spirit" (*CA*, 95). Since spiritlessness excludes spirit, it also excludes consciousness of anxiety. But anxiety is waiting and will appear as a "profound terror" at the moment of death (*CA*, 96).

Article 2 bears the title, "Anxiety Defined Dialectically as Fate," and deals with paganism as such. Here spirit is no longer excluded, for fate is "a relation to spirit as external" (*CA*, 96). In other words, the pagan submits to fate as it is revealed through external and accidental means (for example, the oracle, which may be based upon interpreting the entrails of an animal or upon anatomical patterns). This dependence upon such ambiguous and external elements makes it impossible for the pagan to arrive at the concepts of guilt and sin, which presuppose an inward relationship to the eternal. Indeed, it is a meaningless contradiction to affirm that one becomes guilty by fate (CA, 97). Haufniensis develops the pagan position in a long discussion of genius, a discussion that is particularly interesting for his use of the inner/outer categories. The genius manifests a significant contradiction between a pagan external dependency upon some "insignificance" through which personal fate is revealed, and the fact that the "outward as such has no significance for the genius. . . . Everything depends upon how he himself understands it in the presence of his secret friend (fate)" (CA, 100).

The final dialectical moment of anxiety in relation to the eternal in time is guilt (article 3). The historical subject here is Judaism. An important distinction is made immediately: Jewish anxiety is over the possibility of guilt, rather than "the positing of an actual [guilty] relation" (CA, 104). The anxiety that characterizes Judaism is more advanced than that of Greek culture, since guilt is more inward than fate, but it still manifests a capitulation to externality. According to Haufniensis, "the profound tragedy of Judaism, analogous to the relation of the oracle in paganism," is the dependence upon sacrificial rituals (CA, 104). That rituals increase rather than relieve anxiety about guilt is demonstrated by the fact that the ritual must be constantly repeated (the same is true in a qualified sense, adds Haufniensis, of Catholicism).

The remainder of this chapter on anxiety over the possibility of actual sin (anxiety for-itself) deals with the relation between religious inwardness and its external expression: "to explain how my religious existence comes into relation with and expresses itself in my outward existence, that is the task" (CA, 105). Haufniensis argues the connection between inwardness and guilt on the basis of Jewish ceremonial law: "In turning toward himself, he [the religious genius] *eo ipso* turns toward God, and there is a ceremonial rule that says that when the finite spirit would see God, it must begin as guilty. As he turns toward himself, he discovers guilt. The greater the genius, the more profoundly he discovers guilt" (*CA*, 107). Thus guilt is the inevitable result of the inward turn, since the turn inward is, by its very nature, a turn toward God. In a comment that shows the extent to which Haufniensis is oblivious to the complex systematic structure within his own analysis, he adds that guilt is the *Ansich* or in-itself of freedom (*CA*, 108). Although he does not develop this dialectical terminology at all, it is likely that he has in mind a dialectic of anxiety as entangled freedom (*CA*, 49) in which the three moments are guilt, sin-consciousness, and faith.

To summarize the development of the dialectic of anxiety thus far: in anxiety in-itself, anxiety is not yet self-conscious. It can apprehend itself only through self-projection onto non-human and human others. Once the self realizes that the other about which it is anxious is really identical with itself, it advances to anxiety as a condition of the individual life. This is anxiety-for-itself, and Haufniensis traces its three historical expressions, all of which reveal that the self has not yet abandoned the search for itself (now, the eternal) in something external. The continuity between the first two movements can be stated as follows: in anxiety in-itself, the self seeks itself in another that is external; in anxiety for-itself, the self turns to something external in search of the eternal, which is really the Moment or the divine other.

The internal development of anxiety for-itself follows the familiar pattern: the first moment is Christendom,[17] a state in which the consciousness of the eternal has been repressed, and with it consciousness of anxiety over the need for the eternal. Anxiety must, in such a person, wait for the fear of death, which will certainly stimulate such a sense of need. The pagan does not repress the need for the eternal but seeks it externally. Thus the pagan lives in anxious self-contradiction: the inner need for and relation with the eternal as one's own fate is acknowledged, but the knowledge of that fate is available only externally, in the ambiguous oracle. Judaism overcomes the opposition between Christendom and paganism in that it internalizes the cause of alienation of the self from the eternal. By positing the possibility of guilt, Judaism admits anxiety (with paganism) but focuses that anxiety on the self (as Christendom focuses on the self in indifference to the eternal). But, in attempting to atone for guilt by the performance of rituals, Judaism seeks an external reconciliation with the eternal, an outward solution to an inner problem. This effort is doomed to failure, for, as the Jew has already discovered, freedom is to be found only by "turning inward" (*CA*, 108), since guilt "never has an external occasion, and whoever yields to temptation is himself guilty of the temptation" (*CA*, 109).

C. Anxiety as Inward Constitution
by the Eternal

In chapter IV, anxiety as the consequence or consciousness of sin in the single individual at last appears. Haufniensis stresses that this appearance cannot be reduced to a causal chain. Like freedom, sin must never be understood as in any sense necessary, for then the freedom would be unfree and the sin would not be sinful: "the circle of the leap [would be made] into a straight line" (*CA*, 112). Nevertheless, there is clear dialectical transition from anxiety for-itself to this final movement, anxiety in-and-for-itself.

The simplest way to express this transition is in terms of the relation of inwardness to externality. In the first movement, there is a dialectic of self and other but no distinction between the temporal and the eternal. That distinction takes place in anxiety for-itself, where the temporal self is determined by its external relations to the eternal. In this third movement, the eternal appears inwardly, in the self's relation to itself. Although this appearance of "the eternal in man" (*CA*, 151) is not explicit until the second moment, it is implicit in the first moment, anxiety about evil.

Another striking development at this point, and the one that Haufniensis himself emphasizes, is the transition from anxiety about the possibility of actual sin to anxiety about actual sin. For the first time, "the object of anxiety is a determinate something and its nothing is an actual something" (*CA*, 111). Here the equivocations of Judaism come to an end: the individual is a sinner. Sin is posited as "an annulled possibility," that is, as an actuality.[18] The question is no longer whether one is in sin, but what, if anything, can be done about it.

That consciousness would like to do something about it is immediately clear from the passage with which article 1 ("Anxiety about Evil") opens: "The posited sin is indeed an annulled possibility, but it is also an unwarranted actuality, and as such, anxiety can relate itself to it. Since sin is an unwarranted actuality, it is also to be negated. This work anxiety will undertake" (*CA*, 113). It appears that the very realization of sin as a fact brings with it the hope—and the anxiety—of becoming free from it. Thus this first moment begins with "the ingenious sophistry of anxiety," for the actuality of sin immediately proclaims freedom on the one hand and "the eloquence of illusion" on the other (*CA*, 113). This phase is followed by a second, in which anxiety sees the possibility of the continuation of sin and tries to strike a compromise with it: anxiety "wants to have the actuality of sin continue—but note, only to a certain degree" (*CA*, 114). The sophistry of anxiety and the impotence of compromise are united in repentance, which both hopes for freedom and impotently confesses sin: "Repentance is reduced to a possibility in relation to sin; in other words, repentance cannot cancel sin, it can only sorrow over it."[19] The repentant self has no strength on which to draw. Conquered by sin, the anxiety of the individual "throws itself into the arms of repentance" (*CA*, 115), which Haufniensis implicitly compares with death:

The only thing that is truly able to disarm the sophistry of sin is faith, courage to believe that the state itself is a new sin, courage to renounce anxiety without anxiety, which only faith can do; faith does not thereby annihilate anxiety, but, itself eternally young, it extricates itself from anxiety's moment of death. Only faith is able to do this, for only in faith is the synthesis eternal and at every moment possible. (*CA*, 117)

The synthesis referred to has many applications—physical and psychical, finite and infinite, temporal and eternal, and so on—but one in particular is relevant here. In confessing sin, the self, for the first time, becomes conscious of itself in all its inwardness. No longer is there any external power to tell the self its fate or to absolve it, for awhile, of its guilt. The self is guilty, and no recourse is open to it other than repentance, a death of the self in which the only remaining anxiety is over the possibility of deliverance from sin. Repentance is also the *Aufhebung* of the previous two phases, in that it restores confession of sin as an unwarranted actuality at the same time that it acknowledges its own impotence to cancel sin. Repentance alone, no matter how profound, can never bring freedom (*CA*, 116).

In this final movement, anxiety in-and-for-itself, the first moment is anxiety about evil, in which anxiety is revealed as a "moment of death," for in it inwardness appears as total self-negation. The next moment introduces the demonic, which might seem startling after the discussion of repentance, but which in fact is dialectically coherent: the demonic negates the self-negation of repentance in a last effort at self-assertion. Rather than protest against the evil of sin, the demonic self protests against the good that has revealed sin to be sin: "The bondage of sin is an unfree relation to the evil, but the demonic is an unfree relation to the good" (*CA*, 119). When a person sees that the only way to appropriate the good is to confess and repent of sin, a hostile reaction to the good can occur. Then "freedom is lost" (*CA*, 123), for the demonic individual denies the sinfulness of sin, rejects the rejection of sin, and negates the self-negation of repentance.

It is not possible to do justice here to Haufniensis's lengthy discussion of the demonic (*CA*, 118-154). Despite the obvious irony in his remark that "for me the principle thing is to have my schema in order" (*CA*, 137),[20] it is precisely the structure, as a dialectical development of the experience of anxiety, that I shall analyze. There is less textual basis here than in previous sections of *The Concept of Anxiety* for a systematic analysis of phases. Nevertheless, it is possible to discern a dialectical development within the demonic also.

The first phase of the demonic treats it abstractly, as a theoretical concept. Haufniensis discusses three methods by which the demonic can be approached: aesthetic-metaphysical, ethical, and medical-therapeutic (*CA*, 119-123). The first sympathizes with the demonic determined by fate, the second condemns it, and the third treats it as a physical problem (in contemporary terms, a matter of body chemistry). A number of characteristics of the demonic follow, each of which is discussed in some detail (*CA*, 135). The first is "withdrawnness," which "closes itself up within itself."[21] The withdrawn personality has not returned to external determinations; rather, inwardness here is given the intense perversity of one who rejects God, for "one cannot be withdrawn in God or in the good."[22] The other two characteristics of the demonic—"the sudden," and "the contentless, the boring" (*CA*, 129-133)—are described as new expressions for withdrawnness. Thus there are three methods and three characteristics within the definition of the demonic, but no dialectical progression in either triad. For that, it is necessary to examine the ways in which demonic loss of freedom can be expressed.

The first way is "somatically-psychically," by which Haufniensis means what are now called psychosomatic conditions. He gives a number of examples, among them hysteria and hypochondria, and mentions very briefly that demoniacs often form extremely dependent relationships with one another, such that "no friendship has an inwardness that can be compared with it" (*CA*, 137). Even more illuminating is his description of how the psychosomatic demonic deviates from a healthy relation to the good: "The body is the organ of the psyche and in turn the organ of the spirit. As soon as the serving relation comes to an end, as soon as the body revolts, and as soon as freedom conspires with the body against itself, unfreedom is present as the demonic" (*CA*, 136). The striking phrase here is: "freedom conspires with the body against itself." This idea can be illuminated by recalling the place of the demonic within the dialectic of anxiety. The self has already achieved the inwardness of repentance, understood as the freedom that comes from encountering in God the good by which the self realizes its own sinfulness. All of that was accomplished in the first moment within anxiety in-and-for-itself. Then comes the demonic, which is the negation of that encounter, not by a return to externality but by a perversion of inwardness, namely, a withdrawnness of the self from God or the good. Rather than rest in the painful freedom of repentance, the self strives for independence from God. Thus the demonic self is inwardly at war with itself, pitting its own autonomy against the freedom of the good, and it is this battle that allows freedom to conspire with the body against itself. The result is that the self's freedom appears to be lost psychosomatically, in some sort of debilitating nervous disorder. This inward self-alienation is the demonic for-itself, in contrast to the abstract definition of the demonic in-itself.

The other way in which the demoniac loses freedom is "pneumatically": freedom conspires not with the body but with the mind. The serving relation here is destroyed by the lack of consistency between the beliefs that the self espouses and the behavior that reflects the self's genuine inwardness: "truth is for the particular individual only as he himself produces it in action" (*CA*, 138). In a passage that is as typical of Haufniensis's convoluted style as it is expressive of his anti-Hegelian distinction between concrete existence and the philosophical "pure self-consciousness," he writes:

> The most concrete content that consciousness can have is consciousness of itself, of the individual himself—not the

pure self-consciousness, but the self-consciousness that is so concrete that no author, not even the one with the greatest power of description, has ever been able to describe a single such self-consciousness, although every single human being is such a one. This self-consciousness is not contemplation, for he who believes this has not understood himself, because he sees that meanwhile he himself is in the process of becoming and consequently cannot be something completed for contemplation. This self-consciousness, therefore, is action, and this action is in turn inwardness, and whenever inwardness does not correspond to this consciousness, there is a form of the demonic as soon as the absence of inwardness expresses itself as anxiety about its acquisition. (*CA*, 143)

By means of a number of examples, Haufniensis illustrates what he means by this demonic anxiety over inwardness. In each of them, the basic conflict within the self is between passivity and activity. Thus, when the demonic self-inconsistency is one of unbelief versus superstition, passivity and activity can be understood in their dialectical relation as equally lacking in inwardness: "unbelief is passive through an activity, and superstition is active through a passivity. . . . Superstition is unbelieving about itself. Unbelief is superstitious about itself " (*CA*, 144). In all of these formulations, self-reflection is shown to be in contradiction with the action of inwardness. The person who espouses unbelief on the grounds of a humanistic philosophy of action is rendered passive by virtue of a superstitious belief in the autonomy and capacity of the self. Conversely, the superstitious self appears to be passive, but its refusal to see its own active role as interpreter of the omens (like the pagan receiving the oracle) constitutes a profound form of unbelief. Haufniensis mentions two other internal struggles between belief and action: "hypocrisy is offense at oneself, while offense is hypocrisy to oneself," and "[p]ride is a profound cowardice. . . . [cowardice] is a profound pride" (*CA*, 145).

Haufniensis's concluding remarks on the demonic illuminate its dialectical role within anxiety in-and-for-itself. In his view, the demonic rejection of the good is a loss of inwardness, since inwardness is "eternity or the determination of the eternal *in* a man."[23] The pneumatic demoniac is one who intellectually conceives of countless evasions of the eternal, whereas the psychosomatic demoniac rejects the eternal by allowing the body to revolt against the soul and spirit, thereby making inward consciousness of the eternal impossible. Thus the demonic constitutes a negation of the inwardness of repentance, which means that it is self-assertion over against the inwardness of the eternal, the good. In this sense, Haufniensis is consistent in calling the demonic a loss of inwardness. But it is not a return to the externality of anxiety for-itself, which is a total lack of consciousness of sin. As a rebellion against God and a repudiation of the fact of sin, the demonic is an attempt to assert the self's independence of the good, not by virtue of an external relation to it but in unremitting opposition to it. Without the consciousness of the eternal and of sin, there could be no demonic. For this reason, I prefer to call it a perversion of inwardness rather than an absence of inwardness. The demonic is a futile attempt to sustain inwardness and freedom without the good, which is their origin and only sustaining power. As such, it is a false inwardness and a form of unfreedom.

It is more difficult to trace the vague dialectical development of phases within the demonic. Such as it is, that structure substantiates the claim that the demonic is not so much absence as it is perversion of inwardness. The demonic in-itself is first defined as withdrawnness, in which the self acknowledges no relational determinations. It closes in upon itself in the illusion of self-sufficiency. In the demonic for-itself, that abstract unity of withdrawnness is sundered, for the self finds itself at war with its own body. This battle may be utterly internal, but it is nevertheless violently divisive for the self. For the psychosomatic, the body becomes the external expression of an inner illness. The pneumatic demonic reconciles this division, in the sense that the expression of inward self-contradiction can no longer be identified with the "external" body; now it is the self's action, a manifestation of inwardness no less than of consciousness, that reveals the self demonically at war with itself.

The demonic, as anxiety about the good, stands in opposition to anxiety about evil, which resulted in repentance. Their dialectical culmination is accomplished by anxiety as saving through faith, which is the subject of chapter V. The primary argument in this short chapter is that through faith it can be seen that anxiety is educative, for it is anxiety over possibility that leads the self along this difficult path to faith, a path on which every finite definition of the self is exposed as illusion until at last the self accepts itself as determined by the eternal (CA, 155-156).

An interesting and significant aspect of Haufniensis's analysis of faith illustrates its dialectical development with striking clarity: the phases of faith recapitulate the moments of anxiety over the possibility of sin (chapter III). Haufniensis first discusses the case of the person who has never been conscious of anxiety, that is, spiritlessness (CA, 157). If such a one is indeed "educated by possibility," then the possibility of faith will also appear: "Then the assaults of anxiety, even though they be terrifying, will not be such that he flees from them. For him, anxiety becomes a serving spirit that against its will leads him where he wishes to go" (CA, 158-159). This is the positing of anxiety as educative (in systematic terms, of faith in-itself). It is followed by a second phase, faith for-itself, in which anxiety discovers fate: "but just when the individual wants to put his trust in fate, anxiety turns around and takes fate away, because fate is like anxiety, and anxiety, like possibility, is a 'magic' picture" (CA, 159). Fate, of course, is the second moment within anxiety over the possibility of actual sin. Whereas the pagan remains shackled by fate, the Christian learns that anxiety can also lead beyond it: "With the help of faith, anxiety brings up the individuality to rest in providence" (CA, 161). Finally, anxiety discovers the guilt that lies beyond fate. Here the lesson of faith is that "he who in relation to guilt is educated by anxiety will rest only in the atonement" (*CA*, 162).

The dialectic here is as follows: faith in-itself posits anxiety as saving through faith; faith for-itself is the last flicker of negation and otherness, in which salvation is identified with providence in a relatively external manner; and faith in-and-for-itself is the at-one-ment of the self with the eternal, in which "the eternal in man" is fully realized.

The concept of the eternal in man thus points toward the internalization of consciousness of the divine eternal other. God is known only inwardly, although he remains other to human inwardness. This conclusion, together with the crucial role played by sin-consciousness, confirms also that *The Concept of Anxiety* deals primarily with the religious stage. Finally, the systematic dialectical structure of Haufniensis's argument should by now be clear. All that remains is to describe briefly how that structure is manifest within the final movement (anxiety over the actuality of sin) and among the three movements of the text as a whole. Following that description, Chart 4 will outline the entire structure, giving both the character of each movement, moment, and phase and their respective correlations with the chapters and sections of *The Concept of Anxiety* (in brackets).

Faith is the third moment of the third movement, which is anxiety in-and-for-itself. The way in which this dialectic unfolds can be described as follows: in anxiety about evil, inwardness is posited as a "moment of death," a confession of sin and an impotent repentance that constitute the self's negation of itself before the goodness of the eternal. The demonic opposes this self-negation by its denial of the hegemony of the eternal, which is a form of self-assertion. The reconciliation of these two moments in faith can be characterized as a self-affirmation of the self as dependent upon God. With the first moment, faith acknowledges the self's dependence upon God; with the second, it affirms the self; the two moments are *aufgehoben* in such a way as to negate the abject self-negation of the first moment and the proud self-assertion of the demonic (the second).

Finally, the structure of *The Concept of Anxiety* as a whole demonstrates that it does indeed reflect a systematic development of inwardness. In anxiety in-itself, inwardness is still in an embryonic form, for the self's anxiety is projected onto external others—whether indeterminate, the created world, or the erotic other. Consciousness of inwardness first appears as the consciousness of the self over against or in relation to the eternal as externally manifest. This is anxiety for-itself, in which the eternal is never fully internalized; it is ignored (Christendom), externally determined (paganism), or externally expressed (Judaism). In anxiety in-and-for-itself, the eternal as the determination of inwardness is revealed in the dialectic of self-negation (confession and repentance of sin), self-assertion (the demonic), and self-affirmation in dependence upon God (faith). Thus the three movements of the dialectic of anxiety can be analyzed as follows: an initial, abstract unity in which the self has not yet consciously distinguished itself from its external world; a negative dialectic of opposition between the self as inner and an external power that determines it; and a final reconciliation, in which the determining power is inwardly revealed and appropriated, and the self finds in faith the culmination and fulfillment of its dialectical education by anxiety.

This analysis, I hope, has substantiated my three claims: that there is a systematic dialectical structure of inwardness in *The Concept of Anxiety*; that in it the eternal does not remain external; and that the internalization occurs as a movement that must be characterized as religious. *The Concept of Anxiety* is, according to Haufniensis, a merely psychological study, not a dogmatic treatise. As such, it explores the development of anxiety as an anthropological phenomenon. However, Haufniensis does not treat anxiety apart from the problem of sin and the relation between the individual self and the eternal. As reflected in human consciousness, that relation undergoes a development that can be analyzed in terms of its dialectical

CHART 4.
The Dialectic of Inwardness in
The Concept of Anxiety

A. Anxiety posited as origin and result of sin
  1. Dreaming anxiety: self seeks itself in indeterminate other [I]
  2. Objective anxiety: self projects anxiety onto nonhuman other (creation) [II.1]
  3. Subjective anxiety: self finds itself in relation to human other [II.2]
     a. Modesty: alien erotic (self not related to its other)
     b. Propagation: comic erotic (self related to its other)
     c. Christianity: suspended erotic (self identical with its other)

   ANXIETY IN-ITSELF:
   SELF'S INNER ANXIETY PROJECTED
   ONTO EXTERNAL OTHER

B. Anxiety over the possibility of actual sin [III]
  1. Spiritlessness in Christendom: anxiety waiting (consciousness repressed) [III.1]
  2. Dialectic of fate in paganism: inner anxiety about external oracle [III.2]
  3. Dialectic of guilt in Judaism: inner anxiety expressed in external sacrifice [III.3]

   ANXIETY FOR-ITSELF:
   DIALECTIC IN WHICH SELF IS DETERMINED
   BY EXTERNAL RELATION TO THE ETERNAL

C. Anxiety over the actuality of sin
  1. Anxiety about evil: inwardness as self-negation [IV.1]
     a. Sin posited as unwarranted actuality (sophistical claim of freedom)
     b. Compromise with sin (impotence to achieve freedom from sin)
     c. Repentance of sin (impotent sorrow in hope of freedom)
  2. Anxiety about good: demonic self-assertion [IV.2]
     a. Withdrawnness into self
     b. Psychosomatic externalization of self
     c. Spiritual self-contradiction within self
  3. Anxiety as saving by means of faith: self-affirmation in dependence on God [V]
     a. Spirit as the eternal within the self (versus spiritlessness)
     b. Providence as the eternal over the self (versus fate)
     c. Atonement reconciles the eternal with the self (versus guilt)

   ANXIETY IN-AND-FOR-ITSELF:
   SELF CONSTITUTED INWARDLY BY THE ETERNAL

structure. But as a direct encounter, as the meeting of the temporal and the eternal, the human and the divine, it resists this sort of analysis, for the assertion that there can even be such a meeting is profoundly paradoxical. This paradox is frequently alluded to in *The Concept of Anxiety* and constitutes the fundamental theme of *Philosophical Fragments*.

PHILOSOPHICAL FRAGMENTS

Although Johannes Climacus is the pseudonym in whom interpreters most often feel they can see Kierkegaard's own views expressed, considerable confusion surrounds him. He is sometimes credited with writing the early novel, *De Omnibus Dubitandum Est*,[24] but in fact he is the subject, not the author, of that work. As mentioned at the beginning of this chapter, Climacus's *Philosophical Fragments* has been viewed as a spiritual work on the revelation from above to below; yet it is also true that the name Johannes Climacus means John the Climber, and that this character loves logic more than God.[25] Climacus gazes from below at the paradoxes of faith, never claiming for a moment to be a Christian. In his own eyes, he is just a humorist and dialectician. The dialectic that he propounds and illustrates in *Philosophical Fragments* is one of relentless paradox: a thoroughgoing repudiation of mediating, systematic dialectics that is based upon a strident apologia for the principle of contradiction (*PF*, 136-137). In this case, analysis of the dialectical structures in the essay supports that position and also demonstrates again that a distinctive mark of faith is inwardness as "the determination of the eternal in man" (*CA*, 151).

In his Preface, Climacus immediately announces his anti-Hegelian intentions: "The present offering . . . does not make the slightest pretension to share in the philosophical movement of the day" (*PF*, 3). Both the system[26] as a whole and the particular brand of dialectics that accompanies it are targets of his sarcasm: "the concept all the while like an acrobatic clown in the current circus season, every moment performing these everlasting dog-tricks of flopping over and over, until it flops over the man himself" (*PF*, 5). In contrast, Climacus is a man of resignation who approaches his subject with a unique blend of earnestness and humor: "I have disciplined myself and keep myself under discipline, in order that I may be able to execute a sort of nimble dancing in the service of thought, so far as possible also to the honor of the god, and for my own satisfaction" (*PF*, 6).

Chapter I, "A Project of Thought," opens with a "Socratic" question: "How far does the truth admit of being learned?" The logical conundrum behind this question is that, if a person is ignorant of the truth, then it is impossible to learn about the truth, for there must be some knowledge of the truth both to know how to seek it and to be able to recognize it as the truth. However, if one already has knowledge of the truth, then it is equally impossible to *learn* it. It follows that the truth cannot be learned. Socrates' claim, argues Climacus, is that the truth can only be recollected: "Thus the truth is not introduced into the individual from without, but was within him" (*PF*, 11). This claim presupposes that truth is a form of self-knowledge in which "each individual is his own center" (*PF*, 14). In this scheme, a teacher functions only as a midwife, one who assists in delivering a truth that is already emerging by a natural process. The historical circumstances surrounding this birth are of no consequence to the truth itself: "The temporal point of departure is nothing; for as soon as I discover that I have known the truth from eternity without being aware of it, the same instant this moment of occasion is hidden in the eternal" (*PF*, 15-16).

Climacus then turns to an alternative possibility: "Now if things are to be otherwise, the Moment in time must have a decisive significance . . . because the eternal, which hitherto did not exist, came into existence in this Moment."[27] In contrast to the reasonableness of recollection, this notion involves a paradox: that which is external and eternal must enter the internal and temporal realm, it must *become*. Just as Haufniensis argues in *The Concept of Anxiety*, the Moment occurs when the eternal breaks in upon time.

The dialectic of the Moment differs in every respect from that of recollection (*PF*, 16-18). Rather than mere ignorance, in which the individual already possesses the sought-after truth but must make it conscious, the Moment is decisive precisely because it cannot be possessed unconsciously. If a person has not encountered and appropriated the Moment, then that person lacks any relationship whatsoever with the truth; this antecedent state is one of error, pure and simple. Since the individual has no inner resources for encountering the Moment, there must be some external factor, a teacher, who will bring about that encounter and who will actually create in an individual the condition necessary to learn the truth. Such a teacher, however, must be "the god himself" (*PF*, 19), for no human being can create the condition for learning in other humans.

Climacus, the climber, has actually made a logical leap from the dilemma of one who would come to know the eternal to the paradoxical notion of a god who enters time. He writes as though the problem itself forced this "project in thought" upon him, but the suspicion is inescapable that he could not have arrived at this second alternative by philosophical reason alone. The historical source of his line of thinking is illuminated by the further claims that the teacher/god will reveal the individual's previous error to have been sin and himself as the savior, redeemer, atoner and judge (*PF*, 19-22). The Moment is "filled with the eternal" and therefore deserves the name of "*fulness of time*" (*PF*, 22). This obviously Christian language continues in the final section, "The Disciple." Transformation from a person in error into a knower of the truth is said to render one a "new creature." It is conversion, requiring repentance and leading to a "rebirth."[28] This process results in a disciple, one who is the exact opposite of the Socratic pupil. Whereas the Socratic pupil "forgets the world in his discovery of himself," the disciple "forgets himself in the discovery of his teacher" (*PF*, 24).

The organization of chapter I does not make entirely clear that it suggests a contrast not simply between Socratic and

Christian modes of relating to the truth but also between two types of dialectical reason. In Socratic recollection, the antecedent state is ignorance, the teacher and moment of recollection are merely accidental, and the result is self-knowledge. From an initial immediacy in which there are no distinctions between inner and outer or self and other, there emerges a brief encounter with an external other, but this opposition and otherness prove to be unessential, for the resulting recollection is a return to self in which that other is forgotten as accidental. Such self-knowledge does not attempt to take the other up into itself; it abolishes the otherness of the other by its belief that the truth is eternally in all persons, and that the only task is for everyone to be made aware of it.

In contrast, the Christian dialectic involves three parallel moments that work to establish the fact of otherness all the more firmly. The antecedent state is here viewed as the error of sin, an awareness that is possible only on the basis of an encounter with the teacher in a decisive Moment. The disciple unites sin with salvation in a way that never denies the otherness of the teacher. In fact, the disciple is an example of the paradox of internalized otherness.[29] Repentance presupposes a new sense of otherness in relation to the "old" self. In rebirth as a saved sinner, there is the sense of living by virtue of the divine other, who is now inwardly present. Thus the disciple represents a paradoxical unity of inner and outer, self and other, old and new, in which the opposition between these terms is heightened rather than annulled. Because of the difficulty of grasping such paradoxes, Climacus remarks that they will be thinkable only for the person who has actually experienced this rebirth.

In chapter II, the dialectical tension is between divine and human rather than inner and outer. The theme is the difficulty of understanding a revelation when there is such a total incommensurability between the eternal (divine) and the temporal (human). The Moment in which the eternal enters time is an "incommensurable occasion" (*PF*, 30), for the god who becomes human for the sake of humans must nonetheless suffer an unhappy love, "for how great is the difference between them!" (*PF*, 31). The assumption here is that mutual understanding is possible only between equal partners, that the incommensurability of the divine with the human must be overcome in order for their mutual estrangement to end. Climacus expresses this as the god's determination "to bring [the learner] to equality with himself" (*PF*, 34).

Three possible modes of revelation are suggested, which again follow the dialectical pattern of chapter I. First, the divine-human union might be accomplished "by an elevation of the learner" (*PF*, 35). Climacus criticizes this possibility, according to which the learner would simply forget the previous estrangement from the god as sheer deception. What he does not point out is that the deception involved is similar to that of the Socratic attitude. In both cases, the opposition between the divine and the human is denied by means of divinizing the human. It is salvation by apotheosis. The learner simply forgets his error and sin; they are shown to be of no more consequence for the relation with the divine teacher than were historical occasions for the Socratic learner. In short, apotheosis begs the question; it denies the very problem that the possibility of revelation poses.

The second possible mode of revelation is a clear allusion to Old Testament theophany: "The union might be brought about by the god's showing himself to the learner and receiving his worship, causing him to forget himself over the divine apparition" (*PF*, 36). Climacus appeals to the Jews themselves for his refutation of this mode: "There once lived a people who had a profound understanding of the divine; this people thought that no man could see the god and live.—Who grasps this contradiction of sorrow: not to reveal oneself is the death of love, to reveal oneself is the death of the beloved!" (*PF*, 37). Here the opposition is affirmed in the greatest possible degree. The god is, as it were, totally other and cannot be revealed to mere humans. With the logical rigor of an Apollinaris, Climacus asserts the incapacity of human nature to host the divine. As in chapter I, where the learner is impotent to create the condition for overcoming ignorance but has not yet been reborn from above as a disciple, this is the dialectical moment when consciousness can only grieve over the "contradiction of sorrow" (*PF*, 37).

Once again, however, there is a third moment: "Since we found that the union could not be brought about by an elevation it must be attempted by a descent. . . . the god will therefore appear in the form of a *servant*" (*PF*, 39). This section develops the idea of the god's desire for equality with the disciple. It also fulfills the promise of the chapter's title— "The God as Teacher and Savior: A Poetic Essay"[30]—for Climacus waxes lyrical over the sufferings that true love must endure for the beloved. But the dialectical moment must not be obscured by that lyricism. When, in the manner of the kenosis in Phillipians 2, the god descends to become the servant of the beloved, then their "equality . . . in earnest and truth" is shown (*PF*, 39). But this equality in no way denies their difference. The god remains divine, even in human form, and the human as such does not thereby become divine. The humanity of god is a paradoxical unity, neither a Hegelian *Aufhebung* nor a mere contradiction. The kenosis reveals a god who is God as-a-man, just as the Lord is said to be Lord *precisely as* the servant of those over whom he is Lord.

Dialectically, chapter II is thus another aspect of the paradoxical dialectic of Christian revelation. Kenosis is not a sublation of apotheosis and theophany, although it does paradoxically accomplish the equality of the former without jeopardizing the asymmetry of the latter. Furthermore, no systematic progression relates the dialectic of sin-teacher-disciple to the three types of revelation. The paradox displays neither the oscillation of reciprocity nor any progressive development. That this is very much Climacus's intention is made clear in chapter III, "The Absolute Paradox."

Despite its whimsical subtitle, "A Metaphysical Crochet," this chapter develops a serious argument, namely, that the god is the unknown and that the unknown is "the limit to which the reason repeatedly comes" (*PF*, 49, 55). Because the difference between the divine and the human is absolute, reason cannot grasp it. The very effort to grasp the difference would destroy it, for, Climacus assumes, in knowledge "like and unlike finally become identified with one another, thus sharing the fate of all such dialectical opposites" (*PF*, 56). Yet this negative aspect of the paradox is not the whole story: since the god wants so much for man to understand him, he has given the paradox a positive aspect also, "by wanting to sublate the absolute likeness into absolute unlikeness."[31] The presence of these two aspects together in the paradox is not, Climacus stresses, something that reason is able to conceive.

In an Appendix to chapter III, Climacus explains why reason makes the mistake of thinking that it is in a position to comprehend and judge the paradox. The paradox is not a passive subject that is available to rational inspection. In "its most abbreviated form," it is the Moment (*PF*, 64). Thus the paradox is the agent in the encounter with human reason. As the Moment, it breaks into time. As the paradox, it defies comprehension. This divine action serves to negate the independent existence of both time and reason. It passes judgment upon them, but reason mistakenly tries to set itself up as judge over the paradox. When it does so, it declares the paradox to be an offense, never realizing that this judgment is nothing more than an echo ("acoustic illusion") of the judgment already passed on it by the paradox: "The expression of the offended consciousness is to assert that the Moment is folly, and that the paradox is folly, which is the contention of the paradox that reason is the absurd, but now reverberating like an echo out of the offended consciousness."[32]

Although the argument of chapter III does not follow the same paradoxical pattern as that in chapter II,[33] its statement of the radical otherness of the divine in fact reinforces the claim that the structure of *Philosophical Fragments* is a series of paradoxes. The point of departure is the absolute difference between human reason, which tries to mediate oppositions, and divine truth. The concept of absolute paradox negates this absolute difference, for it ironically counterposes to the absolute unlikeness of sin the concept of revelation as the *Aufhebung* of absolute unlikeness into absolute likeness. This reconciliation, which would constitute the third systematic moment in a Hegelian dialectic, is here nothing more than the second—a negation of the posited absolute difference. Furthermore, that negation remains inconceivable for human reason. All efforts to grasp the paradox result in an acoustic illusion. It is the paradox that grasps reason, not vice versa. That is why the notion of an absolute paradox in which the absolutely unlike become absolutely alike is a metaphysical crochet, a whimsical concept from the point of view of philosophy.

Climacus's heavy emphasis upon otherness might imply that truth is only external, in opposition to the Socratic position. That this is not the case is clear from chapter IV, where Climacus moves from his metaphysical concerns to epistemological issues.[34] Here, again, the pattern seems to be one in which the contradiction between a merely internal and a merely external view of the truth is resolved by the concept of an internalized other. (However, in chapter I the inner state—sin—precedes the encounter with the external teacher, whereas in chapter IV the external moment precedes the internal.)

The epistemological problem of the last half of *Philosophical Fragments* can be simply stated: given the paradoxical nature of the Moment when the truth comes to the learner as the divine teacher in human form, what difference does one's historical relation to the Moment make? Is it an advantage to be contemporary with the Moment, to be able to see and hear the teacher in person? For Climacus, the epistemological difficulties in the concept of revelation involve the problems of time and history, and so he now addresses the questions he had placed on the title page: "Is an historical point of departure possible for an eternal consciousness; how can such a point of departure have any other than a merely historical interest; is it possible to base an eternal happiness upon historical knowledge?"

Here the dialectic is cast in terms of the opposition between the historical and the eternal. As soon as a historical point of departure for an eternal consciousness is posited, then comes the paradox. True to form, Climacus insists that "we do not ask that he understand the paradox but only understand that this is the paradox" (*PF*, 72). He first imagines a contemporary who would spare no effort in investigating the historical circumstances surrounding the appearance of the teacher, and then supposes another contemporary whose sole concern would be the teacher's doctrine. These two lines of reflection result in a familiar opposition:

> For the first contemporary, the life of the teacher was merely an historical event; for the second, the teacher served as an occasion by which he came to an understanding of himself, and he will be able to forget the teacher (Chapter I). As over against an eternal understanding of oneself, any knowledge about the teacher is accidental and historical only, a mere matter of memory. As long as the eternal and the historical are external to one another, the historical is merely an occasion. (*PF*, 74-75)

A word of warning is in order here. Although the second contemporary understands the eternal and the historical as external to one another, it is the first contemporary who seeks the truth in merely external circumstances, namely, historical events. Climacus denies adequacy to both positions—to positivist externalism and equally to an inwardness that denies significance to everything external or historical. Without implying any reconciliation or identity between them, he insists that "the paradox unites the contradictories, and is the historical made eternal, and the eternal made historical" (*PF*, 76).

Parallel to the themes of historical externality, ahistorical inwardness, and their unity in the paradox, there runs a similar theme that is more properly epistemological: the theme of faith. The first contemporary is so busy chasing after the teacher that no question of self-awareness ever arises. The second is content with self-certainty, independent of contextual relations. It is again the third position, faith as the appropriation of the paradox, that unites these contraries. In Climacus's analysis of faith and reason, it is clear that faith is neither objective certainty nor provisional uncertainty; it is the radical uncertainty of a reason that has been negated by the paradox.

Faith occurs, writes Climacus, "when the reason sets itself aside and the paradox bestows itself" (*PF*, 73). The object of faith is the teacher (rather than the teaching), who is a paradox and can never be comprehended due to the absurdity of the claim that "the eternal is the historical" (*PF*, 76). Neither is faith an act of will. No, faith arises as a "happy passion" (*PF*, 73) after the death of a reason that has failed to create an adequate basis for faith out of historical or doctrinal knowledge. Climacus recapitulates this dialectic in relation to the learner's quest for "immediate contemporaneity" with the teacher. Only in faith, he argues, can one move beyond such immediate contemporaneity to become a "real contemporary" (*PF*, 83): "But such a contemporary is not in the immediate sense an eye-witness; he is contemporary as a believer, in the autopsy of faith. But in this autopsy every non-contemporary (in the immediate sense) becomes a contemporary" (*PF*, 87).

The notion of real versus immediate contemporaneity raises the question of the nature of historical knowledge, which Climacus discusses in the relatively long and densely argued "Interlude." A main point of this section is that Hegel's claim to reconcile possibility and actuality in necessity is false, for necessity is a logical category, having nothing to do with existence, where all change occurs in freedom. Leaving aside the question of how well Climacus understands Hegel on this matter,[35] the important point is that Climacus's real concern over the necessity of historical knowledge turns out to be his uneasiness with any notion of certainty. Contemporaries do not, he observes, perceive events as necessary. Only the distance of the centuries creates that illusion, "just as distance makes the square tower seem round" (*PF*, 98). Indeed, all historical knowledge is so problematical that uncertainty is in its very nature: "The historical cannot be given immediately to the senses, since the *elusiveness* of coming into existence is involved in it" (*PF*, 100). Thus "the organ for the historical must have a structure analogous with the historical itself; it must comprise a corresponding somewhat by which it may repeatedly negate in its certainty the uncertainty that corresponds to the uncertainty of coming into existence" (*PF*, 100-101).

This explanation brings Climacus back to faith, which he now defines as just such a "negated uncertainty, in every way corresponding to the uncertainty of coming into existence. Faith believes what it does not see" (*PF*, 101). Belief looks to the elusive coming into existence, whereas its opposite passion, doubt, is "a protest against every conclusion that transcends immediate sensation and immediate cognition" (*PF*, 105). In this way, faith appears as the paradoxical unity of external, historical knowledge and ahistorical self-certainty. The first contemporary seeks certainty about the historical life of the teacher but lacks self-certainty. For the second contemporary, self-certainty is the goal, and certainty about the teacher's historical actuality is irrelevant. Faith unites certainty with uncertainty in its passion for the paradox, for it affirms the absurdity of the paradox and thus allows reason to remain constantly uncertain; and yet, by virtue of that absurdity—namely, that the paradox does bestow itself—faith is in fact certain of it. Faith is not, it should be emphasized, certain of itself. It is certain of the paradox, and its very certainty about the paradox makes it all the more uncertain about its own knowledge and resources as an independent self.[36]

The final chapter applies Climacus's notion of real contemporaneity to the issue of the necessary conditions for receiving faith. In particular, the question arises about the effect of the passing of centuries: if all who did not walk with the teacher while he was on earth are "secondary disciples," then is there any advantage to belonging to the first generation of secondary disciples? Or to the last? The answer is no. The first generation hears the gospel proclaimed by eyewitnesses, but it has a very strange sound; therefore their "advantage is entirely dialectical, like the aroused attention itself" (*PF*, 117). Climacus means that the gospel's strangeness does provoke a reaction in the first "secondary" generation, but one that is more likely to be hostile than friendly. Thus the gospel creates opposition and negativity, either between it and the hearer or between the hearer and the world, and the advantage of belonging to that generation is thereby rendered "dialectical."

The last generation enjoys even less advantage, for, after eighteen centuries, the fact of the paradox no longer seems strange. It has been naturalized, and faith is thought of as second nature. This assumption, asserts Climacus with good evangelical fervor, is nonsense: "the notion of being born with faith is as plausible as the notion of being born twenty-four years old" (*PF*, 121). Thus the ease of becoming a Christian in the last generation is precisely the difficulty, and "this new difficulty will correspond to the difficulty of the fear confronting the first generation, and it will be gripped as primitively by awe and fear as the first generation of secondary disciples" (*PF*, 124).

These conclusions are hardly surprising, for in the previous chapter Climacus has already insisted upon real rather than immediate contemporaneity for all faith, thus rendering all immediate circumstances irrelevant to faith. Now he returns to that dialectic in order to show that "there is not and never can be a disciple at second hand" (*PF*, 128). This time he presents the dialectic in terms not of the epistemological process but of the object of faith, the fact of the Moment. If the Moment were a historical fact, contemporaneity would be an advantage; if it were an eternal fact, immediately available to all generations, it could not be the Moment. In reality, however, it is an "absolute fact," by which he means that it is a historical fact that cannot be "essentially differentiated by time" (*PF*, 125). This paradox can be apprehended only in faith, and the condition for faith can be given only by the god. The conclusion follows: there is no disciple at second hand.

The dialectic of historical and eternal facts thus culminates

CHART 5.
The Dialectic of Paradox in
Philosophical Fragments

Chap. I:	Sin	Encounter with teacher	Disciple (internalization)
Chap. II:	Apotheosis	Theophany	Kenosis
Chap. III:	Absolute difference	Absolute paradox	Acoustic illusion
Chap. IV:	Historical certainty (externality)	Ahistorical self-certainty (inwardness)	Faith as negated uncertainty (internalization)
Chap. V:	Historical fact	Eternal fact	Absolute fact

in the absolute fact, which paradoxically unites them without in any way overcoming the contradiction between them. In so doing, it is still another instance of the same dialectical logic that Climacus has used throughout *Philosophical Fragments*, and which is graphically summarized in Chart 5.

There are several ways in which this series in *Philosophical Fragments* illuminates the nature of paradoxical dialectics. First, it demonstrates that paradoxes are not a matter of mere alterity, an endless oscillation of binary oppositions; rather, they are unities of opposites in which the opposition is not diminished by the unity. Secondly, because of this unity, paradoxes appear very much like the third moment (the *Aufhebung*) within a mediating dialectic. Indeed, one of the lessons of the paradoxes in *Philosophical Fragments* is a heightened awareness of the paradoxical element in every claim for dialectical unity. This insight will be made even clearer in *Concluding Unscientific Postscript*. Finally, this series of paradoxes illustrates the fundamental difference between the two types of dialectic. Paradoxes accentuate the very oppositions they momentarily overcome, whereas mediations incorporate and thereby mute oppositions within a larger whole. This incorporation is accomplished by the unfolding development in a mediation, the progression from abstract, simple unity through opposition to a unity that is both concrete and complex.

A convenient way to characterize the difference between paradoxes and mediations is to use mathematical analogies. Kierkegaard's paradoxical dialectics are frequently described as "algebraic," which means "the compact, abstract, dialectical form of such works as *The Concept of Anxiety, Philosophical Fragments*, and *The Sickness unto Death*."[37] But, as the preceding analysis has shown, the differences between the first two texts are far too great to conflate them in this manner. Rather, one of the elements in algebraic equations, substitution, seems to be an appropriate metaphor for a series of paradoxical dialectics, in which the three moments are the positive, the contradictory, and the paradoxical. In every case, $p + -p = P$. In contrast, because of the development within *The Concept of Anxiety*, it would not be possible algebraically to reduce the logic within the third movement (anxiety in-and-for-itself) to that within the first (anxiety in-itself). In a mediating dialectic the third movement or moment contains earlier movements and moments within itself, and thus it is, as it were, built upon them. The mathematical analogy that suggests itself for this Hegelian sort of structure is geometry. Rather than stating one formula over and over again, a geometric dialectic builds a complex configuration of relations; each part can be understood only in its relation to the whole. No simple formula can express the structure of that whole.

Because of this difference between *The Concept of Anxiety* and *Philosophical Fragments*, both of which deal dialectically with the religious stage, it is not yet possible to claim for either the honor of representing *the* dialectic of the religious. Although the themes of self/other and inner/outer appear in *The Concept of Anxiety*, they do not develop in such a way as to overcome their opposing presentations (contradiction versus reciprocity) in the aesthetic and ethical stages.[38] The one definite advance this work makes is in the internalization of otherness. For the aesthete, the other is an object to be manipulated and exploited. Aesthetic internalization never accepts the other as other; it is only a strategy for dominating the other. The ethical type seeks harmony with the other, but also fails to appreciate adequately the extent to which the other is really other and not merely an instrument for ethical self-realization. It is the religious self who seeks genuine unity with the other, for here that unity is predicated upon the other's otherness to the self and the self's otherness to the other. This acceptance accords with the Christian model of the divine other who takes the form of a human self in order to make that human self divine. In *Concluding Unscientific Postscript* this paradoxical dialectic is stated in a form that is itself paradoxical—as the systematic culmination of the dialectic of the stages.

SIX

The Dialectic of Religious Inwardness

IT IS NOT UNUSUAL for interpreters to treat *Concluding Unscientific Postscript* as the definitive statement of Kierkegaard's religious philosophy. Such a procedure could be adopted in a study of his dialectic of inwardness also, for *Postscript* is the text in which that dialectic reaches its culmination. Furthermore, its pseudonymous author, Johannes Climacus, continues here the polemic against mediation that he began in *Philosophical Fragments* and argues strenuously that Christianity can be understood only in terms of paradox. Unlike *Fragments*, however, *Postscript* is also susceptible to systematic analysis: embedded within the attack upon systematic thought is a systematic dialectical structure of religious inwardness. Thus it is true that the different types of thinking found in the earlier peusdonymous works are brought together in a unique way in *Postscript*.[1]

As will shortly become evident, the systematic structure within *Postscript*, as in the earlier pseudonymous texts, is not sufficiently obvious to be explained as conscious irony. Climacus is certainly partial to irony, as his title demonstrates, and he prides himself on being a humorist.[2] But the systematic dialectic of religious inwardness is not something that either he or his creator seems to understand and espouse. Once again, my analysis must be structural in the twofold sense of attempting to identify a structure that is present without having been consciously created by the text's author.

If there is any theme that captures the essential argument of *Postscript*, it is that truth can be truth for existing individuals only when they *appropriate* it in their own lives. *Fragments* poses the question: How can an eternal happiness be based upon historical knowledge? In *Postscript*, that question becomes: How can an eternal happiness based upon historical knowledge be appropriated by an existing individual?

The first book of *Postscript* argues briefly against the opposing view, namely, that the truth of Christianity is objectively knowable on the basis of evidence. The evidence considered is of three sorts: the truth of the Bible, the confession of faith in the Church, and the witness of the centuries. Climacus does not deny that each of these can be construed as evidence for the truth of Christianity. Rather, he points out that in each case there is only an approximation of the truth, subject to scholarly debate and constant revision. Thus the believer is asked to place all hope for an eternal happiness in an objective belief that can never become objectively certain. Even worse, all such objective arguments for the truth of Christianity presuppose a "self-adequate subject" (*CUP*, 45), whereas the primary problem is precisely the dialectical relation between the individual subject and the object of faith. No so-called evidence for faith stands in an immediate relation to the inquiring subject. Indeed, a major theme of *Postscript* is that, according to Christianity, the subject is not, never has been, and never will be self-adequate: "Christianity is spirit, spirit is inwardness, inwardness is subjectivity, subjectivity is essentially passion, and in its maximum an infinite, personal, passionate interest in one's eternal happiness" (*CUP*, 33). In contrast, the Bible, the testimony of the Church, and the witness of the centuries are merely external phenomena, from which no leap can be made to the internal appropriation of Christianity as truth. It is the same with the speculative point of view. Climacus concedes that "the Hegelian principle, that the external is the internal and the internal the external . . . is highly original," yet he rejects it as false (*CUP*, 52). A speculative mediation of a truth that is external, phenomenal, and quantitative cannot abolish the leap that is required to reach the inwardness, hiddenness, and qualitative difference of faith.

In book two, the first part treats Lessing's claim that between the eternal truths of reason and the contingent truths of history there exists a ditch over which reason cannot leap.[3] For Climacus, this notion raises the problem of the relation between thought and existence, a relation that he describes as a double reflection or reduplication.[4] However dense his discussion of these terms might be, Climacus does make clear that thought and existence are inseparable yet opposed within every individual: "The reflection of inwardness gives to the subjective thinker a double reflection. In thinking, he thinks the universal; but as existing in this thought and assimilating it in his inwardness, he becomes more and more subjectively isolated" (*CUP*, 68). This dialectic between universalizing reflection and the particularity of existence considerably complicates the process of communication, for there the double reflection is between two persons rather than within one individual. In either case, however, the process is a reflective universalizing of existence and then a return from reflection to one's particular inwardness, a process that can be defined as "a thinking mode of existence" (*CUP*, 69). From this discussion it should be evident that Climacus in no way advocates "the destruction of thinking."[5] The reflection of inwardness is just that—a mode of reflection. What Climacus wishes to destroy is the sort of thinking that tries to identify by an abstract mediation what in reality remains distinct: "The systematic idea is the identity of subject and object, the unity of thought and being. Existence, on the other hand, is their separation" (*CUP*, 112).

A. Concrete Thought

Having criticized all claims to "objective" faith, and having argued that existence divides thought and being, Climacus next turns to the problem that occupies *Fragments*. Prior to addressing that problem directly, however, he devotes three chapters to the question of the subjective nature of truth. Here Climacus spells out his understanding of "a thinking mode of existence," that is, a subjectivity that is genuinely reflective

CHAPTER SIX

rather than merely a private emotionalism or a dogmatic subjectivism.

"The Task of Becoming Subjective" is the subject of chapter I, and it is clearly stated by Climacus in terms that recall a central theme of this study:

> The longer he lives, and the more the activities of the existing individual involve him in the warp and woof of life, the more difficult becomes the task of separating the ethical from the external; and the more readily may the metaphysical principle seem to be confirmed, that the outward is the inward, the inward the outward, the one wholly commensurable with the other. But this is precisely the temptation to be met and conquered; and hence the ethical becomes day by day increasingly difficult, in so far as the ethical precisely consists in that true hypertension of the infinite in the spirit of man, which constitutes the beginning, where it is therefore also most clearly apparent. (*CUP*, 123)

According to Climacus, the task of becoming subjective is the task of separating the ethical from the external, rather than, in the manner of Judge William, ethically choosing to reconcile them. Climacus's admission that the inner and outer might be commensurable for God (*CUP*, 126) is an indirect criticism of the presumptuousness of the Judge's point of view, although his main argument—that an ethics indifferent to the task of becoming subjective inevitably leads to despair (*CUP*, 119)—echoes the Judge's counsel to the young aesthete (cf. *E/O*,II, 212-213). Such an indifferent "ethics," or, more precisely, such a non-ethics, is what Climacus sees at the heart of the Hegelian philosophy of history. In terms that recall his discussions of objective faith and Lessing's ditch, he puts forward five arguments against Hegel (*CUP*, 126ff.): (a) the realm of world-historical meaning is based upon a quantitative dialectic; (b) it is a form of approximation knowledge; (c) it is concerned with the collective/abstract level rather than with the individual/concrete; (d) it is unable to explain individual

184

existence at all; and (e) it is generally of less significance than the ethical task of becoming subjective. Climacus concludes that, unlike speculative knowledge, "the ethical is not merely a knowing; it is also a doing that is related to a knowing, and a doing such that the repetition may in more than one way become more difficult than the first doing" (*CUP*, 143). The examples he offers of the knowing/doing of inwardness are: prayer, attitudes toward death, views of immortality, giving thanks to God, and getting married. All of these are existential situations in which objective knowledge is of no use; only subjective knowing can provide an adequate foundation for the ethical doing of life. Appropriately, Climacus closes the chapter with a parody of J. L. Heiberg's claim that he experienced a miraculous conversion to "the Hegelian philosophy which assumes that there are no miracles" (*CUP*, 163). The irony here is wonderful, for, according to Climacus's interpretation of Hegel, Heiberg is asserting that he has had a subjective awakening to the truth as objectivity![6]

Of course, that will not do. In what may well be the most radical statement of this theme in the Kierkegaardian corpus, Climacus defends the proposition that "truth is subjectivity" (chapter II). To understand this formula, it is important to distinguish between subjectivity and subjectivism. In subjectivism, the opinions of the finite self are held to be the only "truths." This can lead to solipsism or even madness, which Climacus defines as an "absence of inwardness" (*CUP*, 174). But subjectivity (inwardness) is not this sort of rejection of objective reality. It is, rather, the individual's struggle inwardly to become rightly related to reality; it is "the specific inwardness of the infinite" (*CUP*, 174n). Thus Climacus assumes that, just as objective reflection is to be faulted for making the subject accidental and existence a matter of indifference (*CUP*, 173), so also subjective reflection must never make the true object accidental or the infinite a matter of indifference. But the accent certainly falls here on the criticism of objective reflection. If the subject does not strive to appropriate the infinite, resting content with the indifference of objectivity, then it is not possible to make a beginning toward faith. This is why the "how" takes precedence over the "what," why the one who worships an idol with all the passion of the infinite can be said to pray "in truth to God," while the person who "prays falsely to the true God . . . worships in fact an idol" (*CUP*, 180-181). To believe that one comprehends the true God objectively is to substitute an idol for God, but to approach an idol with objective uncertainty and subjective passion is the beginning of faith. For this is Climacus's definition of truth: "*An objective uncertainty held fast in an appropriation-process of the most passionate inwardness is the truth*, the highest truth attainable for an *existing* individual" (*CUP*, 182). To affirm such an objective uncertainty as the truth is to admit that the truth is paradoxical (*CUP*, 183). The remainder of this chapter develops the notion of discovering the paradox and holding onto it with passion (*CUP*, 209), over against all claims for mediation.[7]

The subjectivity of knowledge of God recalls the theme of the inwardness of the divine other. Climacus explicitly affirms that "God is a subject," and therefore any knowledge of God by another subject will necessarily be relational rather than objective (*CUP*, 178). Faith is an action that is better described in social than in cognitive terms.

Another familiar element here is the emergence of a contradiction within the continuity of these first two chapters. The obvious continuity consists in the fact that both argue the incommensurability of inwardness and externality, and locate truth on the side of inwardness. Within this agreement, however, there is a significant difference. In chapter I, the demand is for the separation of the ethical self from all externality, whereas chapter II calls for subjective appropriation of objective uncertainties. Such appropriation is not a return to commensurability, but it does stand dialectically over against the radical opposition required by the prior separation. In chapter III, the opposition between separation and appropriation is overcome, as Climacus argues again that the difficulty he is addressing is that of "penetrating the concrete particularity with thought" (*CUP*, 267).

Of course, that difficulty is not to be underestimated. Thought has a tendency to "abrogate"[8] existence, thereby changing it in the act of trying to know it (*CUP*, 274). The reason for this is clear from Climacus's discussion of faith in the paradox of the existence of the God-man: "But existence involves first and foremost particularity, and this is why thought must abstract from existence, because the particular cannot be thought, but only the universal" (*CUP*, 290). In order to think the universal, thought must become abstract, detached, and disinterested with regard to existence; ultimately it is "thought without a thinker" (*CUP*, 296; cf. 278).

In contrast, concrete thought is "thought with a relation to a thinker" (*CUP*, 296). This is the heart of Climacus's notion of a subjective thinker, the person who actually maintains the double reflection while thinking: "An existential thinker must be pictured as essentially thinking, but so that in presenting his thought he sketches himself" (*CUP*, 319). Concrete thought does not abrogate or annul the opposition between thought and existence, it holds them together in tension: "The subjective thinker is an existing individual and a thinker at one and the same time; he does not abstract from the contradiction and from existence, but lives in it while at the same time thinking" (*CUP*, 314). Thus the concrete thinker holds the opposites of existence and thought together and, in so doing, fulfills the ultimate task of the subjective thinker, which is "to transform himself into an instrument that clearly and definitely expresses in existence whatever is essentially human" (*CUP*, 318). Although this cannot be done without passion, there is no hint of emotionalism here. Passion implies not only emotion and suffering,[9] but also the intensity of *thought*, for it is only in thought that the individual manages to cling to uncertainty, contradiction, and paradox. In the words of Climacus, "ethical reality is the only reality which does not become a mere possibility through being known, and which can be known *only through being thought*; for it is the individual's reality" (*CUP*, 284).[10]

Concrete thought is not only the ultimate task for the subjective thinker; it is also the dialectical *Aufhebung* of the previous two moments. In the first moment, the task of becoming subjective is posited as a separation of the ethical or inward from the external. This separation leads to an affirmation of truth as subjectivity. However, that very affirmation involves a subjective appropriation of external uncertainties. Thus appropriation stands as a moment over against the moment of separation. It is, as it were, the self-othering or self-sundering of that initial concept of subjectivity as withdrawal from objectivity. It reveals that subjectivity cannot ignore the issue of objectivity altogether, for whatever it is to appropriate must be objectively uncertain in order for the subjective choice in passion to have any significance. This tension between inner-outer separation and inner appropriation of the outer is overcome (*aufgehoben*) in concrete thought, in which both moments perish and are preserved. The separation perishes, because concrete thought holds the abstract externality of thought together with the concrete inwardness of existence; and it is preserved, because concrete thought simultaneously maintains the radical incommensurability of the very thought and existence that it is trying to hold together. Conversely, the for-itself moment of appropriation also perishes in that incommensurability, even as it is preserved in the act of holding together. In short, concrete thought reconciles the paradoxical unity-in-contradiction of subjectivity's separation from and appropriation of externality. In this sense, the concrete thinker is a paradox, a person who, like the knight of faith in *Fear and Trembling*, makes two apparently opposite movements at the same time.

These three moments together constitute the in-itself movement of religious inwardness. Given the opposition between the aesthetic and the ethical stages, it is hardly surprising that this first movement of the religious stage posits a theory of truth embracing elements of both aesthetic incommensurability and ethical commensurability. That is precisely the paradox of concrete thought, in which both the separation (incommensurability) and the appropriation (commensurability) stand as opposing moments without one overwhelming the other.

B. *Religiousness A*

The movement of religious inwardness for-itself is what is commonly known as religiousness A.[11] In his opening remarks to this section (*CUP*, 323-342), Climacus continues to complain that speculative philosophy has totally misrepresented Christianity, for it fails to appreciate that "Christianity is not a doctrine but an existential communication expressing an existential contradiction" (*CUP*, 339). At last the problem of *Fragments* is to be discussed directly, not in terms of an objective definition of Christianity but as the problem of how an existing individual can become a Christian. This problem, in turn, brings Climacus back to the incommensurability of externality and inwardness: the less of one, the more of the other, he insists. But he also acknowledges that an absence of externality may not reflect inwardness at all: "The external is the watchman that arouses the sleeper. . . . the absence of externality may mean that it is the inwardness itself that summons the individual inwardly; alas, it may also mean that the individual has ceased to have an inwardness" (*CUP*, 341). This ambivalence about the significance of the negative relation between inwardness and externality is the key to religiousness A, in which inwardness attempts to exploit the paradoxical unity of incommensurability and commensurability and thereby implicitly undermines or negates it.

In his short introduction to the problem itself, Climacus distinguishes between pathetic and dialectic factors within the problem of basing one's eternal happiness upon a historical relation to the eternal. The pathetic factor is the culmination of human passion and constitutes religiousness A.[12] In religiousness B, "the eternal happiness, to which the individual is assumed to have a pathetically correct relationship, is itself made subject to a dialectic by the addition of further determinations, which again react so as to excite passion to the highest pitch" (*CUP*, 345). However, as Climacus twice warns in the introduction, the difficulty is less one of understanding the pathetic and the dialectic individually than it is a matter of grasping their relationship. That difficulty is precisely where a systematic, structural analysis can be of help.

The three moments of religiousness A are resignation, suffering, and guilt. Each of these is an expression of existential pathos. As the initial expression, resignation posits an absolute respect for the absolute *telos* in the existing individual:[13]

> In relation to an eternal happiness as the absolute good, pathos is not a matter of words, but of permitting this conception to transform the entire existence of the individual. Aesthetic pathos expresses itself in words, and may in its truth indicate that the individual leaves his real self in order to lose himself in the idea; while existential pathos is present whenever the idea is brought into relation with the existence of the individual so as to transform it. If in relating itself to the individual's existence the absolute *telos* fails to transform it absolutely, the relationship is not one of existential pathos, but of aesthetic pathos. (*CUP*, 347)

Two ideas are central here, one qualitative and the other quantitative. Qualitatively, the issue is whether the pathos in question involves a change in the individual's concrete existence. If not—if the interest in the idea is merely a matter of words—then, no matter how deep the self-identification with the idea may be, the pathos is only aesthetic. Likewise, even in the case of pathos that is a result of the action of the idea or absolute *telos* upon the individual's existence, if it is still quantitatively incomplete and remains a partial transformation, then it is merely an aesthetic pathos.

The remainder of the section on resignation develops these two ideas. The importance of clearly distinguishing between the existential spheres is stressed by Climacus, and an essential difference between the aesthetic and the religious is said to be that the latter "should have passed through the ethical" (*CUP*, 347). This qualification leads to further distinctions:

> Ethically the highest pathos is interested pathos, expressed through the active transformation of the individual's entire mode of existence in conformity with the object of his interest; aesthetically the highest pathos is disinterested. When an individual abandons himself to lay hold of something great outside him, his enthusiasm is aesthetic; when he forsakes everything to save himself, his enthusiasm is ethical. (*CUP*, 350)

Thus the ethical and religious modes of pathos are distinguished from the aesthetic by virtue of their involvement in concrete existence, their passionate interest in the absolute *telos*, and their ultimately *inner* objective—salvation. But this movement, which Climacus believes to be the culmination of the ethical,[14] requires that the individual forsake *everything*, every one of those external objects of interest that attract the aesthetic type. Thus the relation of the religious individual with the absolute *telos* is one of utter inwardness, a relation, writes Climacus, in which all immediacy has been submitted to "the inspection of resignation" (*CUP*, 353).

To become religious, the individual must embrace ethical resignation totally: it is impossible to resign only part of one's immediacy. When the individual chooses among the external objects of interest or decides for a degree of resignation, the process is one of selection, not resignation. With resignation, a new attitude enters: the individual relinquishes *all* rights to everything external or immediate. In Climacus's view, the common opinion avoids this radical resignation by appeal to the principle of mediation of opposites (*CUP*, 354). This view is expressed by the interlocutor, familiar from *Philosophical Fragments*, and Climacus answers it here, as there, with a denial of the possibility of mediation between the individual and an eternal happiness in time (*CUP*, 355). Mediation involves only that which is relative, never the absolute *telos*.[15] Moreover, mediation looks for some sort of finite advantage from the relationship with the absolute *telos*, a further indication of the extent to which it muddles important distinctions:

> In the finite sense there is nothing whatever to gain, and everything to lose. In the life of time the *expectation* of an eternal happiness is the highest reward, because an eternal happiness is the highest *telos*; and it is precisely a sign of the relationship to the absolute that there is not only no reward to expect, but suffering to bear. (*CUP*, 360)

This reference to suffering could provide a convenient transition to the next section, but Climacus goes on at length about the difficulty of resignation and the evils of mediation. A new point is introduced in relation to monasticism (*CUP*, 362-363), which Climacus praises for its passion but criticizes for its commitment to "a distinct and special outwardness." The task for the religious individual is to live like others outwardly, while inwardly submitting everything to that "inspection of resignation" in every moment, thereby maintaining a relative relationship with the relative world and an absolute relationship with the absolute *telos* (*CUP*, 365).[16] In terms that echo Johannes de Silentio's *Fear and Trembling*, Climacus writes of this principle as a "double-movement" (*CUP*, 366). Anticipating his own later discussions, Climacus says the individual is a "stranger in the world of the finite, but does not manifest his heterogeneity. . . . He is incognito" (*CUP*, 367). The person who fails to make this double-movement throughout each and every day, who relates to the absolute only on Sunday and is "otherwise immersed in the manifold business of life, readily produces an illusion by means of the aesthetically foreshortened perspective" (*CUP*, 372). Throughout all of these discussions and digressions, a single theme reappears: resignation must be absolute; there can be no qualifications or mediation or outward expresssion; it is an inward "venturing everything absolutely" that alone can lead the individual into a relationship with "an eternal happiness as the absolute good" (*CUP*, 382).

In resignation, the individual renounces the realm of immediacy in order to gain the eternal. Dialectically, this action represents a negation of the paradoxical unity of inner/outer commensurability and inner/outer incommensurability. Resignation has no room for the commensurability thesis; it is committed to purging the self of everything immediate and temporal and does so under an incognito that externally hides its inward heterogeneity.[17] As an absolute respect for the absolute *telos*, resignation aims at nothing less than the inward death of the finite self. This is the first moment of religious inwardness for-itself.

Suffering is a "dying away from immediacy" (*CUP*, 412, 414) that continues the process of resignation. Yet suffering is also the essential expression of existential pathos, a for-itself moment within religiousness A that in some sense negates the in-itself moment of resignation. How this negation works is again a matter of the relation between the incommensurability and the commensurability of inner and outer.

Religious suffering is "action in inwardness" (*CUP*, 388), but not all suffering is religious. For example, aesthetic suffering "keeps itself at a distance from existence," whereas the religious suffering under discussion "becomes more and more concrete through acting to transform existence." According to Climacus, the fact that this is an action rather than a passive enduring should not be construed to mean that it is not suffering. For "it becomes evident here again, as the sign of the religious sphere, that the positive is signaled by the negative."[18] A helpful footnote illustrates what he means: "A revelation is signalized by mystery, happiness by suffering, the certainty of faith by uncertainty, the ease of the paradoxical-religious life by its difficulty, the truth by absurdity" (*CUP*, 387n). Elsewhere he cites St. Paul's famous thorn in the flesh as the sign of the reality of his journey to the third heaven (*CUP*, 407; cf. 2 Cor. 12). It is this inverted or negative expression that constitutes the "essential" form or moment of religiousness A: "the positive is constantly wrapped up in the negative, and the negative is its criterion" (*CUP*, 467).[19]

Suffering is the negative (and therefore essential) expression of the fact that an individual exists in the sphere of religious pathos. However, such an individual cannot be identified by others on the basis of that suffering. To develop this point, Climacus returns to the contrast between the aesthetic and the religious as one of outwardness versus inwardness. Acting to transform existence, he insists, is genuinely religious suffering only when it is inner existence that is transformed (*CUP*, 387). He admits that this definition rules out the apostolic suffering portrayed in the New Testament (Acts 5:41), and even complains that the New Testament has very little to say about religious suffering (*CUP*, 405). The sources of religious suffering are two: the contradiction between the internal and the external, and the ambiguity of the God-relationship.

In his discussion of suffering, Climacus considerably deepens his treatment of the theme of inwardness versus externality: "But herein lies the profound suffering of true religiousness, the deepest thinkable, namely, to stand related to God in an absolutely decisive manner, and to be unable to find any decisive external expression for this (for a happy love between human beings expresses itself externally in the union of the lovers)" (*CUP*, 440). The religious individual (like the lover) ardently desires to express the relationship with the absolute *telos* (or beloved) externally, in the realm of immediacy. Immediacy and relativity are vital constituents of human nature, and so the task of dying away from immediacy is bound to result in intense suffering. Climacus also characterizes this suffering as a consciousness of impotence. Immediate consciousness, not being dialectical in itself, strives for power over external reality. But the individual's awareness of being "nothing before God" means that the sine qua non of religiousness is "consciousness of impotence" in all situations (*CUP*, 412).[20] This consciousness initiates true inwardness before God: "But he transforms his outward activity into an inward matter, inwardly before God, by admitting that he can do nothing of himself, by severing every teleological relation to his activity in the outward direction and cutting off every resultant in the finite world, although he labors to the limit of his powers" (*CUP*, 452). The religious individual experiences impotence in all external relations, in every effort at self-transformation, and especially when there is the temptation to "annul" the pain in so-called religious joy. Climacus denies that the New Testament notion of rejoicing over suffering is genuinely religious, for there suffering has an external origin (*CUP*, 405). For suffering to be religious, it must be both inward and total, which means that it requires both a sense of total impotence before God and the "persistence of suffering" (*CUP*, 397).[21]

Indeed, for the religious sufferer, the relation with God is fraught with ambiguity. It is not that the contradiction between inner existence and outer expression renders the individual ambivalent toward God or that this "martyrdom" (*CUP*, 453) causes any sort of resentment: "No, when the individual is secure in his God-relationship and suffers only outwardly, then this is not religious suffering."[22] The implications of this statement are startling. According to Climacus, the deepest suffering experienced by the religious individual is not the loss of the world or even the consciousness of impotence; it is the sense of insecurity in the God-relationship itself. That is why the only "security" that one has in the God-relationship is precisely the persistence of suffering. To become secure in relation to externals is to put an end to religious suffering (*CUP*, 406). And to become secure in relation to God by means of the striving of resignation and suffering is also to fall into self-deception—the aesthetically foreshortened perspective by which one presents an aesthetic position as if it were religious. The absolute remains elusive in a world of relative relationships. Thus, within the context of religiousness A, the sole sign of a relationship with God is insecurity and inner suffering. It is certainly true that this inverted dialectic is "the paradoxical logic of inwardness."[23]

The notion that suffering is a negative sign of the positive relation with God brings Climacus to the concept of spiritual trial (*Anfægtelse/ Anfechtung*). For the most part, his discussion emphasizes that such trials are religious and from above, in contrast to ethical temptations from below. This notion echoes the idea, familiar from *Fear and Trembling*,[24] that a spiritual trial is the temptation to escape the paradox of faith. Climacus, however, adds another dimension to that concept in his analysis: "Spiritual trial therefore originates first in the genuinely religious sphere, and occurs there only in the last lap, increasing quite rightly with the degree of religiousness, because the individual has discovered the boundary, and spiritual trial is the reaction of the boundary against the finite individual."[25]

This surprising claim—that spiritual trial is not simply the individual's experience but is also the reaction of the boundary itself against the finite individual—can be understood by reference to the acoustic illusion that is discussed in *Fragments*.[26] Just as offense at the paradox is in fact determined by the paradox itself, so also spiritual trial is determined by the boundary that separates the eternal from the temporal. The point in both cases is the same: the paradox of faith is not one created by the religious individual; rather, it is the result of the nature and action of God. God is the paradox, the infinitely incommensurable one who both encourages and rejects all human efforts to become commensurable through resignation and suffering. Spiritual trial is the temptation to escape from this paradox into mere incommensurability or mere commensurability.

The concept of spiritual trial provides a transition to the final expression of religious suffering: "consent to the finite" (*CUP*, 423).[27] This consent is not a return to the identification with the finite that has been resigned in suffering by the religious individual. Rather, it is a double-movement in which the finite is constantly and simultaneously both renounced and accepted for what it is—the medium of human existence. Thus Climacus can assert that "in the living-room must the battle be fought, not fantastically in the church . . . for the victory consists precisely in the living-room becoming a sanctuary" (*CUP*, 416). It also explains why he devotes so many pages to the problem of whether the religious individual can participate in such a finite activity as a picnic in Deer Park. His conclusion is that, unless one would enter the cloister, it is appropriate to go on the picnic and enjoy oneself, for that is the ordinary human thing to do (*CUP*, 440-441). Ultimately, it is not the finite as such that is to be renounced, but only that false consciousness that treats the finite as the locus of infinite meaning.

It is in this context that Climacus's claim to be a humorist can be clarified. He discusses the relation between humor and the religious frequently, in part because he believes that they are not sufficiently distinguished in the present age (*CUP*, 403). Humor he argues, is the lower boundary of the religious and therefore an incognito that the religious may wish to adopt, just as irony is the lower boundary and potential incognito of the ethical (*CUP*, 448). Both humor and irony are based upon contradiction: irony upon the contradiction between inner existence and outer expression, and humor upon the contradiction between the greatness of God and the finite realm in which God is sought. The humorist exploits that contradiction without being, like the religious person, related to God "in his inmost consciousness" (*CUP*, 451).[28] Whereas the ironist will conceal pain and suffering, the humorist will jokingly exaggerate them (*CUP*, 400-401). Humor, therefore, does not fully consent to the finite, does not take its pain and suffering with ultimate seriousness. This is why Climacus, who identifies himself as a humorist, also characterizes himself as "almost . . . in earnest" (*CUP*, 210).

The religious individual is utterly earnest about everything. Although humor may be useful as an incognito, there is nothing about resignation and suffering that makes them seem amusing to the genuinely religious person. On the contrary, the religious individual is preoccupied with the quest for God, a quest that is severely complicated by a labyrinth of contradictions. In resignation, the posited reconciliation of aesthetic incommensurability with ethical commensurability has been contradicted. Now suffering contradicts that contradiction, for it shows the individual that the external realm of immediacy must be consented to even as it is renounced. Corresponding to this, the moment of suffering reveals a new understanding of incommensurability that, in effect, renders it inversely commensurable: the positive is now recognizable in the negative, happiness in suffering, and so on. This paradoxical notion exploits the incommensurability of opposites by suggesting that the opposition is itself the sign of an indirect relation. That means the incommensurability of inner and outer is a sign of their inverted commensurability. And, in existential terms, the true renunciation of immediacy and externality is manifest in the consent to them. If one is looking for a religious individual, look not in the churches on Sunday morning; look in Deer Park on a lovely Sunday afternoon, and look only among those who are thoroughly enjoying themselves.

The third moment, and the dialectical culmination within religious inwardness for-itself, is guilt. As the *Aufhebung* of resignation and suffering, it must take up into itself the opposition between the denial of inner/outer commensurability in the former and the inverted commensurability implicit in the latter. Another opposition here is between resignation's focus upon the object that it renounces and suffering's attention to the subject that it affirms (as impotent). In guilt, which is the decisive expression of existential pathos (religiousness A), both of these oppositions must be dialectically overcome.[29]

One way to sharpen the issue is to examine the relation between existence and guilt. There has been so much discussion of the need to renounce immediacy and to suffer as a finite individual that it is little wonder that one scholar reaches the conclusion that, according to Climacus, "[e]xistence is guilt: this is the outcome of the individual's attempt to become himself by means of the absolute venture of religion."[30] Climacus himself, however, warns against such an interpretation of religiousness A:

> But how can the consciousness of guilt be the decisive expression for the pathetic relationship of an exister to

an eternal happiness. . . ? One might think that this consciousness is an expression of the fact that one is not related to it. . . . The answer is not difficult. Precisely because it is an exister who is to relate himself, while guilt is at the same time the most concrete expression of existence, the consciousness of guilt is the expression of the relationship. The more abstract the individual is, the less is he related to an eternal happiness, and the more remote he is from guilt. . . . The difficulty is really a different one; for the fact that guilt is accounted for by existence seems to make the exister guiltless, it seems as though he could throw the blame upon the one who had placed him in existence, or upon existence itself. In this case the consciousness of guilt would be nothing else but a new expression for the suffering of existence, and the investigation would have got no further than #2, wherefore #3 ought to fall out, or be treated as an appendix to #2. (*CUP*, 470)

The difficulty here is to understand how guilt can be the most concrete expression of existence without making the exister guiltless and thereby collapsing guilt into suffering as the exister's response to an "externally" determined situation (in particular, a spiritual trial from God). To say that existence is guilt implies that the exister is not responsible for being guilty; yet, lacking a sufficiently dialectical context, the notion of a guiltless guilt is nonsense.[31]

Another aspect of this issue is the "totality of guilt" (*CUP*, 471). In resignation, there is both a qualitative task (dying to immediacy) and a quantitative demand (absolute respect for the absolute *telos*). The task is developed in suffering, but it is guilt that reveals the demand. The logic of guilt, like that of resignation, is distressingly simple: it can never be partial. The slightest fall from innocence, and a person is guilty. It is impossible to be somewhat guilty. The absoluteness that was sought in the relation of respect is now found in the relation to oneself as totally guilty.

But guilt-consciousness also represents a qualitative advance beyond suffering's dying to immediacy. Because of the complexity of this dialectic, it is useful to state it first in its most obvious terms and then to restate it in terms of the dialectic of commensurability and incommensurability. Those simplest terms are an abstract schema of the relation between subject and object. In resignation, the object of consciousness is the realm of externality and immediacy that must be renounced in order for the self to relate to the eternal. Suffering shifts the focus to the subject, to the self who suffers in the act of trying to die to immediacy and externality. The tension between being oriented outward and looking inward is sublated in guilt-consciousness, for there the subject becomes the object of consciousness, since it is the self that must be resigned. This is the first appearance of a fully self-reflexive consciousness in the entire dialectic of inwardness.

There are several ways in which Climacus indicates the importance of this shift to consciousness as the self's relation to itself. One is his emphasis upon the self-identity of the individual in guilt-consciousness: "the identity of the subject consists in the fact that it is he himself who becomes conscious by putting guilt together with the relationship to an eternal happiness" (*CUP*, 475). (This is in sharp contrast, he adds in a footnote, to religiousness B, where that self-identity is broken.) Again, in noting the difference between aesthetic externality and ethico-religious inwardness, Climacus comments that the latter is a matter of self-annihilation (*CUP*, 498). These remarks show that a key characteristic of guilt is its self-reflexivity.

The concept that expresses this new self-reflexivity most clearly is "eternal recollection" (*CUP*, 476). Guilt-consciousness is an endless process in which the self recollects its own inadequacy, its failure to establish a right relationship with the eternal. The self's relationship with the eternal has become repellent. Suffering is the direct reaction of that relationship, whereas the self-negation of the guilty consciousness is a "repellent reaction of a repellent relationship" (*CUP*, 474). This repellent reaction is an eternal recollection, for it moves backward rather than forward, always digging "deeper into existence" (*CUP*, 469). The retrogression is due to the fact that the guilty self is attentive to its past, in contrast to the focus of resignation upon the future and that of suffering upon the present. The sequence in this retrogressive dialectic (future-present-past) is an implicit rejection of progressive dialectics, a rejection that also receives expression in Climacus's insistence that eternal recollection cannot be mediated in any way. Mediation distracts the individual from self-reflexivity with all sorts of external determinations, but guilt, at least in its highest form (eternal recollection), can never be mediated or satisfied at all (*CUP*, 481). The consciousness of guilt does not move forward, but backward and deeper into the self.

Nevertheless, in terms of the dialectical structure, that very retrogression is an advance. The dialectic of subject and object, in which guilt-consciousness is the *Aufhebung* by which the subject becomes object and the object becomes subject in *self*-resignation, is such an advance. So also is the dialectic of incommensurability and commensurability. Resignation, as the initial expression of existential pathos for-itself, denies the unity of incommensurability and commensurability. Suffering does not reinstate that unity, but it dialectically negates the denial by affirming a direct correspondence in which the positive is recognizable by the negative. This is the inverted dialectic. The *Aufhebung* of resignation and suffering in guilt is as follows: by turning totally inward in eternal recollection, guilt is a self-consciousness that ignores everything external and thereby takes the moment of resignation up into itself. At the same time, consciousness is now self-consciousness, existing in relation not to the external but only to itself as a self that would relate itself to God. Although there can be no external expression of this intensely inward self-reflexivity, it is, like suffering, a relation in which a form of commensurability can be detected. Without denying the inverted dialectic, which is said to characterize the entire religious stage, guilt reveals the commensurability of the guilty self with itself.

In eternal recollection, the self manifests this commensurability by the fact that it is both the subject and the object of its reflection. The identity of subject and object is not, in this case, a doctrine of speculative philosophy; nor is it merely the implication of self-consciousness as such. On the contrary, the emphasis throughout Climacus's phenomenological analysis of religiousness A is upon concrete existence,[32] and the identity of subject and object within this context is the result of the dialectic of guilt-consciousness.[33]

There is one other way in which guilt-consciousness manifests the notion of incommensurability. In addition to the incommensurability of inner with outer, which is expressed in the indifference of guilt to externality, there is the incommensurability of the inward self-consciousness with the inwardness of God. This is the final result of religiousness A. Self-recollection may be eternal, but it is not a consciousness of the eternal. The guilty self is estranged from God no less than from itself. It is imprisoned in itself yet divided against itself and unable to find God. It is in the midst of this despair that the leap—which is also a progression in the dialectic of inwardness—to religiousness B can occur.

One of Climacus's favorite terms for religiousness A is "immanence." The preceding analysis shows that the immanence he has in mind is not that of a pantheistic spirit; nor is it the paradoxical notion of a God-in-time, which he reserves for religiousness B. By immanence, Climacus means the self: in seeking a relationship with the eternal *within* the resigned-suffering-guilty self, the religious individual is assuming that the eternal is accessible to the self, that it is immanent in the self. This failure to distinguish adequately between the self and God is the reason for the guilt of the self. Guilt cannot be identified with existence, only with that individual who would search for God within the existing self. Thus guilt confirms resignation's initial task by demonstrating the impossibility of achieving an absolute respect for the absolute *telos* and a relative respect for everything relative.

To summarize the dialectical structure up to this point: in

its in-itself movement, religious inwardness is posited as paradoxically both incommensurable and commensurable with externality. This paradox is expressed as concrete thought, which sublates the moments of separation from and appropriation of the external. The question now arises: In what sense does the for-itself movement negate that paradoxical unity? As the preceding analysis has shown, resignation denies that unity by rejecting commensurability. If the task calls for a sharp distinction between absolute and relative, there is a fundamental incommensurability. Suffering, however, restores commensurability (in indirect or inverted form) by positing the negative as the sign by which the positive is recognizable. Guilt, in its turn, takes both of these moments up into itself. As a self-reflexive consciousness within immanence, guilt resigns not only externality but the finite self itself as incommensurable with the eternal. Yet as eternal recollection, guilt discovers a commensurability from which it cannot escape: the circle of the identity of subject and object within self-consciousness. In this way, guilt fulfills resignation's initial denial of the unity of incommensurability and commensurability, for it is an inward commensurability of the self with itself that is in tension with the self's incommensurability with God. Religiousness A shows that the paradoxical unity of these two poles, although posited as concrete thought, is not something that human consciousness can achieve. Indeed, the deeper the self goes into inwardness in search of the eternal, the greater the distance between it and the eternal. And yet, according to the dialectic of religious inwardness, it is only by pursuing this religious task with all possible passion that there is any hope of being delivered from its inevitable contradictions.

C. Religiousness B

Kierkegaard scholars generally agree that religiousness B presupposes (rather than simply opposes) religiousness A.[34] Climacus describes the transition from pathetic to dialectical religiousness as a leap, yet also insists that there can be no awareness of B without first grasping A (*CUP*, 494) and that B can be understood as a "sharpened pathos" (*CUP*, 516). ⁵⁸³ Once again, a systematic structural analysis will help to clarify this transition. Such an analysis shows that Climacus's view of the religious as paradoxical reveals itself (paradoxically!) to be a systematic development of religious inwardness.

In the eternal recollection of the consciousness of guilt, religiousness A culminates as self-reflexivity—a dialectic of inward transformation. The posited reconciliation of inner/outer incommensurability with inner/outer commensurability is thereby negated, and the movements of religious inwardness in-itself and and religious inwardness for-itself stand in contradiction to one another. Religiousness B accomplishes their *Aufhebung* by uniting the incommensurability of the dialectic of inward transformation with a paradoxical commensurability that is attested in Christian revelation. Moreover, religiousness B can also be analyzed in terms of its own internal moments of development.

In contrast to religiousness A, Climacus's analysis of religiousness B is very brief. He describes it as "not merely deeper dialectical apprehensions of inwardness, but . . . a definite something which defines more closely the eternal happiness" (*CUP*, 494). Thus it is "dialectical in the second instance" (*CUP*, 496): the dialectic of inward transformation is the first instance; the second is the encounter with the dialectical paradox of Christianity. As in *Philosophical Fragments*, Climacus argues that the existence-communication of Christianity requires a leap from understanding into believing "against the understanding" (*CUP*, 504). This leap is not one into ecstatic or enthusiastic devotionalism; any claim to glimpse God undermines the incommensurability between the divine and the human even more than speculative philosophy (*CUP*, 500-501). Yet this radical incommensurability no longer leads to a turning away from everything external:

> Aesthetically, the holy resting place of edification is outside the individual, who accordingly seeks the place; in

the ethico-religious sphere [religiousness A] the individual himself is the place, when he has annihilated himself. This is the edifying in the sphere of religiousness A. . . . In religiousness B the edifying is something outside the individual, the individual does not find edification by finding the God-relationship within himself, but relates himself to something outside himself to find edification. The paradox consists in the fact that this apparently aesthetic relationship (the individual being related to something outside himself) is nevertheless the right relationship; for in immanence [religiousness A] God is neither a something (He being all and infinitely all), nor is He outside the individual, since edification consists precisely in the fact that He is in the individual. The paradoxical edification [religiousness B] corresponds therefore to the determination of God in time as the individual man; for if such be the case, the individual is related to something outside himself. The fact that it is not possible to think this is precisely the paradox. (*CUP*, 498)

This passage is fascinating for its clear statement that paradoxical religiousness (B) is a return to externality.[35] In this case, however, the external is neither finite nor temporal. It is God, the infinite and the eternal, who is determined "in time as the individual man." This notion of the eternal-in-time may be unthinkable, but it is also the object of Christian faith.

The first moment of religiousness B is entitled: "The dialectical contradiction which is the breach: to expect an eternal happiness in time through a relationship to something else in time" (*CUP*, 505). What this title does not specify is that the "something else in time" is not an indeterminate something in time. It is the eternal in time, which is generally known in Christian discourse as the incarnation. This identification is clear from Climacus's several rankings of the different spheres as existence-communications.[36] Only the briefest description of these rankings is possible here. There are four of them, each cast in terms of a different question: (1) How are the "here" and the "hereafter" distinguished? (2) How is existence understood? (3) How dialectically is inwardness understood? And (4) how are the contradictions of existence understood? Aesthetic understanding is not mentioned for (1) and (2) but affirms a dialectic of inwardness and a contradiction of existence that are both external to the individual. Speculative philosophy denies any distinction between the "here" and the "hereafter," discounts existence, and is not mentioned for (3) and (4). Ethical understanding, like the aesthetic, is not mentioned for (1) and (2) but locates both inwardness and contradiction inwardly "within self-assertion." This concept corresponds to what I have called the ethical negation of incommensurability (that is, of aesthetic contradiction). The understanding of religiousness A consistently reduces the distinctions—"here" from "hereafter," actuality from eternity, inward self from God, time from eternity—to dimensions within the immanence of the suffering and self-annihilating self; and religiousness B intensifies those very distinctions by virtue of its paradoxically external break with immanence.

Climacus's complex ranking of the four existence-communications is helpful in several ways. First, it demonstrates that he also understands the stages as a structural (although not systematic) progression. True, the inclusion of speculative philosophy disrupts efforts at systematic interpretation, but Climacus admits that it is really not an existence-communication at all (*CUP*, 505). Therefore, speculative philosophy should not be ranked with the aesthetic, ethical, and religious spheres.[37] Second, his emphasis upon the contrasts between religiousness A and B supports the claim that the "three moments of the Christian dialectic . . . contradict the three expressions of existential pathos."[38] Thus, in this first moment, incarnation contradicts resignation, for resignation gives up the temporal in order to attain the eternal, whereas the incarnation is the union of the eternal with the temporal. Finally, this contrasting of A and B points to the fact that religiousness

B takes up into itself the dialectical opposition between concrete thought and religiousness A. For concrete thought also posits a paradoxical unity of incommensurability and commensurability, a unity that is negated by the dialectic of inwardness in religiousness A. The externality of the incarnation reinstates the paradoxical unity initially posited by concrete thought, for it affirms that the radically incommensurable *became* commensurable in a particular man. Thus the incarnation is the first or in-itself moment of religious inwardness in-and-for-itself.

The second or for-itself moment of religiousness B is: "The dialectical contradiction that an eternal happiness is based upon something historical" (*CUP*, 508). The issue here is the knowledge of God, and the contrast with religiousness A is again clear: "As opposed to the man whose suffering is the negative sign of his positive God-relationship, the Christian directly relates himself to an historical deity."[39] Climacus stresses in this section that the approximation process, which had earlier proven to be so inadequate for objective knowledge of history, here serves as a basis for a subjective and passionate belief in the incarnation. The incommensurable is revealed through the commensurable. The dialectical contradiction is, therefore, to relate to eternity through a particular moment in history, "a thing which can be done only when one has *in oneself* no eternal determinant."[40] By taking this leap of faith, each and every Christian is "nailed to the paradox" (*CUP*, 512). The necessity for this leap demonstrates that religiousness B is in no way *merely* external; it is the inward appropriation of an externally revealed truth that is believed to be the only means to an "eternal happiness."

The third and final moment is: "The dialectical contradiction that the historical fact here in question is not a simple historical fact, but is constituted by that which only against its nature can become historical, hence by virtue of the absurd" (*CUP*, 512). The incarnation is "an eternal historical fact" (*CUP*, 513), not in the sense of a fact that is eternally becoming (which would be a return to immanence), but in the paradoxical sense that the eternal became a particular historical fact. This formulation is reminiscent of the concept of absolute fact in *Fragments*: the concept is paradoxical to the point of being absurd. Precisely that absurdity is the culmination of religiousness B and the entire dialectic of inwardness.

Climacus seems almost to suggest that the dialectical contradiction of an eternal historical fact takes up the two previous dialectical contradictions into itself. Protesting against those who would turn it into a myth (that is, understand it eternally rather than historically), he writes: "Instead of noticing that there are two dialectical contradictions, first, the basing of one's eternal happiness upon the relation to something historical, and then the fact that this historical datum is compounded in a way contradictory to all thinking, they leave out the first and explain the second away," with the result that "religiousness B is done away with, 'all theology is anthropology.' "[41] Climacus has reversed the order here—his "first" is really the second moment (revelation), and his "second" refers to the first moment (incarnation)—but the idea is nonetheless correct: the paradox, however absurd, can be dialectically understood as the *Aufhebung* of incarnation and revelation. And so it is. Incarnation posits the objective, external, historical event as the Moment in which the incommensurable eternal makes itself commensurable within time. Revelation requires a subjective appropriation of that objective event, the inward establishment of a relation to eternal happiness on the basis of that event. Finally, the paradox of the absurd is the common structure that the two prior moments share, for they both present an incommensurable commensurability. The paradox is both the objective fact and its subjective appropriation. It is the eternal in existence, both as the historical incarnation and in the life of the believer. How fitting yet ironical that Climacus, who so often praises paradox and ridicules systematic dialectics, culminates his own dialectic of religious inwardness with a paradox that is also a systematic *Aufhebung*!

Before recapitulating the dialectical structure of religious inwardness, it should be noted that, in an Appendix to B,

Climacus offers a more existential understanding of religiousness B as a dialectic of sharpened pathos. Whereas the primary analysis treats the movement in terms of inwardness and externality, this second one employs categories that are more closely related to the dialectic of self and other. The structure is parallel, however, and embraces three moments: sin-consciousness, the possibility of offense, and the smart of sympathy.

Sin-consciousness is the existential break with the self-identity of guilt-consciousness. In a word, the individual can acquire true self-knowledge only by looking to another:

> Hence the individual is unable to acquire sin-consciousness by himself, as he can guilt-consciousness; for in guilt-consciousness the identity of the subject with himself is preserved, and guilt-consciousness is an alteration of the subject within the subject himself; sin-consciousness, on the other hand, is an alteration of the very subject himself, which shows that outside of the individual that power must be which makes clear to him the fact that in coming into life he has become another than that he was, has become a sinner. This power is the deity in time. (*CUP*, 517)

Sin-consciousness does away with that "fellow-feeling" for all others that is based upon the assumption that they also can be eternal, replacing it with the equally universalistic belief that all are in sin, even though relatively few may have received consciousness of that fact by being brought into relation with the deity in time (*CUP*, 518).

Two striking ironies permeate Climacus's analysis of sin-consciousness. One he shares with Haufniensis: sin comes *after* guilt. In contrast to the common-sense view, which says that one must sin in order to become guilty, Kierkegaard's two pseudonyms understand guilt as the final consciousness of possibility prior to consciousness of sin as actuality (Haufniensis), or as the last moment of self-reflexive consciousness before the self is shown by an external power that it has become a sinner

(Climacus). The second irony involves the contrast between sin-consciousness and resignation. In resignation, the individual seeking an eternal happiness embraces the task of dying to immediacy. Immediacy is a positive fact for such a person, a fact to which the person reacts negatively. In contrast, sin-consciousness is a negative immediacy, a new immediacy of a negative nature, but one that the individual positively affirms. Thus the consciousness of sin is, in effect, the dialectical converse of resignation.

Of course, the individual may not, in fact, affirm sin-consciousness, and this possibility constitutes the second existential moment in the dialectic of religiousness B. This is what Climacus calls the "possibility of offense" (*CUP*, 518), which is so important in *Philosophical Fragments*. Offense is the negative reaction of an individual to the paradox of the deity in time, especially to the scandal of the deity suffering in time. That is why there are essentially only two responses possible: belief or mockery. Thus Climacus asserts that "Christianity is the only power which is able truly to arouse offense," and that, "[f]or the believer, the offense is at the beginning, and the possibility of it is the perpetual fear and trembling in his existence" (*CUP*, 518-519).

Finally, when the believer once again affirms the consciousness of sin, he does so despite the mocking of those who are offended. This opposition to the world leads to the "smart of sympathy," for the fellow-feeling with all humanity that had been enjoyed in religiousness A is now replaced with a sympathetic bond among Christians and a corresponding pain[42] in relation to those who reject Christianity. Moreover, the smart of sympathy emphasizes that the Christian self is constituted by its relationships both to God and to other human beings, and not simply by the intensely introspective dialectic of eternal recollection in guilt-consciousness.

The existential dialectic of religiousness B can accordingly be summarized as follows: sin-consciousness shatters the self-identity of the eternal recollection of guilt; the possibility of offense stands as the negation of sin-consciousness, a moment in which the self mocks faith and thereby asserts itself one last, desperate time; and the smart of sympathy takes up into itself both a positive bond (with other sin-conscious Christians in faith) and a negative position (in relation to those who reject Christianity).[43]

THE CHRISTIAN is not determined simply by relations with other Christians or non-Christians. The most significant other for a Christian is God—not simply God as an external power or historical datum, but God as the ground and source of all inwardness:

> This paradoxical inwardness is the greatest possible, for even the most paradoxical determinant, if after all it is within immanence, leaves as it were a possibility of escape, of a leaping away, of a retreat into the eternal behind it; it is as though everything had not been staked after all. But the breach makes the inwardness the greatest possible. (*CUP*, 507)

Climacus insists that the externality of revelation is not a return to immanence or a denial of inwardness. It is a transcendent inwardness constituted by God as the divine other. Faith is the paradox of a self that is other to itself (as sinner) and yet is also a new self by virtue of its relation to a divine other. Yet God remains transcendant, even in relation to this new self. There is never any "escape" from Christian revelation into the paganism of divine immanence.

The self-other dialectic in religiousness B draws attention to the fact that the entire dialectic of religious inwardness can be transposed into comparable terms. Within the in-itself movement, this transposition yields three moments: separation of the ethical self from the external other; inward appropriation of the divine other as an external uncertainty; and the paradox of a divine other that is inwardly known yet remains other, which is the self-other parallel to concrete thought. Religiousness A loses touch with the otherness of the other, just as it devalues externality. Resignation posits the unity of the self with the inward divine other; suffering is the inversely dialectical sign of that unity; and guilt finally abandons hope of such unity, for it finds itself unable to transcend its own immanent self-identity. It is this self-identity that sin-consciousness negates. If it survives the threat of offense, religiousness B emerges as the paradox in which both the self and the divine other are both inward and external. This acme of paradox is thus also the culmination of the systematic dialectics of inner/outer and self/other, and can be schematically summarized as a dialectic of religious inwardness (Chart 6).

CHART 6.
The Dialectic of Religious Inwardness

A. Truth as inwardness (subjectivity) in the concrete thinker

1. Separation of self from the external	1. Separation of self from external others
2. Inner appropriation of external uncertainty	2. Appropriation of inner divine other
3. Concrete thought as paradox: separation *and* appropriation	3. Divine otherness internalized

RELIGIOUS INWARDNESS IN-ITSELF:

POSITED UNITY OF AESTHETIC INCOMMENSURABILITY AND ETHICAL COMMENSURABILITY OF INNER/OUTER	DIVINE OTHER POSITED AS INWARD YET OTHER

B. Religiousness A as immanent dialectic of inward transformation

1. Resignation of temporal/external to gain eternal	1. Resignation posits the unity of self with inner divine
2. Suffering as inverted sign of inner happiness	2. Self-negation as sign of unity with inward divine other
3. Eternal recollection of guilt as resignation to painful self-reflexivity	3. Unity with inward divine other revealed as merely immanent self-identity in guilt

RELIGIOUS INWARDNESS FOR-ITSELF:

INCOMMENSURABILITY OF INNER/OUTER AS INVERTED COMMENSURABILITY	DIVINE FOUND INWARDLY BUT OTHERNESS OF THE DIVINE LOST

C. Religiousness B:

Transcendent Revelation	*Sharpened Pathos*
1. Incarnation of the eternal as Moment in time	1. Sin-consciousness negates self-identity of guilt
2. Leap of faith as inward appropriation of the incarnation	2. Possibility of offense negates sin-consciousness
3. Paradoxical revelation as common structure of incarnation and faith	3. Smart of sympathy as positive bond in sin-consciousness and negative relation to world

RELIGIOUS INWARDNESS IN-AND-FOR-ITSELF:

INCOMMENSURABILITY PARADOXICALLY REVEALED IN AND THROUGH COMMENSURABILITY	RECONCILIATION OF SELF AND THE DIVINE IN PARADOX OF INWARD *AND* EXTERNAL OTHERNESS

SEVEN

The Dialectical Structure of Consciousness: The Anti-Climacus Writings

OF ALL THE major pseudomyms, Anti-Climacus is the thinnest, the least developed, the one whose identification with Kierkegaard himself seems least open to question.[1] Kierkegaard writes that he intended to publish *The Sickness unto Death* and *Practice in Christianity*[2] under his own name, and only at the last minute decided to use the pseudonym and relegate himself (on the title page) to the position of one "responsible for publication."[3] His explanation of this decision focuses upon his concern for security in the future and thus deflects attention from the literary and conceptual ambiguity of the two works.

Formally, the Anti-Climacus works appear to be part of the "second literature,"[4] those largely nonpseudonymous works that were written after *Concluding Unscientific Postscript* was published in 1846.[5] However, *The Sickness unto Death* has a literary and conceptual nature that leads to its inclusion in many studies of the pseudonymous authorship,[6] whereas *Practice in Christianity* never finds a place in such works. Nevertheless, Kierkegaard conceived these works as parts of a whole,[7] wrote them both 1848, and, as this structural analysis will demonstrate, made them interdependent by completing in *Practice in Christianity* the systematic dialectic begun in *The Sickness unto Death*.[8] Moreover, the similarities between this dialectic and those examined in earlier chapters are thematic as well as formal, for this one can also be analyzed in terms of the inner/outer and self-other[9] relations.

THE SICKNESS UNTO DEATH

A. Despair In-Itself as Implicit Consciousness

In his Introduction to *Sickness unto Death*, Anti-Climacus explains that the title of the work is taken from Jesus' response to the news that Lazarus was ill: "This sickness is not unto death" (John 11:4). Since Lazarus did in fact die, Anti-Climacus concludes that Jesus meant by "death" something other than physical death, namely, the death of the spirit. In part one, section A, he defines the sickness unto death as the despair of a self who remains unconscious of having a self, or who *despairingly* wills either to be or not to be itself. In a passage that is as dense as it is famous, the self is characterized as self-reflexivity within a relation of opposites:

> A human being is spirit. But what is spirit? Spirit is the self. But what is the self? The self is a relation that relates itself to itself or is the relation's relating itself to itself in the relation; the self is not the relation but is the relation's relating itself to itself. A human being is a synthesis of the infinite and the finite, of the temporal and the eternal, of freedom and necessity, in short, a synthesis. A synthesis is a relation between two. Considered in this way, a human being is still not a self. (*SD*, 13)

The self is a consciousness that is conscious of itself as a synthesis of opposites. Furthermore, that self does not create itself. It is "a derived, established relation," and therefore the self that is not in despair can be described as follows: "in relating itself to itself and in willing to be itself, the self rests transparently in the power that established it" (*SD*, 13-14). This rest is enjoyed only by Christians, although the possibility of despair is universal and is the demonstration of "man's superiority over the animal" (*SD*, 15). A person in despair suffers from the sickness unto death. Ironically, that sickness is also characterized as the inability to die to life in this world — Bultmann and be reborn in eternity. It appears that death is inevitable. The only questions are when and to what one will die. Indifference to this issue is of no avail, since no one can be rid of the eternal within, and spiritual death results in being condemned to one's despairing self for all eternity (*SD*, 21).

Section B develops the idea that since "all immediacy is anxiety," despair must be universal. Therefore the appearance of happiness in immediacy is in fact a sign of despair in the self, whether or not the self has become dialectically aware of its despair (*SD*, 25-26). Ignorance of despair does not mean an absence of despair, any more than ignorance of anxiety indicates freedom from anxiety.[10] This close relation between despair and anxiety can be understood as a reflection of the fact that both are related to the inner disrelationship between human beings and God (namely, sin).[11] However, it is important to note also the differences between them, the most obvious of which is that anxiety is only the condition of sin, whereas despair is sin itself. This distinction is related to a second and more complex difference, namely, that anxiety is an inward immediacy that reflection can contemplate as a possible or actual object, whereas despair, as a form of *self-consciousness*, cannot be an object to itself in this way.[12]

With section C in part one, the dialectic of despair really begins. This first movement deals with the forms of the sickness, by which Anti-Climacus means the elements or opposite poles to be synthesized in the self, but without regard to consciousness of the self as a self-relation. Two such oppositions are treated: finitude/infinitude and possibility/necessity. In both cases, the dialectic is binary rather than progressive: whether consciousness is viewed as infinite or finite, it will fall into despair if the other is lacking, just as possibility and necessity are "equally essential to becoming" (*SD*, 35). At this point in his analysis, Anti-Climacus implies that dialectical thought is nothing more than a matter of oppositions: "No form of despair can be defined directly (that is, undialectically), but only by reflecting upon its opposite" (*SD*, 30).

A typological method is employed by Anti-Climacus to

explicate these opposite poles.[13] Infinitude's despair is characterized by the fantastic, which appears in various mystical and ascetic types depending upon whether it is rooted in feeling, knowing, or willing. In each case the self loses itself in uncontrolled imagination, so that eventually all sense of the finite factor in the synthesis is lost. In contrast, finitude's despair is a narrowness that has no sense of the infinite, of the fact that the self is constituted by God: one is merely a number, not really a self (*SD*, 33-34). In Anti-Climacus's view, people who are utterly preoccupied with temporal goals "have no self, no self for whose sake they could venture everything, no self before God—however self-seeking they are otherwise" (*SD*, 35).

A similar typology is used for despair as defined by possibility/necessity. Possibility's despair occurs when one is unable "to obey, to submit to the necessary in one's life" (*SD*, 36). This takes two primary forms: hoping for or fearing the possible, types that respectively adumbrate the manic and the depressive in contemporary psychiatric terminology. Conversely, necessity's despair is over the lack of possibility and appears in the types of the fatalist and the pragmatist.[14] The fatalist is in despair due to a lack of faith in God and possibility, whereas the pragmatist's despair lacks imagination, with the result that "he lives within a certain trivial compendium of experiences as to how things go, what is possible, what usually happens" (*SD*, 41).

B. Despair For-Itself as Explicit Consciousness

From despair without regard to whether it is conscious [A], Anti-Climacus goes on to the second movement [B], "Despair as Defined by Consciousness."[15] Here binary oppositions are no longer treated in abstraction. Now the self is present, emerging in the dialectical progression of moments. Superficially, however, there is still a dichotomous organization, for section B is divided into two sections, a and b, the second of which is also subdivided into two subsections, *alpha* and *beta*.

To complicate matters further, there are two parts, (1) and (2), within *alpha*. Thus it is evident that whatever trichotomous systematic dialectic can be found in the text will not correspond to its overt organization.

Section a is entitled: "Despair That Is Ignorant of Being Despair, or the Despairing Ignorance of Having a Self and an Eternal Self." This first moment is spiritlessness, a total lack of concern for spiritual truth. The individual is given over to a life of sensuousness and immediacy, or perhaps finds an identity "in some abstract universality," such as the state or nation, rather than in God (*SD*, 46). Anti-Climacus judges this search for the self in externals to be the most common form of despair in the world, since it is one shared by paganism and Christendom (which is paganism in Christian garb). But he does affirm a distinction suggested by Haufniensis: pagan spiritlessness is at least oriented toward spirit, whereas Christian spiritlessness is apostasy from it.[16]

The Sickness unto Death contains an ambiguity about the direction of the development of despair. On the one hand, Anti-Climacus insists that despair is a sickness, not a cure (*SD*, 6). This notion leads to the conclusion that the intensification of despair pushes the self further away from the truth.[17] On the other hand, the dialectic of despair now becomes a dialectic of consciousness, in which the increase in consciousness of despair is clearly equated with "a rise of the consciousness of the self" (*SD*, 49). Anti-Climacus never resolves this ambiguity, but he does succeed in stating it clearly:

> However, it is in only one sense, in a purely dialectic sense, that the individual who is ignorant of his despair is further from the truth and deliverance than one who knows it and yet remains in despair, for in another sense, an ethical-dialectical sense, the person who is conscious of his despair and remains in it is further from deliverance, because his despair is more intensive. (*SD*, 44)

Despite this ambiguity, it soon becomes clear that Anti-Climacus's primary concern is with an "advance over pure immediacy" (*SD*, 54). The direction is that of a dialectical progression, even if the "progress" is, at this point, into a deeper consciousness of despair. Whereas the first movement [A] deals with binary oppositions without regard to consciousness (despair in-itself), the second [B] is despair as consciousness (despair for-itself). Within this second movement, the first moment [a] is a despair that seeks the self in externals and is therefore really spiritless or unconscious of having a unique self at all. Conscious despair remains, in this moment, in-itself, an abstract potential. Only with conscious despair for-itself does a genuine negation of immediacy appear, for this second moment is the despair of not willing to be oneself, which Anti-Climacus calls "Despair in Weakness" [b. *alpha*].

The distinction between the first moment [a] and the first phase of the second moment [b. *alpha* (1)] is not an obvious one in Anti-Climacus's analysis and is therefore sometimes ignored or denied by interpreters, as if both were forms of spiritlessness.[18] However, this moment, which is the negative moment of conscious despair for-itself, represents both a crucial dialectical advance and, according to Anti-Climacus, that which alone is "indispensable" for that "truer conception of despair" that the pagan lacks (*SD*, 47-48). The key to this distinction can be stated as follows: unlike spiritlessness, despair over something earthly results from the inability of a person to return to immediacy after an extremely unfortunate, or even fortunate, event: "immediacy is dealt such a crushing blow that it cannot reproduce itself" (*SD*, 51). The event serves as an external motivation, and the resulting despair seeks an external remedy. It is this externality that makes the despair over something earthly appear similar to spiritlessness. Yet the difference must also be noted: spiritlessness is despair without any consciousness whatsoever of being a self; the self is merely a member of an abstract universal such as the nation. In contrast, despair over something earthly manifests an inchoate consciousness of selfhood as the problem, a consciousness that appears in imaginative fantasies about the self one would like to be. Anti-Climacus's understanding of this is summed up in the following definition: "This form of despair is: in despair not to will to be oneself. Or even lower: in despair not to will to be a self. Or lowest of all: in despair to will to be someone else, to wish for a new self. Immediacy actually has no self, it does not know itself; thus it cannot recognize itself and therefore generally ends in fantasy" (SD, 52-53).

The second dialectical phase within despair—as weakness—does not receive a distinct section in Anti-Climacus's text, but it is designated by him as a "modified" form of despair in weakness, namely, a despair in which *immediacy is assumed to have some reflection* (SD, 54). Here the self is still mired in immediacy, but a quantitative (rather than infinite) reflection enables it for the first time to distinguish itself in a limited way from that immediacy. Appropriately, reflection appears for the first time in this *for-itself* phase of the for-itself moment (despair in weakness) within the for-itself movement (despair as consciousness). The self no longer wishes to be another self, although its inability to accept itself is demonstrated by the fact that it is still looking for an external deliverance from its despair. The self cannot yet make the total break with external immediacy that is required for true inwardness. It is incapable of the degree of self-reflexivity necessary to break through to the "naked abstract self" that is "the first form of the infinite self and the advancing impetus in the whole process by which a self infinitely becomes responsible for its actual self with all its difficulties and advantages" (SD, 55).

From the first to the second phase of despair in weakness, according to Anti-Climacus, an important dialectical advance can be discerned. Although they appear to be identical expressions of despair, the first is despair over something earthly, a particular earthly thing; the second is over the earthly as such: "its infinite passion changes this particular thing, this something, into the world *in toto*." However, continues Anti-Climacus in a Kantian vein, "the category of totality inheres in and belongs to the despairing person." This, in turn, is "a dialectical initial expression for the next form of despair," in which the particularity of despair over something earthly and the universality of despair over the earthly as such will be sublated in the infinity-within-finitude of self-reflection: "Despair of the Eternal and over Oneself" [b. *alpha* (2)], which is "the formula for all despair" (& 60).

With Haufniensis, Anti-Climacus assumes that the eternal is first encountered in inwardness. The fact that despair is now for the first time characterized as "of the eternal" indicates that despair over oneself is the first flicker of consciousness in the self that it even has an inner dimension. The inwardness of the self can never be satisfied (or commensurable) with temporal externality, and that incommensurability gives the self the capacity to universalize something earthly into the earthly as such. Thus "all despair is *of* the eternal," for only the eternal offers inner deliverance from despair (*SD*, 60n),[19] a fact that enters consciousness only in this final phase.

Despair of the eternal or over oneself is the third phase of despair as not willing to be oneself (weakness). The relation between this and the previous two phases is described by Anti-Climacus in terms that reveal both his progressive understanding of the dialectic of despair and his lack of concern for the triadic systematic structure as such: "This despair is a significant step forward. If the preceding despair was *despair in weakness*, then this is *despair over his weakness*, while still remaining within the category: despair in weakness as distinct from despair in defiance (*beta*). . . . The person in despair himself understands that it is weakness to make the earthly so important, that it is weakness to despair" (*SD*, 61). In this passage, a contrast is drawn between despair in weakness and despair over weakness. The former embraces both of the first two phases, a consciousness that Anti-Climacus has already ridiculed as similar to that of a man who thinks he is discussing and pointing to the town hall—even though it is directly behind him (*SD*, 52). The latter is the dawning awareness of the self that the real root and object of its despair is itself, not something external. For the first time, consciousness is in

–despair *over* its weakness and thereby advances beyond despair –that is merely *in* weakness.

Yet this distinction between despair *in* and *over* weakness does not do justice to the triadic nature of Anti-Climacus's actual analysis of despair in weakness, as presented above. The systematic dialectic of that moment is as follows: despair as weakness, as not willing to be oneself or self-rejection, is the for-itself moment that negates despair as spiritlessness, in which the self dissipates any possible consciousness of self in externality. That negation unfolds in three phases. In the first phase, weakness in-itself, the self despairs over something earthly in which it seeks itself. This self-seeking reflects a new self-consciousness that posits a negation of mere spiritlessness. In the second phase, weakness for-itself, that self-consciousness takes the form of conscious reflection, thereby intensifying the negation of spiritlessness. But it also negates the particularity of despair over something earthly, for it totalizes the object _ of its despair into the earthly as such. The third phase, weak- – ness in-and-for-itself (despair over oneself), is what Anti-Cli- –macus calls withdrawnness.[20] As the *Aufhebung* of the two previous phases, it unites the focus of the first upon one external object with the focus of the second upon the ability of the reflecting subject to universalize the object of its despair. Like –despair over something earthly, withdrawnness is a conscious- –ness of one "object" of despair—the self. And like despair over –the earthly as such, withdrawnness is a consciousness of the –inwardness of despair, of despair as a problem *in* the self and –not simply a problem that the self has with the external world. –This self-consciousness is the culmination of the moment of –despair as weakness and completes this for-itself moment as a –negation of the external, unreflective moment of spiritlessness.

Despair *over* one's own weakness also moves beyond the passivity of the previous forms of despair. In contrast to spir- itlessness and despair over something earthly or over the earthly as such, here the self actively seeks solitude in withdrawnness and "has a great contempt" for external immediacy (*SD*, 63). –This withdrawnness is neither a yielding of the self to the eternal nor a necessary breaking of the self; it is a passionate clinging to the self in pure negativity, in despair over the weakness of the self. None of this inward despair shows externally, of course, for any communication of it would shatter the withdrawnness. Such isolation can produce "a restless spirit who wants to forget" its despair, or even a suicidal personality (*SD*, 66). As in earlier forms, one can try to turn back, or one can advance in the dialectic of consciousness. If one does advance, then withdrawnness will become intensified to the point where it manifests the primary characteristic of the next form of despair: defiance.

At the very beginning of his discussion of despair as weakness, Anti-Climacus observes that there is really only a relative contrast between weakness and defiance, for each always includes an element of the other. That relation is developed in a long footnote on weakness as feminine despair and defiance as masculine despair, in which it is admitted that "only ideally is this distinction between masculine and feminine despair altogether true" (*SD*, 49n). Nevertheless, the distinction between weakness and defiance is another crucial step in the dialectical progression. In withdrawnness, the self despairs over its own weakness and thereby becomes conscious that despair is of the eternal. Defiance takes up into itself the degree of self-consciousness that has been attained in despair as weakness, but rejects both the idea of weakness and the notion that the self is dependent upon the eternal. In a desperate effort to recapture the simple unity of the moment of spiritlessness, the self in defiant despair attempts to claim the eternal as a characteristic or possession of its own. It claims infinitude for itself, it tries "to be master of itself or to create itself" (*SD*, 68). This attitude toward the power that established it is the distinguishing mark of the defiant self. And, like the earlier advances, its achievement is very ambiguous: "just because it [defiance] is despair through the aid of the eternal, in a certain sense it is very close to the truth; and just because it lies very close to the truth, it is infinitely far away" (*SD*, 67). Awareness of the eternal qualifies defiance as inwardness, but the rejection of help from God shows that its withdrawnness is "what could be called an inwardness with a jammed lock" (*SD*, 72). With an outer appearance of indifference and a withdrawn inward-ness, the defiant self lives in an isolated and spiritualized despair that is rooted in its estrangement from God.

According to this analysis, defiance is the dialectical *Aufhe-bung* of spiritlessness and despair as weakness.[21] Together, they constitute the three moments within despair as consciousness. In terms of the dialectic of internal and external, despair has advanced from the abstract concept of despair in-itself, where inner and outer and all such determinations of consciousness are irrelevant, to despair for-itself, which is despair determined as consciousness. This awareness, in turn, developed from ex-ternality (spiritlessness) through dawning self-reflexivity (weakness) to self-assertion in inwardness (defiance). The mid-dle moment (weakness) is further developed in three phases: despair over some external earthly thing, despair over the earthly as such, and despair over oneself for having invested the earthly with such importance (withdrawnness). These three phases are the beginning of self-reflexivity. The third phase is a direct transition into the third moment, defiance, which sublates the reflective consciousness of weakness with the re-jection of (or indifference toward) the eternal that characterizes spiritlessness. Thus inwardness is born of despair, and con-sciousness advances only through this profoundly negative re-lation with the realm of externality. But deliverance from this despair cannot come simply by turning inward. On the con-trary, rather than opening the self to the eternal, defiance finds itself utterly isolated: inwardness for its own sake is a jammed lock.

This dialectic can also be traced in terms of self and other. In spiritlessness, there is not yet any essential distinction be-tween the self and others. Despair as weakness is the gradual disillusionment of the self with external others, first with particular others and then with others in general. This leads to the defensive posture of withdrawnness. Here the self realizes that it seeks the eternal, but, rather than submit to it, the self becomes defiant, attempting to deny its dependence upon an other (the eternal) that is out of its control. Since the divine other is also that which establishes the self, defiant alienation from God is a self-assertion that is simultaneously self-alienation. As degrees of self-awareness, the three moments of despair as consciousness are: self-ignorance, self-rejection, and self-assertion (as self-alienation). This progression also supports Anti-Climacus's claim that consciousness is "decisive with regard to the self. The more consciousness, the more self; the more consciousness, the more will; the more will, the more self" (*SD*, 29).

This structural analysis of despair as a systematically dialectical development avoids the problem of distinguishing between a higher and a lower self. That problem arises from the contrast between despair as weakness, where despair is the refusal to be the self, and defiance, where the self arrogantly wills to be the self. It would appear that the first "self" is the ideal, toward which one ought to aspire; and that the "self" in defiance is the actual self, from which one needs to be liberated.[22] But the self in both cases is the same: "the relation's relating itself to itself" (*SD*, 13). In weakness, the self denies itself as a self-relation, first by turning exclusively outward and then by withdrawing into itself. In defiance, the jammed lock of isolated inwardness attempts to affirm itself as an autonomous self-relation. In this sense, defiance one-sidedly wills the same self-relating self that weakness one-sidedly avoids.

Defiance is, as it were, a perverse *Aufhebung* of externality and inwardness, for it is the attempt to embrace all externality and otherness within the closed circle of the self. This is not just a withdrawal from externality—it is an attempt to conquer it through internalization. But this affirmation of the self as a self-relating relation is false, since the self, by Anti-Climacus's definition, "rests transparently in the power that established it" (*SD*, 14). The infinity of self-reflexivity within defiant despair is, to use a Hegelian term, a spurious infinite, precisely because it attempts to be an autonomous and total *Aufhebung*. The irony here is that Anti-Climacus has implicitly turned Hegel's concept of a spurious infinite against the Hegelian effort to unite the inner and the outer in infinite self-reflexivity. The realization by consciousness that this infinite unity is false can come only when consciousness advances to the self-consciousness in which despair is recognized as sin.

C. Despair In-and-For-Itself as Absolute Consciousness

There can be no doubt about the importance that Anti-Climacus attaches to the formula, "despair is sin," which he uses for the title of both part two and section A within part two. His concept of sin, and with it the dialectical transition from despair as consciousness to despair as self-consciousness, is best explained in terms of the relation between the self and the divine other. In the initial movement of despair, when the elements of the synthesis are examined without regard to consciousness, there is not yet either self or other. They emerge together in the dialectical struggle between externality and inwardness within the movement of despair for-itself (despair as consciousness). The culmination of that struggle is the withdrawn inwardness of defiance, in which a negative relation exists between the self and everything that remains other. The systematic task of despair in-and-for-itself is to reunite self and other in a new relationship in which both their difference and their unity receive adequate expression. This accomplishment brings the self into full self-consciousness as the self it really is, namely, a self that is both alienated from God by sin and reconciled to God by grace.

The phrase that occurs again and again in the first moment within this final movement is "before God." Indeed, the very definition of sin adapts the earlier definition of despair to this new context: "Sin is: *before God, or with the conception of God, in despair not to will to be oneself, or in despair to will to be oneself.* Thus sin is intensified weakness or intensified defiance: sin is the intensification of despair" (*SD*, 77). Anti-Climacus stresses that this in no way externalizes either despair or the God-relationship. God is not something external, like a policeman (*SD*, 80). God is the inward divine other by which and before which the self is established. Thus despair can no longer be a mere consciousness that the self possesses, as when the self is understood "within the category of the human self." Rather, the self now becomes conscious of itself "directly before God," and this leads to a realization that was already implicit in the earlier dialectic: the self always exists only in relation to others. As Anti-Climacus puts it: "The criterion for the self is always: that directly before which it is a self" (*SD*, 79).

Anti-Climacus's discussion of sin is divided into three chapters. In the first, he explains the implications of the God-relationship for consciousness of selfhood: "Despair is intensified in relation to the consciousness of the self, but the self is intensified in relation to the criterion for the self, infinitely when God is the criterion" (*SD*, 80). Consciously to be in relation to God intensifies one's sense of self, and therefore one's despair. According to this conception, sin is not a matter of misdeeds; it is a misrelation to God. Likewise, faith, as the opposite of sin, is not merely belief in an external deity; faith is the right relation that exists between God and a self that has been delivered from despair: "the self in being itself and in willing to be itself rests transparently in God" (*SD*, 82). In an Appendix to chapter 1, Anti-Climacus develops this relational understanding of the self in terms of the possibility it offers for offense. Just as a relation "between man and man" can be one of either admiration or envy, so also that between God and man will be either adoration or offense.[23]

Chapter 2, which discusses the Socratic definition of sin, functions dialectically to negate the relational concept of self, and with it the entire concept of sin. By defining sin as ignorance, Socrates denies the notion of sin as consciousness and quite logically concludes that "there is no such thing as a person's knowing what is right and doing wrong, or knowing that something is wrong and going ahead and doing wrong" (*SD*, 89). Thus the self is putatively once again a mere self-relation, an unconsciousness or preconsciousness that does not

relate to other subjects so much as it attempts to gain knowledge of external objects. In contrast, Christianity insists that
the self is a self-consciousness before God and that sin is a
matter not of ignorance or knowledge; it is an ethical matter
of the will (*SD*, 93). Sin itself cannot be an object of knowledge
for anyone, since everyone is in sin. According to Christianity,
we can become aware of the fact of sin only by means of a
revelation from God (*SD*, 95). It is God alone who can reveal
the misrelation between himself and his creatures. Thus the
definition of faith can be cast also in terms of sin: "sin is—
after being taught by a revelation from God what sin is—
before God in despair not to will to be oneself or in despair
to will to be oneself" (*SD*, 96).

Chapter 3 explores the dialectical ramifications of the idea
that knowledge of sin can be gained only from a revelation.
The claim stated in its title, "Sin is not a Negation but a
Position," was already implicit in the argument against Socratic ignorance, which is the negation of knowledge, and in
the Christian notion of the sinful will, which is a position over
against God and not merely a moral failing or mistake. The
complexity of Anti-Climacus's attitude toward dialectics is
clear in this chapter. In affirming sin as a position, he is
negating it as a Socratic negation—a highly dialectical ma-
neuver! At the same time, he argues strenuously against the
claim of speculative dogmatics (and that of Martensen in particular) that the position of sin can be comprehended.[24] That
claim sets comprehension higher than sin, beyond its power,
which implicitly negates sin. Over against this view, Anti-
Climacus insists upon "the Christian teaching that sin is a
position—yet not as if it could be comprehended, but as a
paradox that must be believed" (*SD*, 98). The positive element
in sin is not that it is a foil for speculative comprehension but
that it is the self's true position before God (*SD*, 100). The
Appendix to A repeats the point that sin is the position of
every person before God, regardless of the fact that, within
Christendom, most people remain spiritlessly unaware of it.

This chapter completes the in-itself moment of despair as

sin. Three phases have appeared within that moment, corresponding to the three chapters in section A: in the first, the self is posited as constituted by its relation to God, which intensifies the self's despair over its misrelation to God (sin-consciousness); in the second, the Socratic notion of sin as ignorance negates the relational understanding of sin-consciousness; finally, the third phase restores sin as a misrelation to God, but on the basis of Christian revelation, which is a paradox to be believed rather than understood. In this way, the immediate knowledge of the first phase and the negative ignorance of the second are reconciled in the third, which is thereby shown to be the in-and-for-itself phase within the in-itself moment of despair as sin. This moment has established that the self is a relation before God that is a misrelation and that therefore the self is in sin. The second moment will be an attempt to deny that confession, with the result of inadvertently confirming it.

The title of section B is "Continuation of Sin."[25] Anti-Climacus opens with a brief discussion of sin as the continuous and self-consistent existence of a demonic person, not just the sum of particular sins. Sin's continuity is also conveniently discussed in three sections, each of which deals with one phase in the development of the dialectic of despair. The first phase is the sin of despairing over one's sin:

> To despair over one's sin indicates that sin has become or wants to be internally consistent. It wants nothing to do with the good, does not want to be so weak as to listen occasionally to other talk. No, it insists on listening only to itself, on having dealings only with itself; it withdraws into itself, indeed, locks itself inside one more enclosure, and protects itself against every attack or pursuit by the good by despairing over sin.[26]

Although Anti-Climacus himself draws the parallel between despair over one's sin and withdrawnness, it is important also to note the significant difference between them. Their similarity lies in the fact that both are a despair *of* the power that could deliver the self from despair—of the eternal in the case of withdrawnness, and of the good in the case of despair over one's sin.[27] The difference is that withdrawnness as such has no awareness of sin; it is a despair of the eternal that is over one's own weakness, but the withdrawn consciousness does not see itself as standing before God and withdrawing from God. In despair over one's sin, it is precisely the God-relation that makes the crucial difference, for this withdrawnness into self is a turning away from God, away from the relational self that is established by and in God. Here the self burns its bridge, to use Anti-Climacus's metaphor, to the good. It breaks away from the good not once but twice: first when it sins; and again when it so despairs over that sin that it withdraws itself from "everything called repentance and grace," rejecting them as "empty and meaningless" (SD, 109).

Anti-Climacus understands this first phase of demonic despair as the self's desperate attempt "to become internally consistent" (SD, 109). Despair over one's sin is the realization that one cannot attain self-consistency through striving for the good; it is "an effort to survive [that is, to be consistent] by sinking even deeper" (SD, 110). It also reflects a certain resentment toward God for having let one succumb to temptation. Rather than romantically deceive ourselves, Anti-Climacus lectures, about how "deep" those natures are who despair over their sin, we ought to realize that they are motivated only by selfish pride and self-love, by the desire to be above reproach and repentance in relation to God.[28] The self in despair over its sin refuses to forgive itself, but the demonic truth of this despair is that it really refuses to be forgiven by God. It embraces the darkness of despair in order to avoid humbling itself before God.

The second phase within the continuation of sin is the sin of despairing of the forgiveness of sin, or taking offense at God. The "intensification of the consciousness of the self" that takes place here is "the knowledge of Christ, a self directly before Christ." Anti-Climacus explains this as the culmination of the development of consciousness from a total ignorance of having an eternal self to a limited knowledge of the eternal to a final position of standing before God, which is "the basis for the definition of sin" (SD, 113). Only now does the despairing self find itself before Christ in its despair.

A brief recapitulation demonstrates the dialectical appropriateness of this development. In the first phase within the moment of despair as sin, the self is posited in relation to God. This relation is negated by Socratic ignorance, but the opposition between them is overcome in the Christian revelation of sin, which reinstates the position of sin and also affirms that the self remains ignorant of the truth (of sin) apart from faith. Thus, in that first moment, the correlative ideas of the self before God and of faith as the opposite of sin are posited. The second moment, the continuation of sin, negates those ideas. The demonic self withdraws from both the relation with God and the divine forgiveness offered to faith and isolates itself in a desperate self-consistency. Left to its own devices, the self could never return from that withdrawnness.

It is at this point that the second phase of the second moment begins, which is the fact of God coming to the despairing self in Christ. Anti-Climacus puts it this way: "A self directly before Christ is a self intensified by the inordinate concession from God, intensified by the inordinate accent that falls upon it because God allowed himself to be born, become man, suffer, and die also for the sake of this self" (SD, 113). In Christ, God negates the demonic withdrawnness of the previous phase and reestablishes the relationship with the sinner in despair. He does this by offering forgiveness of sins through the life and death of Christ. The self's refusal of forgiveness is the further sin of offense, a sin that implicitly acknowledges the reestablishment of the relationship but rejects reconciliation with God in favor of continued and intensified enmity with him.

Without remarking the dialectical complexity of this phase in relation to structural development, Anti-Climacus points out that it involves a reversal of an earlier pattern. On the assumption that every form of despair "must be classifiable"[29] in terms of either weakness or defiance, he remarks that these two rubrics no longer correspond respectively to despairingly willing not to be or to be oneself. Those formulas were fine when the self involved was merely the consciousness of despair, which could accordingly either weakly look for an external remedy or defiantly affirm itself. When the self is a sinner *who rejects the forgiveness of sins*, however, then to will despairingly not to be oneself (that is, the sinner one is) becomes defiance; to will despairingly to be oneself (again, the sinner one is) is weakness. It is demonic defiance to will to overcome sin apart from the forgiveness of sins, and it is demonic weakness to deny forgiveness of sins by giving oneself over to sin.

The discussion of the sin of despairing of the forgiveness of sins (offense) gives Anti-Climacus another opportunity to attack Christendom, not only because it is guilty of taking offense but also because in it "the qualitative difference between God and man is pantheistically abolished" (*SD*, 117). Christendom's speculative philosophy cannot grasp "the category of individuality" and therefore cannot even think the thought of sin (*SD*, 119). But sin is precisely that which establishes the single individual as fundamentally related to God, even when the individual's response to that relationship is offense at the forgiveness offered by God in Christ.

The third and final phase of the continuation of sin is: "The Sin of Dismissing Christianity *Modo Ponendo* [Positively], of Declaring it to be Untruth." "This," declares Anti-Climacus, "is sin against the Holy Spirit" (*SD*, 125). Whereas offense had been defensive, a rejection of the offer in Christ, sin now goes on the offensive, in the sense of consciously opposing God and actively declaring Christianity "to be a lie and untruth" (*SD*, 125). The basis for this intensification of offense is, once again, the "infinite qualitative difference" between God and man (*SD*, 126). This appears in three graduated forms of offense at Christianity: indifference, agnostic fascination, and active opposition (*SD*, 129-131). Opposition is "the highest intensification of sin," for it is a self-conscious and explicit rejection of faith, which is again defined as follows: "in relating itself to itself and in willing to be itself, the self rests transparently in the power that established it" (*SD*, 131).

The sin of dismissing Christianity is the dialectical culmination of the continuation of sin. In this final phase, as in the first, the self reaffirms its own self-consistency as withdrawn from and independent of God. But the second phase (offense at Christ) is also taken up into the rejection of Christianity in a more intensified form, for it is Christ who is rejected—not simply the idea of God's grace but the historical person in whom God made that grace actual. Thus the sin against the Holy Spirit is self-conscious opposition to Christ as savior from sin. This rejection is also an implicit denial of the very fact of sin, that is, of the position—that despair is sin—established in the first moment. The opposition between these moments is extreme: on the one hand, Christianity reveals the fact of sinfulness to be the fundamental character of human self-consciousness; on the other, the demonic self-consciousness rejects Christ and Christianty entirely in order to deny the self-alienation of sin and thereby maintain its own self-consistency.

Here *The Sickness unto Death* ends. There is no deliverance from this tension, no reconciliation of the dialectical opposition. If it were only a matter of structural interpretation, this inconclusiveness might indicate that the dialectic in this work is really not systematic after all, that part two is not to be read as the third movement that culminates the movements of despair without regard to consciousness and despair as consciousness in part one. But such an approach fails to satisfy for two reasons: first, there are too many clearly systematic triads of moments and phases within the movements already analyzed to settle for a nonsystematic conclusion; second, and much more compelling, there is the sense that the "sickness unto death" must have a cure and that the cure must be more fully developed than is the mere definition of faith with which *The Sickness unto Death* closes. A possible solution, one that offers not only a cure but also a structural conclusion, is to turn to the other work by Anti-Climacus, *Practice in Christianity*.[30]

PRACTICE IN CHRISTIANITY

Before attempting to identify the dialectical phases in *Practice in Christianity*, which also differ from the organization of the text, it is necessary to describe briefly the text as it stands. Part I is a discussion of Matt. 11:28: "Come to me, all who labor and are heavy laden, and I will give you rest." The first section discusses the "invitation" expressed in this verse, emphasizing that, although Christ invites people to come to him, "it is he in fact that comes to them" (*TC*, 21). Surprisingly, the people to whom he comes halt before his invitation. Section II explores the reason for that halt, which, according to Anti-Climacus, is nothing less than the nature of the inviter (*TC*, 25). The halt stems from both the humble appearance of the historical person who does the inviting—it was Christ in humiliation, not in glory (*TC*, 26)—and the fact that "it is not permissible to accept the invitation and reject the inviter" (*TC*, 43). The person of Jesus is discussed from the point of view of those of his contemporaries who objected to him, a striking contrast with the contemporaneity with Christ called for in the Invocation to part I. Further objections, in particular to Christ's teaching about sin, are considered in section III. Section IV explains that to be a Christian requires contemporaneity with Christ—not an external, historical relationship, but the realization that Christ's historical existence is a matter of inwardness (Luther's "for thee" is cited): "for Christ's life on earth, sacred history, stands for itself alone outside history" (*TC*, 68). This inwardness and absolute respect toward God can find expression only in the consciousness of sin (*TC*, 71-72).

Part II turns to verse 6 in Matt. 11: "And blessed is he who takes no offense in me." The familiar theme of offense is presented here in several ways. An opposition is stated between offense at Christ's loftiness and offense at his lowliness (*TC*, 84). But the discussion really begins with offense at Christ as an individual man who dares to attack the established order (section A), an implicit criticism of the holistic view of the state advanced by Hegel[31] and of the related notion of the commensurability of inner and outer. Here Anti-Climacus introduces the idea that Christ offended the Pharisees by teaching that piety is absolute inwardness, and then paid the merely external tax in order to avoid giving offense—doing so by performing a miracle. By this miracle, he shows himself to be the God-man, an occasion that introduces the first essential cause for offense (section B), that is, Christ's loftiness as an individual man who displays divine power. In addition to miracles, another such display is the demand that followers eat his flesh and drink his blood (John 6). Most outrageous (from the Pharisees' point of view) is that Jesus dares to forgive sins. In section C, the other essential cause for offense is discussed, namely, Christ's lowliness as the Son of God whose entire life was a story of humility and suffering. This paradox of loftiness and lowliness in the God-man leads Anti-Climacus into a long digression on the necessity for God to communicate indirectly in order to be able to maintain his incognito, even while he expresses the paradox sufficiently to create the possibility of offense (*TC*, 122-144).

In part III, Anti-Climacus takes up John 12:32: "And I, when I am lifted up from the earth, will draw all to myself." Seven "expositions" occur in this part, all of which explicate the claim that redemption is accomplished by Christ alone. Christ will draw all who remember him "from on high" [I]; Christ is a self who enables other selves to choose him freely, as "a unity of two contraries" (*TC*, 161) [II]; to follow Christ will always require suffering and humiliation [III]; such suffering is due to the cruelty of the world, and its opposition to God means that even exaltation will always appear in it as lowliness and humiliation [IV]; although direct expression of Christian inwardness is impossible, Anti-Climacus argues against hidden inwardness and for indirect recognition of the Christian by the opposition suffered in the world [V]; whereas admiration induces self-forgetfulness, to follow Christ as one's pattern results in heightened self-absorption [VI]; and the interpretation of "lifted up" as a reference to the crucifixion confirms the paradoxical claim that exaltation means humiliation in this world [VII].

This brief outline of the contents of *Practice in Christianity* suffices to show that there is no obvious structural relationship between it and *The Sickness unto Death*. Once again, the structural relations, like geological strata, lie beneath the surface, in the unfolding of a sytematic dialectic. In these two works, the dialectic is the development of consciousness through despair. It remains to be shown how *Practice in Christianity* constitutes the third and culminating moment of the third movement within that dialectic and, further, how that culmination offers a cure for the sickness unto death which is despair.

The third movement of Anti-Climacus's dialectic is despair as the self-consciousness of sin. The first two moments of that movement have already appeared in *The Sickness unto Death*: the self is posited as a sinner before God (the in-itself moment), and the self demonically negates sin-consciousness by affirming the continuation of sin (the for-itself moment). In terms of self-consciousness, the positing of sin represents the realization that one has betrayed oneself and God, while the demonic rejects that notion in the interests of self-consistency, and does so by repudiating Christ and Christianity. In relation to this dialectic, *Practice in Christianity* is the final moment, in which the demonic negation of Christ is overcome and Christianity is revealed as the *Aufhebung* of sin-consciousness.

As the *Aufhebung* of the consciousness of sin, this final moment takes up into itself aspects of both the preceding moments and discards other, purely negative aspects. From the in-itself moment, the claim that the self stands before God as a sinner is affirmed, but the conclusion that this position leaves the self in a state of incurable self-alienation is rejected. That rejection in turn shows that some truth does motivate the demonic quest for self-consistency, but it negates the demonic repudiation of Christianity. Thus Christianity, as the in-and-for-itself or absolute self-consciousness of the sinner, heals rather than fosters self-alienation, a point that somewhat undermines the charge that Kierkegaard's ideal can be identified with what Hegel calls the unhappy consciousness.[32]

The transaction here is not limited to the despairing self-consciousness: it is God who makes the self aware of sin, and God who delivers the self from sin (not, however, from sin-*consciousness*). The absolute self-consciousness of the Christian is that of a sinner who has been redeemed, an individual who has been given a new identity in place of the old vicious circle of self-alienation and self-assertion. This fully developed consciousness is one that never forgets the previous state from which it has been delivered. It is in this sense that Christianity can be called the *Aufhebung* of sin-consciousness and can be claimed by Anti-Climacus as the cure for despair.

This same dialectic can be stated abstractly in terms of the familiar dialectic of self and other. In the in-itself moment, when despair is posited as sin, the self is defined as that which is alienated from the divine other who establishes it; in the demonic continuation of sin, the self negates its dependence upon that other and stands in self-consistent opposition to it; and in Christianity as the *Aufhebung* of sin-consciousness, the self finds a new self-consistent identity by accepting the divine other as its pattern.

The moment represented by *Practice in Christianity* also reveals an (admittedly faint) internal systematic structure. On the level of phases, the initial invitation is opposed by the phase of offense, and their *Aufhebung* is expressed as redemption. The terms in which this dialectic advances are those of otherness and paradoxicality. In the in-itself phase (invitation), the divine other comes to the self in need of help. Offense is the for-itself phase, in which the self rejects God's invitation because of the intolerable paradox of loftiness and lowliness in Christ. Redemption preserves the otherness of God and the paradoxicality of Christ, yet it also negates the empty sense of need by satisfying it, just as it overcomes the intolerableness of the paradox by revealing Christ as the pattern for anyone who is willing to share in his sufferings.

The possibility of discerning three dialectical points[33] within each phase lends cogency to this structure, even though it departs even further from the overt organization of the text. With regard to the invitation, the three points are not too obscure: in the first section, God extends an unsolicited word of invitation; in the second and third sections, those to whom that invitation is addressed halt before it, judging the inviter on historical and objective grounds rather than subjectively responding to him; the fourth section constitutes the third point, for there self-consciousness reconciles the invitation and the inviter in its own sin-consciousness and in the realization that Christ comes only to sinners and only for their salvation.

The dialectic of offense corresponds more closely to Anti-Climacus's organization. Although he seems to think in terms of the bipolarity of loftiness and lowliness, his discussion actually has three sections, dealing in turn with Christ as individual man, Christ as divine man, and Christ as human God. To view these as three points does not require much imagination, for the concept of an individual human God neatly reconciles the offensive human individuality of the first point with the offensive divinity of the second, at the same time considerably intensifying the possibility for offense.

The dialectic of redemption requires the most deviation from the organization of the text, but a vague triadic structure can be discerned there also. The first point emerges in sections I and II, in which redemption by Christ is posited as a relation in which self-consciousness is confirmed in its freedom rather than overwhelmed by the power of Christ to draw all to himself. That divine power of love encounters opposition from the world, which means in turn that receiving Christ in the world will always involve submission to suffering and humiliation; for, unlike God, the world cannot tolerate the freedom of others. Thus Christians will be recognizable by the opposition they incur from the world. This negative relation between the world and Christ/Christians constitutes the second dialectical point and is developed in sections III-V. The third point is the realization that the life of redemption consists in following Christ in the world in such a way that the freedom of self-consciousness (the first point) is fulfilled by following Christ's pattern of enduring opposition from the world (the second point). This freedom-in-conformity (section VI) leads to the paradoxical unity of exaltation and humiliation in the world (section VII).

Admittedly, these dialectical patterns in *Practice in Christianity* do not have the same clarity and persuasiveness that those in *The Sickness unto Death* and several of the other pseudonymous works do. But the presence of even vague patterns helps to demonstrate that *Practice in Christianity* can constitute the third and final moment in the systematic dialectic of despair that is developed primarily in *The Sickness unto Death*. A brief recapitulation will show their continuity.

In the first movement, despair in-itself is posited without regard to consciousness; the second presents despair for-itself as externalized consciousness; and despair in-and-for-itself is the self-consciousness of the sinner before God. Perhaps owing to its level of abstraction, the development here is quite obvious. In despair without regard to consciousness there is as yet no awareness of a distinction between inner and outer or self and other. That awareness first emerges in despair as consciousness. Here the self as mere elements (namely, the binary oppositions of despair in-itself) is negated by the concept of despair as a form of consciousness. However, in this movement consciousness is still of the autonomous human self over against the eternal. As consciousness develops through the phases— spiritlessness, weakness (not willing to be onself), and defiance (willing to be oneself)—the self in despair for-itself remains alienated from its true nature, which is to rest transparently in the power that established it. The recognition of that relation constitutes the first moment within the movement of despair as self-consciousness. The fact that the birth of self-consciousness represents a new awareness of alienation from God determines self-consciousness as sin-consciousness. It is as this sin-consciousness that despair develops through the demonic and is transformed or transfigured by the redeeming practice of Christianity, that is, the acceptance of Christ's invitation to follow him as pattern, which completes the dialectic of despair and the development of consciousness.

STRUCTURAL analysis of the dialectic of consciousness in the works published under the pseudonym of Anti-Climacus helps to illuminate those texts and demonstrates that Kierkegaard's habit of thinking in such patterns did not cease with the publication of *Concluding Unscientific Postscript*. It also combines in an interesting way the categories of externality and otherness, showing once again that they must be distinguished in the religious stage. But the question of the relation between these late works and the dialectical structure of the theory of stages as such is more difficult. There is no obvious way in which *The Sickness unto Death* and *Practice in Christianity* illuminate that theory.[34] They are included here because, like *The Concept of Irony*, they manifest a dialectical structure that is formally and thematically similar to that which characterizes the stages. The systematic nature of that structure is evident in Chart 7.

CHART 7.
Anti-Climacus's Dialectic of Despair

A. Despair Without Regard to Consciousness [*SD*, part one, C, A]
   Binary oppositions: finitude/infinitude, possibility/necessity
   No distinction between inner/outer or self/other

DESPAIR IN-ITSELF:
CONSCIOUSNESS ONLY IMPLICIT

B. Despair as Consciousness [*SD*, part one, C, B]
   1. Spiritlessness: unconsciousness of self, externality [a]
   2. Weakness: not willing to be oneself, self-rejection [b. *alpha*]
      a. Despair over something earthly (external object) [(1)]
      b. Despair over the earthly as such (some reflection)
      c. Despair of the eternal or over oneself (withdrawness) [(2)]
   3. Defiance: despairing self-assertion, alienation from self and God,
      inwardness as a "jammed lock" [*beta*]

DESPAIR FOR-ITSELF:
CONSCIOUSNESS AS ALIENATION

C. Despair as Self-Consciousness of Sinner before God [*SD*, part two]
   1. Despair as sin: self posited before God and sin as self-alienation [A]
      a. Self posited in relation to God, despair posited as sin-conscious-
         ness [chap. 1]
      b. Socratic ignorance negates sin-consciousness of self in relation to
         God [chap. 2]
      c. Christian revelation affirms both sin-consciousness and ignorance
         of God [chap. 3]
   2. The demonic: continuation of sin, rejection of self dependent upon
      God [B]
      a. Sin of despairing over one's sin: self-consistency in sin [A]
      b. Sin of despairing of forgiveness of sin: offense at Christ [B]
      c. Sin against Holy Spirit: rejection of Christianity [C]
   3. Christianity as the *Aufhebung* of sin-consciousness [*TC*]
      a. Invitation: God comes to those in need [I]
         i. God's initiative [I]
         ii. Halt [II, III]
         iii. Sin-Consciousness [IV]
      b. Offense: Christ as paradox of loftiness/lowliness [II]
         i. Arrogant individual [A]
         ii. Divine man [B]
         iii. Human God [C]
      c. Redemption: God-in-Christ draws all from on high [III]
         i. Freedom [I, II]
         ii. Opposition [III-V]
         iii. Exaltation [VI, VII]

DESPAIR IN-AND-FOR-ITSELF:
SELF-CONSCIOUSNESS BEFORE GOD

CONCLUSION

ONE TEST of any critical argument is its ability to illuminate the matter in question. In the case of this book, the matter is Kierkegaard's pseudomymous literature. It is my hope that the preceding analyses will enable readers of that literature to see several dimensions that have previously gone unnoticed.

(1) The pervasive nature of the dialectic of inner and outer commends it as an Ariadne's thread, a common theme that permits the interpreter to relate the various pseudonyms to one another without according to any of them priority over the others.

(2) The dialectic of self and other, although less constant than that of inner and outer, is also central and reveals that Kierkegaard's concept of the self is thoroughly relational, even in the pseudonymous works.

(3) Together, the inner/outer and self/other dialectics provide helpful themes for understanding the theory of stages, for they constitute closely related aspects of the dialectic of inwardness, the systematic development of which can be traced through the aesthetic, ethical, and religious stages.

Kierkegaard's Dialectic of Inwardness

Although the primary purpose of Chapter One was to introduce various types of dialectical thinking and to demonstrate Kierkegaard's systematic abilities as they appear in *The Concept of Irony*, the theme of inner and outer also makes its first appearance there. Interpreted as a treatise on the emergence of subjectivity, the text reveals a progression from the externality of Xenophon and the merely abstract inwardness of Socrates to the concrete but utterly negative subjectivity of the Romantics, and then culminating in the subjectivity of Hegel and Goethe, which embraces both positive actuality and negative irony as moments within itself. Here the inner stands in a systematically dialectical relation to externality, a relation that must be mediated within inwardness (subjectivity). Thus inwardness is not merely inner in this "Hegelian" book: it is a proper relation between the inner and the outer.

Volume I of *Either/Or* appears to attack that implied reconciliation of inner and outer full force (Chapter Two). The contradiction between them is both preached and illustrated throughout its various essays. The irony is that the message of contradiction is stated in a series of essays that embody a systematic dialectic of mediation. The internal dialectic of the first essay is obvious, but its role as the first movement in a larger dialectic is not. As that in-itself movement (A), a trio of Mozart characters ardently pursue women to whom they remain indifferent as persons. This implicit contradiction becomes explicit, or for-itself (B), in the three *symparanekromenoi* essays, where the contradiction is between an indifferent exterior and a passionate yet hidden inner grief. In the last three sections, absolute indifference to the object of desire becomes the goal of self-consciousness, as subjects and objects come to recognize that they are the source of their own self-contradiction. This is contradiction in-and-for-itself (C), where the incommensurability between inner and outer is exploited for the purpose of deception.

Volume II pursues the inner/outer theme, but with this difference: the ethical type is committed to reconciling all aesthetic contradictions (Chapter Three). With his belief in the ethical transfiguration of the aesthetic and his goal of self-revelation, Judge William makes a strong case for commensurability over against incommensurability. In the case of language, the aesthete believes that it will always distort meaning, whereas the Judge finds Danish perfectly adequate to his purpose. His constant efforts to develop a dialectic of reciprocity (for all matters other than ethical choice per se) do not really result in a systematic structure, but it is possible to schematize the most important features of his position as three movements:

(A) transfiguration, (B) resolution, and (C) self-revelation. However, as Kierkegaard points out in *The Concept of Irony*, a dialectic of reciprocity falls short of both genuine dualities and true unities. In the ethical stage, the commensurability of inner and outer never receives a precise characterization. The one clear dialectical point is that the ethical demands repudiation of the aesthete's insistence upon inner/outer incommensurability.

The texts analyzed in Chapter Four all support this emphasis upon the question of the commensurability of inner and outer. In *Repetition*, the young man strives for the ethical commensurability of a husband, much to the dismay of his aesthetic friend, Constantin. As Constantin sees it, the religious is superior to the ethical precisely because it, like the aesthetic, affirms the incommensurability of reality with inwardness. He has no awareness of the role that the ethical plays in becoming religious. In *Fear and Trembling*, the religious also contradicts ethical commensurability, not by disdaining it but by uniting it with the incommensurable movement of faith. This is a paradox that an ethical type such as Johannes de Silentio finds unintelligible. The relation of the earlier stages to the religious is also the subject of " 'Guilty?'/'Not Guilty?' " in *Stages on Life's Way*. There the aesthetic is again portrayed as an inner/outer incommensurability and the ethical as a commitment to self-revelation (commensurability) in marriage. The relation between them is illuminated by a further extension of the inner/outer dialectic: aesthetic incommensurability is criticized as an utterly external contradiction, whereas the ethical is judged to be only somewhat external, insofar as it seeks a "visible" (commensurable) justice. The religious stage, in contrast, is utterly inward. However, Frater Taciturnus, like Constantin and de Silentio, seems unable to penetrate the deeper dynamics of the religious. This is because all three assume that to do so means to comprehend it. All approaches to the religious that would comprehend the incomprehensible must inevitably fail.

The dialectic of inner and outer appears again in the third

chapter of *The Concept of Anxiety* (Chapter Five). As the religious individual seeks the eternal, a development from externality (paganism and Judaism) to inwardness (Christianity) emerges. Although instances of inwardness and internalization also appear within the series of paradoxes in *Philosophical Fragments*, the algebraic nature of those paradoxes precludes systematic analysis.

It is in *Concluding Unscientific Postscript* that aesthetic incommensurability of inner and outer and their ethical commensurability are dialectically united in a systematic *Aufhebung*. The religious is portrayed in *Postscript* as a complex progressive structure composed of three movements, each of which in turn consists in three moments (Chapter Six). The first movement is the religious in-itself (A), in which inwardness (subjectivity) is posited as the incommensurable commensurability of inner and outer. The moments of this movement are as follows: first the self separates itself from the external, which implicitly negates the ethical claim for their commensurability; next the external is appropriated by the self, which implies an (uncertain) commensurability; and finally the self arrives at concrete thought as the simultaneous separation from and appropriation of the external. It is this paradox—this simultaneous affirmation of incommensurability and commensurability—that posits the religious stage as the dialectical *Aufhebung* of the aesthetic and ethical stages. Religiousness A then appears as a for-itself or negative movement (B). Its first moment is resignation of everything external (incommensurability); suffering restores a relation of commensurability, but it is an inverted relation, one in which the negative is the sign of the positive; finally, guilt-consciousness unites the incommensurability of resignation with the inverted commensurability of suffering in a self-consciousness whose eternal recollection cannot escape its own self. This implicit designation of the self as the place where the eternal appears leads Climacus to describe religiousness A as an immanent dialectic. In contrast to its utter inwardness, religiousness B reinstates an element of externality. There a transcendent dialectic of revelation constitutes the culminating in-and-for-itself movement (C) of the religious stage. In its first moment, the paradox of the incarnation of the inward, eternal divine in an external, historical human is posited. Next, attention turns to the subjective appropriation of this fact by faith. Finally, the fact that both incarnation and faith are logically absurd results in the affirmation of paradox as the structure of revelation and the truth of religious inwardness. In religiousness B, the incommensurability of the inner with the outer is demonstrated through a revelation that makes them commensurable! This paradoxical *Aufhebung* determines religiousness B as the culmination of the religious stage and the religious stage as the dialectical fulfillment of the aesthetic and ethical stages.

The dialectic of despair in the works by Anti-Climacus (Chapter Seven) can also be expressed in terms of the relation between inner and outer. That distinction is merely implicit in the first movement, where despair is considered without regard to consciousness. It becomes explicit in the second, where despair as consciousness is precisely the search for self in externals, which results in frustration and the rejection of all externality (defiance, or "inwardness with a jammed lock"). Only as the self-consciousness of sin does despair arrive at a proper balance of inner and outer, and it does so by virtue of coming into relation with the divine other who is inwardly known.

Kierkegaard's Relational Concept of Self

Parallel to this dialectic of inner and outer, many of these works present a dialectical development of the self in relation to its other. In *Stages on Life's Way*, "In Vino Veritas" confirms the ideas and patterns of the aesthetic and ethical stages as represented in *Either/Or*, I, but does so in terms of self and other rather than inner and outer (Chapter Two). The initial movement (A) is the young man's rejection of love, a rejection based upon total unconsciousness of woman as other to man. The next three speeches (B) criticize woman directly, precisely because she is so other, that is, so self-contradictory. In the final speech by Johannes the seducer (C), mutual self-contradiction is matched by reciprocal opposition of self and other. Here the other is distinct, but has significance only in relation to the self. Thus the opposition between self and other has been internalized within the dialectic of deception.

"Various Observations" is an ethical critique of the aesthetic claim that self and other are always opposed (Chapter Three). Transposing the ethical dialectic of inner and outer into these categories, the initial movement (A) posits the other as distinct from yet necessary to the self; the ethical for-itself (B) shows that the self must resolve to be related to the other; and self-revelation is again the expression for the ethical *Aufhebung* (C), in which self and other enjoy a reciprocity such that each chooses to be a self that is distinct from and yet dependent upon the other.

The self/other theme is not prominent in the works that I have treated as approaches to, and varieties of, the religious stage (Chapters Four and Five), although it does make several appearances. Since *Repetition* and the Quidam material have such a strongly aesthetic character, they present the dialectic more in terms of inner and outer than self and other. Johannes de Silentio, however, is an ethical humanist, and one of the paradoxes that concerns him in *Fear and Trembling* is Abraham's inability to speak about his trial to either Sarah or Isaac. The theme of otherness appears in *The Concept of Anxiety* within the in-itself movement, which portrays the self as seeking itself in a sequence of others: first indeterminate, then nonhuman, and finally human. Anxiety for-itself seeks the eternal externally, particularly in oracles and ritual sacrifices. In the final movement, the self is constituted in inwardness by the eternal. This paradoxical concept of an other that is met only inwardly is also expressed in *Philosophical Fragments* by the concept of disciple, that is, a sinner who is saved by virtue of a decisive encounter with an other—the divine teacher.

Once again, however, it is *Concluding Unscientific Postscript* that really illustrates the dialectic of self and other in the religious stage (Chapter Six). This is clear in the third movement, and can be transposed from the inner/outer parallel for the first and second. Thus the in-itself movement (A) posits the divine as paradoxically inward *and* other, over against the merely reciprocal relations of the ethical stage. This inward otherness first appears in the separation of the self from all external others, then in the effort to appropriate the inward divine other, and finally in the internalization of the otherness of the divine. The for-itself movement (B) is what Climacus calls religiousness A. Its moments are as follows: resignation, in its effort to be free of everything external, shows that it assumes a unity of the self's inwardness with the divine other; suffering, however, qualifies that unity by its affirmation of self-annihilation as its inverted manifestation; and guilt-consciousness shows that the final result of such radical inwardness is not unity with the divine other but the infinite recollection of a merely *self*-consciousness. Religiousness B is the in-and-for-itself movement (C) in which the contradiction between the inward divine other and the circle of self-consciousness is overcome. Here the three moments are set out separately from, yet parallel to, those that develop the inner/outer dialectic. The first is sin-consciousness, which negates the mere self-identity of guilt-consciousness. It is in turn opposed by the possibility of offense, which denies the sinfulness of sin. Sin and offense at Christ find their *Aufhebung* in the smart of sympathy, which affirms both the self's sinfulness before God and the offense that the world takes to Christ and to Christians. The resulting bond of sympathy among Christians is nurtured by the pain of persecution, which must be endured. It is this community of selves, united in the love of God, that crowns both the religious stage and the entire development of the theory of stages.

In light of this dialectic of self and other, the notorious rhetoric of solitary selfhood must be set in its structural context. Kierkegaard occasionally portrays the self as utterly alone (the unhappiest man) or alone with God (religiousness A). But that "solitude" is always a moment in a development that embraces interpersonal relations that can be contradictory (the aesthetic stage), reciprocal (the ethical stage), or paradoxically both incommunicable and reciprocal (the religious stage). The relational nature of religious selfhood must especially be emphasized. The knight of faith cannot speak of his dilemma to Sarah and Isaac, but the very pain of that ordeal presupposes a thoroughly ethical relationship with them both. Anxiety is an inner state, yet its resolution comes only when the self realizes that the eternal that it seeks is neither external nor simply the inner self—it is a divine *other* who can be known only inwardly. This inward otherness is also what overcomes the self-annihilation of religiousness A and brings the self into relation with both itself and with others who share the smart of sympathy. In religiousness B, the inverted dialectic of hidden inwardness is implicitly replaced by the sharpened pathos of paradoxical self-revelation (confession), both before God and in the community of Christians.

This paradoxical unity of the self as both other to itself (in sin) and restored to itself by God—in conformity with the pattern of Christ—also structures the works by Anti-Climacus (Chapter Seven). There the notions of inward knowledge of the divine other and the otherness of the inwardly appropriated divine are given classic expression. The dialectic of despair shows that the fundamental self/other relation is that between the individual and God, but that this relation is not to be divorced from the relation between the self and other human beings. As with all of Kierkegaard's pseudonymous literature, these texts appear to glorify existential isolation only if certain passages are taken out of context. Structural analysis shows that they portray the development of selfhood and consciousness as a matter of relations, not of solitude.

The Dialectical Structure of Kierkegaard's Theory of Stages

The dialectical structure of the theory of stages as a whole has already been adequately recapitulated in the preceding two sections. It is a dialectic in which the initial stage is one of contradiction, contradiction is in turn negated by reciprocity, and then contradiction and reciprocity are united in paradox. Because of this formally systematic structure, it is possible to conclude that Kierkegaard continued to think in the Hegelian, mediating terms that he so frequently condemned. It is equally true, however, that the sublated oppositions within the dialectic of the stages are profoundly paradoxical unities. In other words, the demonstration that Kierkegaard's paradoxes are not always merely algebraic series, but are frequently susceptible to geometric or systematic analysis, also conversely shows the extent to which the very concept of systematic mediation incorporates and depends upon paradox. Whether such paradox is in fact a latent and unacknowledged aspect of all efforts to mediate contradictions is a question that cannot be addressed here. However, it is possible to conclude this study with a final chart illustrating the dialectical movements of Kierkegaard's theory of stages.

CHART 8.

The Dialectical Structure of
the Theory of Stages

I. Aesthetic Inwardness

Inner/outer incommensurability

A. Unconscious indifference to objects of apparent desire

B. Apparent indifference toward object of inner desire/grief

C. Absolute indifference to object of desire

Self/other opposition

A. Self-involvement; no consciousness of the other as other

B. Other negated by self as self-contradictory

C. Other distinct from but significant only in relation to the self

INWARDNESS IN-ITSELF:
ABSTRACT CONTRADICTION

II. Ethical Inwardness

Inner/outer commensurability

A. Incommensurability transfigured into commensurability

B. Incommensurability opposed by ethical resolution

C. Self-revelation: rendering the incommensurable commensurable

Self/other reconciliation

A. Interdependence and harmonious communication presupposed

B. Self must resolve to be related to the other

C. Self-revelation: selves distinct from/dependent upon one another by choice

INWARDNESS FOR-ITSELF:
CONCRETE RECIPROCITY

III. Religious Inwardness

Commensurable incommensurability

A. Inwardness posited as both incommensurable and commensurable

B. Inwardness as inversely commensurable incommensurability (religiousness A)

C. Paradoxical revelation of the incommensurable in the commensurable (religiousness B)

Reconciliation in opposition

A. Divine posited as inward yet other (concrete thought)

B. Divine found inwardly but its otherness is ignored (religiousness A)

C. Reconciliation of self and divine in paradox of inward *and* external otherness (religiousness B)

INWARDNESS IN-AND-FOR-ITSELF:
ABSOLUTE PARADOX

NOTES

INTRODUCTION

1. One common example of this tendency is the interpretation of the aesthetic stage through the eyes of Judge William, who represents the ethical stage. This choice is hardly surprising in studies that focus primarily upon the concepts of freedom and selfhood, for example, Louis P. Pojman, "The Dialectic of Freedom in the Thought of Søren Kierkegaard" (Th.D. dissertation, Union Theological Seminary, 1972), pp. 117-118; and Mark C. Taylor, *Kierkegaard's Pseudonymous Authorship: A Study of Time and the Self* (Princeton: Princeton University Press, 1975), p. 128. In both of these works, insightful analyses of the aesthetic define its essense negatively, from the ethical point of view (a lack of responsibility or the absence of decision). Some writers go so far as to treat Judge William's pronouncements on the aesthetic as those of Kierkegaard himself: Harry S. Broudy, "Kierkegaard's Levels of Existence," *Philosophy and Phenomenological Research* 1, no. 3 (March 1941), p. 297; and Howard P. Kainz, "Kierkegaard's 'Three Stages' and the Levels of Spiritual Maturity," *Modern Schoolman* 52 (May 1975), p. 361.

2. The most frequent candidate is Johannes Climacus. Although Kierkegaard insists in "A First and Last Declaration" (appended to *Postscript*) that "in the pseudonymous works there is not a single word which is mine," he grants Climacus the privilege of providing overviews of both the entire authorship and the interrelations among the three stages (*CUP*, 225-266, 505-508). The former leads Gregor Malantschuk to argue that Climacus "directed the course of the authorship from the wings," in *Kierkegaard's Thought*, ed. and trans. Howard V. Hong and Edna H. Hong (Princeton: Princeton University Press, 1971), p. 245; the latter is no doubt responsible for the influence of Climacus on Reidar Thomte's chapter, "The Interrelationship of the Stages," in *Kierkegaard's Philosophy of Religion* (Princeton: Princeton University Press, 1948), pp. 97-109.

3. The most interesting recent attempt to do this is a computer-assisted study by Alastair McKinnon, "Kierkegaard's Pseudonyms:

A New Hierarchy," *American Philosphical Quarterly* 6, no. 2 (April 1969), pp. 116-126. On the basis of complex statistical studies of vocabulary and the like, McKinnon ranks the pseudonyms' styles, with Anti-Climacus winning first place (that is, most like Kierkegaard) and A and Johannes Climacus (in *Postscript*) tied for second. Nevertheless, it should be noted that such words as "paradox" and "absurd," which McKinnon finds prominently in the pseudonymous works and not at all in those published under Kierkegaard's name, are proven by the Journals of 1850 and later to represent Kierkegaard's own beliefs. See Merold Westphal, "Kierkegaard and the Logic of Insanity," *Religious Studies* 7, no. 3 (September 1971), p. 210, as well as *JP* no. 7-12, 3093-3102.

4. One famous example of this, and reaction against it, is in Martin Buber, "The Question to the Single One," in *Between Man and Man*, trans. Ronald Gregor Smith, with an introduction by Maurice Friedman (New York: Macmillan, 1965), pp.40-82.

5. Thus Taylor devotes the conclusion of *Authorship* to "The Solitary Self," and Louis Mackey writes that Kierkegard tends "to absolutize human subjectivity." See Mackey, "The Loss of the World in Kierkegaard's Ethics," in *Kierkegaard: A Collection of Critical Essays*, ed. Josiah Thompson (Garden City, N.Y.: Doubleday Anchor, 1972), p. 282. Other representative titles are Ralph Harper, *The Seventh Solitude: Man's Isolation in Kierkegaard, Dostoevsky, and Nietzsche* (Baltimore: Johns Hopkins University Press, 1965); and Josiah Thompson, *The Lonely Labyrinth: Kierkegaard's Pseudonymous Works* (Carbondale: Southern Illinois University Press, 1967).

6. The interest in Kierkegaard's social and political thought is not new; see, for example, Howard A. Johnson, "Kierkegaard and Politics," in *A Kierkegaard Critique*, ed. Howard A. Johnson and Niels Thulstrup (Chicago: Henry Regnery Company, 1962), pp. 74-84; and Gregor Malantschuk, *The Controversial Kierkegaard*, trans. Howard V. Hong and Edna H. Hong (Waterloo: Wilfrid Laurier University Press, 1980). What is new is the realization that Kierkegaard's theories are not as individualistic as has often been assumed. Perhaps the first major study to explore his thought as a comprehensive social theory was Kresten Nordentoft's *Kierkegaard's Psychology*, trans. Bruce Kirmmse (Pittsburgh: Duquesne University Press, 1978), which was published in Danish in 1972. Kirmmse's own two-volume dissertation is a major contribution to this effort: "Kierkegaard's Politics: The Social Thought of Søren Kierkegaard in Its

Historical Context" (Ph.D. dissertation, University of California, 1977). For compatible studies of the works published after *CUP*, see also: John W. Elrod, *Kierkegaard and Christendom* (Princeton: Princeton University Press, 1981); Sylvia Walsh Utterback, "Kierkegaard's Dialectic of Christian Existence" (Ph.D. dissertation, Emory University, 1975), especially pp. 214ff.; and Merold Westphal, "Kierkegaard's Sociology," forthcoming in the International Kierkegaard Commentary volume on *Two Ages*, ed. by Robert L. Perkins (Mercer University Press). For a contribution to, and a review of, recent developments, see Michael Plekon, " 'Anthropological Contemplation': Kierkegaard and Modern Social Theory," and " 'Other Kierkegaards'—New Views and Reinterpretations in Scholarship," *Thought* 55, no. 218 (September 1980), pp. 346-375.

7. I am aware of four such articles, each of which approaches the topic in a unique and interesting way: James Collins, "Kierkegaard's Imagery of the Self," in *Kierkegaard's Truth: The Disclosure of the Self*, ed. Joseph H. Smith, Psychiatry and the Humanities, vol. 5 (New Haven: Yale University Press, 1981), pp. 51-84; Russell H. Davis, "Kierkegaard and Community," *Union Seminary Quarterly Review* 36, no. 4 (Summer 1981), pp. 205-222; Edward F. Mooney, "Understanding Abraham: Care, Faith, and the Absurd," in *Kierkegaard's "Fear and Trembling": Critical Appraisals*, ed. Robert L. Perkins (University: University of Alabama Press, 1981), pp. 100-114; and Merold Westphal, "Kierkegaard's Politics," *Thought* 55, no. 218 (September 1980), pp. 320-332.

8. James Collins, *The Mind of Kierkegaard* (Chicago: Henry Regnery, 1953), p. 42.

9. The inconsistency is again traceable to the influence of Johannes Climacus, who even disagrees with himself: after announcing that there are three stages (*CUP*, 261), Climacus proceeds to discuss four and even five (*CUP*, 505-508).

10. The tendency to set the Christian stage radically over against the others characterizes many German neo-orthodox interpretations. See Thomte, *Kierkegaard's Philosophy of Religion*, pp. 102-103, for an account of Emanuel Hirsch's criticism of this tendency in *Kierkegaard-Studien*, 2 vols. (Gütersloh: C. Bertelsmann, 1933), pp. 802-805.

11. Stephen Crites puts the matter nicely when he writes: "each stage in what we have called Kierkegaard's phenomenology of spirit places the individual in a progressively more self-conscious position of responsibility for his own life." Crites, *In the Twilight of Christen-*

dom: Hegel vs. Kierkegaard on Faith and History, AAR Studies in Religion, no. 2 (Chambersburg, Pa.: American Academy of Religion, 1972), p. 74. This accent on progress implies continuity rather than radical discontinuity among the stages. It also indicates that the higher stages can embrace the lower, whereas the lower will "grasp" the higher only by distorting them. See Crites's introduction to *CLA*, 40. It is important to emphasize the distinction between systematic, progressive development and the notorious Hegelian claim that a particular line of development is "necessary." Kierkegaard ridicules that claim constantly, and even such a leading Hegelian as J. N. Findlay echoes that criticism in *The Philosophy of Hegel: An Introduction and Re-Examination* (New York: Collier, 1962), p. 78. I am not personally convinced that Hegel ever meant to claim the sort of necessity that is being criticized, but to demonstrate that the issue is really a red herring would require a short book on that subject alone.

12. Kierkegaard's relation to Hegel has been the subject of extensive study and debate, most of which is reviewed by Niels Thulstrup in *Kierkegaards Verhältnis zu Hegel: Forschungsgeschichte* (Stuttgart: Verlag W. Kohlhammer, 1969). For a less polemical overview, although one that is limited to the debate about *CI*, see Lee M. Capel's historical introduction and notes to *CI*, pp. 7-41, 351-434. Good discussions of the question of historical influence can be found in T. H. Croxall, "Assessment," *DODE*, 15-54; and Jean Wahl, *Études Kierkegaardiennes*, 4th ed. (Paris: J. Vrin, 1974), pp. 86-171. In many ways, the most interesting treatments are systematic rather than historical, that is, essays in which scholars attempt to sort out the vital issues that unite and divide Kierkegaard and Hegel. Even the most balanced of these works usually tilt in one direction or the other, thereby bringing down upon their authors the frequently unjustified charge of failing to do justice to the other of the two. Thus Max Bense's *Hegel und Kierkegaard: Eine prinzipielle Untersuchung* (Cologne: Staufen-Verlag, 1948) is far more evenhanded than one would gather from Wilfried Joest's review of it in *Sören Kierkegaard*, ed. Heinz-Horst Schrey (Darmstadt: Wissenschaftliche Buchgesellschaft, 1971), pp. 81-89. American scholars have made significant contributions to this genre. See Crites's *Twilight*, the works of Robert L. Perkins (especially "Kierkegaard and Hegel: The Dialectical Structure of Kierkegaard's Ethical Thought," Ph.D. dissertation, Indiana University, 1965), and Mark C. Taylor's *Journeys to Selfhood: Hegel*

and Kierkegaard (Berkeley: University of California Press, 1980). The assumption underlying some of these works seems to be that Hegel and Kierkegaard represent the primary alternatives between which we moderns must choose, an assumption that is explicitly argued by Richard Kroner in "Kierkegaard or Hegel?" *Revue internationale de Philosophie* 6, no. 1 (1952), pp. 79-96.

13. Thus Capel in the introduction to *CI*, pp. 34-35, and Niels Thulstrup, *Kierkegaard's Relation to Hegel*, trans. George L. Stengren (Princeton: Princeton University Press, 1980), p. 257. Thulstrup's strategy in this book, which was published in Danish in 1967, is to marshall every shred of historical evidence that might support his conviction that "such a shrewd genius as Kierkegaard could [not] possibly have let himself be taken in by Hegel" (p. 214). This conviction expresses his answer to the question posed in his earlier article, "Theological and Philosophical Kierkegaardian Studies in Scandinavia, 1945-1953," trans. Paul Holmer, *Theology Today* 12, no. 3 (October 1955): "One can appropriately raise the issue . . . whether the formal structure Kierkegaard gives his thought in the pseudonymous writings does not, in fact, controvert its religious content. It may be true that Kierkegaard's categories for the determination of the essence of Christianity are not in accord with Biblical writings but are rather in accord with the Hegelian outlook against which he was continually polemizing" (p. 303). Thulstrup goes on to call for a "detailed historical and structural analysis of each point, line, and argument" by Kierkegaard, but his own book, which purports to accomplish that task, is a very weak defense of the position that "Hegel and Kierkegaard have in the main nothing in common as thinkers" (*Kierkegaard's Relation to Hegel*, p. 12).

14. The allusion here to structuralist methods in literary interpretation requires comment. This study shares with such approaches: (1) a commitment to the immanent criticism of texts and a corresponding disregard for the conscious intentions of the author; (2) a strong interest in the formal analysis ("archaeology") of conceptual/ dialectical patterns or structures; and (3) a concern with synchronic relations among those structures. Yet my *structural* analysis differs from *structuralist* works in equally significant ways: (1) the focus on texts implies no rejection of external methods per se; (2) the systematic dialectic (this term is defined in Chapter One) is never simply presupposed but always remains subject to verification by careful inspection of the texts in question (and is, in fact, conspicuously

absent from some of them); and (3) the synchronic dimension is not meant to eclipse the even more pronounced diachronic development in the dialectic of the stages.

15. It is common for Kierkegaard scholars to point out Hegelian elements in Kierkegaard's thought. Recent examples include Westphal's "Kierkegaard's Politics," pp. 321-324, and some of the essays in the anthology edited by Joseph H. Smith, *Kierkegaard's Truth: The Disclosure of the Self*, vol. 5 in Psychiatry and the Humanities (New Haven: Yale University Press, 1981), especially the following: Bruce H. Kirmmse, "Psychology and Society: The Social Falsification of the Self in *The Sickness unto Death*," pp. 167-192; Vincent A. McCarthy, " 'Psychological Fragments': Kierkegaard's Religious Psychology," pp. 235-266; Paul Ricoeur, "Two Encounters with Kierkegaard: Kierkegaard and Evil; Doing Philosophy after Kierkegaard," pp. 313-342; Mark C. Taylor, "Aesthetic Therapy: Hegel and Kierkegaard," pp. 343-380; and Michael Theunissen, "Kierkegaard's Negativistic Method," pp. 381-423. My own previous contribution to this quasi-genre is "Kierkegaard's 'Hegelian' Response to Hamann," *Thought* 55, no. 218 (September 1980), pp. 259-270. Much less common than the simple claim that Hegelian elements can be observed in Kierkegaard's writings is the argument that Kierkegaard remained an ambivalent disciple of Hegel despite his efforts to reject Hegelianism. For their "latent commonality," see Wilhelm Anz, *Kierkegaard und der deutsche Idealismus* (Tübingen: J.C.B. Mohr, 1956), p. 70. Richard Kroner has explored the same issue from the point of view of Kierkegaard's misreading of Hegel in "Kierkegaard's Understanding of Hegel," *Union Seminary Quarterly Review* 21, no. 2, Pt. II (January 1966), pp. 233-244.

16. The most influential American Kierkegaard scholar exemplifies the existentialist, antisystematic approach to the pseudonymous materials: Walter Lowrie, *Kierkegaard* (London: Oxford University Press, 1938). Lowrie's influence is due not so much to the persuasiveness of this book as to the fact that he was instrumental in introducing Kierkegaard's writings to English-speaking readers.

17. The outstanding example of a systematic interpretation of Kierkegaard is Paul Sponheim, *Kierkegaard on Christ and Christian Coherence* (London: SCM Press, 1968), although the "system" Sponheim finds in Kierkegaard (diastasis-synthesis-interpenetration) is not progressive or cumulative in the Hegelian sense. A number of recent studies have treated Kierkegaard in terms of the coherent, if not

fully systematic, development of one or another theme: John W. Elrod, *Being and Existence in Kierkegaard's Pseudonymous Works* (Princeton: Princeton University Press, 1975); Vincent A. McCarthy, *The Phenomenology of Moods in Kierkegaard* (The Hague: Martinus Nijhoff, 1978); Adi Schmüeli, *Kierkegaard and Consciousness*, trans. Naomi Handelmann (Princeton: Princeton University Press, 1971); and Taylor's *Authorship*. Structural interpretations are less frequent, unless "structure" is taken in the broad (phenomenological) sense of any "structure of meaning." I am using it more narrowly to refer to specific dialectical structures that appear and reappear in the pseudonymous literature and constitute the skeleton or architectonic of those works. The only other rigorously structural study of this sort that I have found is André Clair's *Pseudonymie et paradoxe: La pensée dialectique de Kierkegaard* (Paris: J. Vrin, 1976), which examines paradoxical structures in the pseudonymous works.

18. Sylviane Agacinski, *Aparté: Conceptions et morts de Sören Kierkegaard* (Flammarion: Aubion, 1977).

19. This disclaimer is doubly important in light of the fact that the dialectical structures I find in most of Kierkegaard's pseudonymous works are "Hegelian" *only* in a formal or structural sense, not in terms of content, and certainly not as the objective unfolding of spirit in world history.

CHAPTER ONE
Training in Dialectics

1. See the Introduction, note 13. Robert L. Perkins offers a balanced discussion of the Hegelian and non-Hegelian elements in *The Concept of Irony* in "Kierkegaard and Hegel: The Dialectical Structure of Kierkegaard's Ethical Thought" (Ph.D. dissertation, Indiana University, 1965), chap. 1. Perkins does not, however, discuss the systematic structure of the text as such. One interesting irony is that Niels Thulstrup and Mark Taylor, who are diametrically opposed in their evaluations of Hegel and Kierkegaard, fundamentally agree in setting them against each other as mutually exclusive representatives of philosophies of either social responsibility or individual freedom (or, stated negatively, either socialist determinism or arbitrary individualism). This occasionally puts them in agreement on specific issues of interpretation, such as the ironical intention behind the Hegelian elements in *The Concept of Irony*. See Niels Thulstrup, *Kier-*

kegaard's Relation to Hegel, trans. George L. Stengren (Princeton: Princeton University Press, 1980), pp. 173, 257; and Mark C. Taylor, *Journeys to Selfhood: Hegel and Kierkegaard* (Berkeley: University of California Press, 1980), pp. 10, 94.

2. Stanley Cavell offers one of the best short definitions I know, one that points to the association with change that is at least partially responsible for that ambiguity: "Very generally, a dialectical examination of a concept will show how the meaning of that concept changes, and how the subject of which it is the concept changes, as the context in which it is used changes: the dialectical meaning is the history or confrontation of these differences." Cavell, "Kierkegaard's *On Authority and Revelation*," in *Kierkegaard: A Collection of Critical Essays*, ed. Josiah Thompson (Garden City, N.Y.: Doubleday Anchor, 1972), p. 381. For general studies of dialectic (a much neglected field, considering how much the word is used), see: Paul Foulquié, *La Dialectique* (Paris: Presses Universitaires, 1969); Adolf Sannwald, *Der Begriff der "Dialektik" und die Anthropologie* (Munich: Kaiser Verlag, 1931); George J. Stack, "On the Notion of Dialectics," *Philosophy Today* 15, no. 4/4 (Winter 1971), pp. 276-290; and Friedrich Traub, "Zum Begriff des Dialektischen," *Zeitschrift für Theologie und Kirche* 37 (1929), pp. 300-388

3. In *De Omnibus Dubitandum Est*, a novel that Kierkegaard wrote at about the same time as *Either/Or* (1841-1842) but never published, he defines "the problem of consciousness" as the negative relation between immediacy (being) and speech (thought, language). See especially *DODE*, 148. A few years later, Climacus writes of "the doubleness characteristic of existence" (*CUP*, 69). There can be no doubt that Kierkegaard intended to repudiate the Hegelian dialectic of unity: see Hermann Diem, *Philosophie und Christentum bei Sören Kierkegaard* (Munich: Kaiser Verlag, 1929), pp. 91-112, and *Kierkegaard's Dialectic of Existence*, trans. Harold Knight (Edinburgh: Oliver and Boyd, 1959); also Dietrich Ritschl's article, "Kierkegaard's Kritik an Hegels Logik," in *Theologische Zeitschrift* 11 (1955), pp. 437-465. On Kierkegaard's use of dialectic to clarify concepts rather than to describe reality, see James W. Thomasson, "Concepts: Their Role, Criteria and Correction in the Thought of Søren Kierkegaard" (Ph.D. dissertation, Yale University, 1968). For Kierkegaard's concern with the limitations of human intellect, see: David F. Swenson, "The Anti-Intellectualism of Kierkegaard," *Philosophical Review* 25, no. 4 (1916), pp. 567-586; and Merold Westphal, "Kier-

kegaard and the Logic of Insanity," *Religious Studies* 7, no. 3 (September 1971), pp. 193-211.

4. Paul Holmer states this contrast well: "But while Hegel and Marx used 'dialectic' to describe an interpretative method by which both entities and thoughts could arise, oppose one another, and be synthesized, Kierkegaard means something far plainer. For him, dialectic is simply a name for the conceptual scheme, the algebraic rubrics, that will hang matters together." Holmer, "Post-Kierkegaard: Remarks about Being a Person," in *Kierkegaard's Truth: The Disclosure of the Self*, ed. Joseph H. Smith, Psychiatry and the Humanities, vol. 5 (New Haven: Yale University Press, 1981), pp. 9-10. On the "objectivity" of Kierkegaard's paradox, see my discussion of *Philosophical Fragments* in Chapter Five. For an attempt to combine Marxist (objective) and existentialist (subjective) dialectics, see Jean-Paul Sartre, *Critique of Dialectical Reason*, trans. Alan Sheridan-Smith (London: Verso, 1982).

5. Since the relation between Kierkegaard and his pseudonymous writings occupies a central place in so many books on his thought, and because it would require another volume to deal with that problem adequately (especially given the extent to which Kierkegaard himself wrote about it), I will not address the issue directly. On the general problem of Kierkegaard's self-contradictory statements about his own authorship, see Aage Henriksen, *Methods and Results of Kierkegaard Studies in Scandinavia: A Historical and Critical Survey* (Copenhagen: Ejnar Munksgaard, 1951). For a discussion of the questionable reliability of many important entries in the *Papirer*, see Henning Fenger, *Kierkegaard, The Myths and Their Origins: Studies in the Kierkegaardian Papers and Letters*, trans. George C. Schoolfield (New Haven: Yale University Press, 1976). Many scholars argue for the noncorrespondence between Kierkegaard's personal views and those of the pseudonyms. See, for example, Ralph McInerny, "Ethics and Persuasion: Kierkegaard's Existential Dialectic," *Modern Schoolman* 33 (May 1956), pp. 219-239; and Alastair McKinnon, "Kierkegaard's Irrationalism Revisited," *International Philosophical Quarterly* 9, no. 2 (June 1969), pp. 165-176. For Kierkegaard's desire to free the reader from concern for him as author, see "A First and Last Declaration," appended to *CUP*, and the statement in his letter to *Fædrelandet* (February 2, 1843), in *CorA*, p. 16.

6. One famous example of this biographical approach to Kierkegaard's works is Walter Lowrie, who defends this method in

"Translators and Interpreters of S.K.," *Theology Today* 12, no. 3 (October 1955), pp. 312-327. Pierre Mesnard suggests a more sophisticated rationale in terms of Kierkegaard's own existential dialectic, *Le vrai visage de Kierkegaard* (Paris: Beauchesne, 1948), p. 419. Josiah Thompson generally looks to Kierkegaard's personality for the key to his thought, and yet he maintains a literary attitude with regard to the integrity of the pseudonyms: "The Master of Irony," in *Kierkegaard: A Collection of Critical Essays*, ed. Josiah Thompson (Garden City, N.Y.: Doubleday Anchor, 1972), p. 163. The same anthology includes a fine general article on this problem: Stephen Crites, "Pseudonymous Authorship as Art and as Act," pp. 183-229. Henriksen argues that biographical interpretations are justified only when a text cannot be explained in literary terms (*Methods*, p. 86).

7. The third way has already been mentioned in relation to the tendency of some interpreters to elevate one pseudonym over the others (see the Introduction, note 2). The dialectic between the aesthetic and the religious as "poles" of the authorship is argued by Kierkegaard himself (*PV*, 20), even while he repeats that the point of pseudonymity is to free the reader from preoccupation with the author (*PV*, 24-25). Although I try to respect the integrity of each text and pseudonym, and I seek harmony among them only as radically different perspectives within the entire theory of stages, my structural method does require treating the sections of *Stages on Life's Way* in different chapters. This division might appear to violate the unity of that work, but in fact Kierkegaard considered publishing the essays separately; see Josiah Thompson's *The Lonely Labyrinth: Kierkegaard's Pseudonymous Works* (Carbondale: Southern Illinois University Press, 1967), p. 170. In any case, my rearrangement of the parts of *Stages on Life's Way* consists merely in treating each of its sections in the chapter that deals with the stage portrayed in that section. For an example of the new tendency among scholars to distinguish sharply both among the pseudonyms and between them and Kierkegaard, see Johann Tzavaras, *Bewegung bei Kierkegaard (Frankfurt am Main: Peter Lang, 1978)*.

8. The literature on Kierkegaard's concept of paradox is voluminous. Especially useful are: Henning Schröer's *Die Denkform der Paradoxicalität als theologisches Problem: Eine Untersuchung zu Kierkegaard und die neueren Theologie als Beitrag zur theologischen Logik* (Göttingen: Vandenhoeck & Ruprecht, 1960), which distinguishes between ordinary ("sup-

plementary") and meaningful ("complementary") contradictions (pp. 35-46, 88-96, 130-132); André Clair's *Pseudonymie et paradoxe: La pensée dialectique de Kierkegaard* (Paris: J. Vrin, 1976), an exhaustive treatment of the pseudonymous literature in terms of the dialectic of repetition, which is shown to structure all the paradoxes "algebraically" (p. 21); and Sylvia Walsh Utterback's "Kierkegaard's Inverse Dialectic," *Kierkegaardiana* 11 (1980), pp. 34-54, which explores the paradoxical notion of a positive that is visible only in its negative counterpart.

9. The brief formal description of Hegelian dialectic that follows will be intelligible only to those already familiar with it, for it can be grasped only by following its actual development in some phenomenon, not in abstraction from its actuality as a process. Since Kierkegaard's *The Concept of Irony* embodies that process quite well, and simultaneously demonstrates Kierkegaard's talent for Hegelian dialectics, I am, in the interests of economy, using it rather than one of Hegel's own works to illustrate how a Hegelian dialectic actually unfolds. For more on Hegel's dialectical method, see J. N. Findlay, *The Philosophy of Hegel: An Introduction and Re-examination* (New York: Collier, 1962), pp. 55-80; and Charles Taylor, *Hegel* (Cambridge: Cambridge University Press, 1975), pp. 216-239.

10. Robert Heiss is typical when he comments that Kierkegaard's dialectic lacks the development to be found in that of Hegel; see *Hegel, Kierkegaard, Marx: Three Great Philosophers Whose Ideas Changed the Course of Civilization*, trans. E. B. Garside (New York: Delta, 1975), p. 290. A more penetrating argument is Hermann Deuser's claim that Kierkegaard's concept of paradox actually presupposes Hegelian dialectics, in *Sören Kierkegaard: Die paradoxe Dialektik des politischen Christen* (Munich: Kaiser Verlag, 1974). Cf. Theodor Adorno's similar comment in *Kierkegaard: Konstruktion des Asthetischen* (Tübingen: J.C.B. Mohr, 1933), p. 111.

11. The verb "posit" is typical of the tendency to use a technical term in English to convey the philosophical meaning of an ordinary word in Danish or German. The Danish verb is *sætte*, which means to put or place, and its past participle, *sat*, is translated by "posited."

12. This development can be understood only in terms of conceptual dialectical structures, not as a historical progression. As McCarthy observes, when *The Concept of Irony* is viewed historically, it appears to present a series of "abrupt leaps." Vincent A. McCarthy,

The Phenomenology of Moods in Kierkegaard (The Hague: Martinus Nijhoff, 1978), p. 9.

13. Immanuel Kant, *Critique of Pure Reason*, trans. Norman Kemp Smith (New York: St. Martin's Press, 1965), p. 111 (B 106). Even Thulstrup admits that this sort of reasoning, used so cautiously by Kant, resembles Hegel's absolute method (*Relation*, pp. 214-215).

14. The upshot of his lengthy discussion seems to be that the mythical is positive, although it would require too long a digression to support that interpretation here.

15. Although Kierkegaard later criticizes Hegelian mediation, it should not be overlooked that he maintains his preference for trichotomies over mere dichotomies, for the concept of paradox is thoroughly trichotomous. See *DODE*, 151, for his contrast between reflection (dichotomous) and consciousness (trichotomous). Capel gives an interesting quotation from the prominent Danish Hegelian, J. L. Heiberg, on this matter (*CI*, 372-373). For an analysis that demonstrates the trichotomous dimension of Kierkegaard's dialectic, see John Elrod's discussion of paradoxical synthesis in *Being and Existence in Kierkegaard's Pseudonymous Works* (Princeton: Princeton University Press, 1975), pp. 29-71. See also *SUD*, 13-14, where Anti-Climacus defines the self in terms of "the third" (discussed in Chapter Seven).

16. Kierkegaard certainly enjoys poking fun at the Hegelian commentary on Aristophanes by H. Theodor Rötscher (see *CI*, 159n). But such jibes—and they are numerous—diminish neither his genuine admiration for Rötscher's work nor his use of Hegelian structures of thought in *The Concept of Irony*.

17. See Capel's instructive comment in *CI*, 388, note 47.

18. The Danish word translated by "ingenuity" is *Sindrighed* (*CI*, 232; *S.V.* 1:235).

19. Kierkegaard's comment (*CI*, 246) that he is merely offering a "modification" of Hegel's interpretation of Socrates indicates the extent to which he was consciously "Hegelian" in this work (whether or not the comment is ironical). Capel objects (*CI*, 403, n. 31) that the dependence is only in details, not as a "totality," but he does not take into account the structure of the book as a whole.

20. The categories of possibility, actuality, and necessity have not played prominent roles in this analysis, for Kierkegaard's use of them is obscure. The most relevant background is probably again Kant, who discusses necessity as a third concept that can be produced

from the previous two only by "a special act of the understanding" (*Critique of Pure Reason*, p. 116, B 111). Thus, although Kierkegaard ironizes the world-historical significance of Socrates, and despite his later rejection of the concept of historical necessity, here the structure of the categories follows that very pattern suggested by Kant and developed by Hegel.

21. This reappearance of Socrates is coherent dialectically (if not historically; see above, note 12) insofar as it is necessary to account for the transition from subjectivity in-itself to subjectivity for-itself (in this instance from the abstract individual to concrete history). The role of Christianity in this development is described by Jean Wahl, *Études Kierkegaardiennes*, 4th ed. (Paris: J. Vrin, 1974), p. 61, and McCarthy, *Moods*, p. 12. In this paragraph, "abrogated" translates *ophævet* (*CI*, 260; S.V. 1:260).

22. This *Aufhebung* is admittedly less impressive than the parallel development in part one.

23. Kierkegaard's failure to mention Hegel in this concluding section is striking, and certainly represents an expression of his ambivalence. Nevertheless, for all his complaints about Hegel's hostility toward irony (see *CI*, 282), Kierkegaard also clearly credits him, as well as Goethe, with having mastered it (*CI*, 260). For this reason, and also on the basis of the distinctly Hegelian *Aufhebung* in this concluding section, I think it is legitimate to consider both Hegel and Goethe as representatives of the final moment in the dialectic of irony.

24. One can only sympathize with the typesetter who decided to "correct" the text by splitting theanthropic (*theanthropisk*) into two words ("the anthropic") at the bottom of page 341! (*S.V.* 1:331).

25. In stressing the Hegelian structure of Kierkegaard's analysis of irony, I do not mean to imply that there are no differences. Robert L. Perkins states the matter well, agreeing that they both understand irony in terms of the development of subjectivity, but that Hegel expresses this in relation to objective history, whereas Kierkegaard thinks more about the concrete individual. See "Hegel and Kierkegaard: Two Critics of Romantic Irony," in *Hegel in Comparative Literature*, ed. Frederick G. Weiss (Jamaica, N.Y.: St. John's University Press, 1970), pp. 250-251. I agree with this assessment, so long as the importance of actuality in the dialectical development of subjectivity is not overlooked.

CHAPTER TWO
The Dialectic of Aesthetic Contradiction

1. A version of this analysis of *Either/Or*, I, appeared as "The Dialectic of Contradiction in Kierkegaard's Aesthetic Stage," *Journal of the American Academy of Religion* 49, no. 3 (September 1981), pp. 383-408.

2. The distinction between inner and outer is more forceful in Danish (and German) than in English. For us, inwardness and externality are aspects or modes of one existence, whereas Danish has two different words for inner existence or character (*Eksistens*) and ordinary existence in the external realm of change (*Tilværelse*), similar to the German distinction between *Existens* and *Dasein*. Thus every reference to the inner or outer alludes to this fundamental distinction.

3. Aage Henriksen argues that *Either/Or* must be interpreted in terms of the pseudonymous persons rather than as a treatise on the principle of contradiction, on the basis of a note to that effect in the *Papirer* III, 189-190 (B 177), a note that is not included in the English *Journals and Papers*. However, that same note describes the diapsalm on tautology as a statement of the principle of contradiction, which in turn is "expressed by either/or." See Henriksen, *Methods and Results of Kierkegaard Study in Scandinavia: A Historical and Critical Survey* (Copenhagen: Ejnar Munksgaard, 1951), p. 99.

4. Lowrie comments in a note on the problems of translating *den sandselige Genialitet* (*E/O*,I, 55, 447-448; cf. *S.V.* 2:55), where he also indicates a preference for "sensuousness" over "sensuous genius."

5. The irony lies in the parallel drawn between sensuousness and sin. Just as St. Paul affirms that the Law brought knowledge of sin, so also A claims that sensuousness can be known as a principle only in light of the incarnation (*E/O*,I, 59, 62). This parallelism, I might add, somewhat undermines T. H. Croxall's claim that Kierkegaard intends *sanselig* (sensuous) here without the moral overtones that the word can carry (as in the English "sensual"); see *Kierkegaard Studies* (London: Lutterworth Press, 1948), pp. 41-47, and Lowrie's comment in the preceding note.

6. A relevant journal entry from 1840: "Whereas the philosophy of the recent past had almost exemplified the idea that language exists [var til] to conceal thought (since thought simply cannot express *das Ding an sich* at all), Hegel in any case deserves credit for showing that language has thought immanent in itself and that

thought is developed in language. The other thinking was a constant fumbling with the matter." *JP* no. 1590 (III A 37). This notion is echoed by A's comment: "The idea in language is thought" (*E/O*,I, 63; cf. p. 65). For Kierkegaard's use of language, see two articles by Paul L. Holmer: "Kierkegaard and Kinds of Discourse," *Meddelelser fra Søren Kierkegaard Selskabet* 4, no. 4 (1954), pp. 1-5, and "Kierkegaard and Religious Propositions," *Journal of Religion* 35, no. 3 (July 1955), pp. 135-146; also William F. Zuurdeeg, "Some Aspects of Kierkegaard's Language Philosophy," in *Atti del XII Congresso Internazionale di Filosophia (1958)*, vol. 12 (Florence: Sansoni Editore, 1961), pp. 493-499.

7. A blames this negative relation for the hostility that the religious mind feels toward music (*E/O*,I, 69). For a nice discussion of Kierkegaard's view of music, see Croxall's *Studies*, pp. 41-57.

8. E/O,I, 83; *S.V.* 2:81. I prefer "unity" to "synthesis" for the nontechnical *Eenhed*.

9. "Aesthetic indifference" (*aesthetisk Indifferents*) is A's term (*E/O*,I, 88; *S.V.* 2:83) for a consciousness prior to any sense of sin or even any reflection at all.

10. There is precedent for speaking of "inwardness" in relation to the aesthetic stage. In his comments on *Either/Or*, Johannes Climacus distinguishes between the "imaginative inwardness" (*Phantasie-Inderlighed*) of the aesthetic stage and the "existential inwardness" (*Existents-Inderlighed*) of the ethical (*CUP*, 227; *S.V.* 9:212). Also, Inter et Inter, one of the minor pseudonyms, remarks that aesthetic interest begins "when inwardness comes into its own" (*CLA*, 70). Whatever the judgment on aesthetic inwardness might be, clearly it does exist, at least *after* the in-itself movement portrayed in the page, Papageno, and Don Juan.

11. The background for Kierkegaard's neologism seems to be his reading of Lucian; see Gregor Malantschuk, *Kierkegaard's Thought*, ed. and trans. Howard V. Hong and Edna H. Hong (Princeton: Princeton University Press, 1971), p. 173. But it could also be the "dead" body of Abraham (Rom. 4:19) that he has in mind. To my knowledge, this structural analysis is the first to account for the *symparanekromenoi* lectures as a distinct literary unit.

12. "Substantiality" (*Substantialitet*) is A's term (*E/O*,I, 151-152; *S.V.* 2:142). It connotes not only the immediacy but also the objectivity of Hegel's concept of ethical substance (*Sittlichkeit*).

13. An interpretation of art in general would require reference to

the ethical and religious spheres also, a task that A could accomplish only by distorting them to fit his perspective.

14. On dialectical "phases," see Chapter One, p. 12.

15. Although I emphasize the diachronic development in this dialectical analysis, synchronic structures are in evidence throughout. Here, for example, the three phases of reflective grief recapitulate to a striking extent the three moments of desire (no object distinguished; a manifold of objects; and a "union" with the object).

16. Louis Mackey suggests ways in which the *symparanekromenoi* may be a parody of the Christian church in *Kierkegaard: A kind of Poet* (Philadelphia: University of Pennsylvania Press, 1971), p. 305, n. 14. I have counted at least nine allusions to Christ in "The Unhappiest Man."

17. The italics are A's (*S.V.* 2:267), omitted by Lowrie (*E/O*,I, 286). The entire discussion of boredom is one of the best satires of Hegelian dialectics to come from Kierkegaard's pen.

18. I employ "sublate" here to emphasize the satirical style. A uses *ophaeve* (*aufheben*) throughout this paragraph, which Lowrie renders "annul" three times and then "overcome" in the last sentence (*E/O*,I, 286; *S.V.* 2:267).

19. Conversely, Vincent A. McCarthy (" 'Psychological Fragments': Kierkegaard's Religious Psychology," in *Kierkegaard's Truth: The Disclosure of the Self*, ed. Joseph H. Smith, Psychiatry and the Humanities, vol. 5 [New Haven: Yale University Press, 1981], p. 243n) thinks that Johannes is the author of all of volume I and that A is merely his pseudonym. He bases this conclusion upon an unspecified "clue given by Victor Eremita." As interesting as it is for scholars to try to solve the "Chinese puzzle box" (*E/O*,I, 9) of pseudonymity in volume I, the chances of success seem very slim. A similar obscurity surrounds A's relation to "In Vino Veritas." David Swenson argues that he appears in that work as the young man (*Something About Kierkegaard*, ed. Lilian Marvin Swenson [Minneapolis: Augsburg Publishing House, 1956; rpr. Macon, Ga.: Mercer University Press, 1983], p. 169), whereas I see a stronger resemblance between A and William Afham.

20. As a language of deception, aesthetic poetry, like silence itself, is the absence of "communication between persons or genuine self-expression." See Mark C. Taylor, "Sounds of Silence," in *Kierkegaard's "Fear and Trembling": Critical Appraisals*, ed. Robert L. Perkins (University: University of Alabama Press, 1981), p. 178.

21. See above, note 19.

22. See Chapter Four for a discussion of *Repetition*, which was published in 1843, two years before *Stages on Life's Way*. For the sake of consistency with *Kierkegaard's Writings*, I will also follow the Danish in writing Constantius's given name "Constantin" rather than "Constantine."

23. Although English convention requires two sets of quotation marks when quoting from quoted material (such as speeches), there are no quotation marks at all in the Danish, and so it seems excusable to follow the simpler procedure of using a single set here.

24. That this is a Christological allusion is confirmed by the description of filial piety as remaining "hidden in the father" (*SLW*, 58; cf. Col. 3:3).

25. The Danish for annihilation is *tilintetgøre* (*S.V.* 7:62), not the dialectical term for abrogation, *ophæve*. Kierkegaard's use of "reduplication" (*Reduplikation*) is confusing, to say the least; see Mark C. Taylor's helpful discussion in *Kierkegaard's Pseudonymous Authorship: A Study of Time and the Self* (Princeton: Princeton University Press, 1975), p. 49. It is used twice in *Stages on Life's Way* to mean the negation of or withdrawal from immediacy (pp. 75, 387; *S.V.* 7:62, 8:224). Johannes Climacus uses it in *Postscript* (p. 297; *S.V.* 10:36) when he writes that "reduplication of the content in form is essential to all artistry." The most famous uses in English are attributed to Johannes Climacus but do not, in fact, occur in the Danish. Thus *Fordobling* (*PF*, 94; *S.V.* 6:70) is translated by Swenson and Hong "reduplication," and Lowrie uses "reduplication" for *Tanke-Tilværelsens Dobbelthed* in a famous but difficult section of *Postscript* (*CUP*, 69; *S.V.* 9:64). The first of these passages refers to the actualizing of possibilities, the second to the double relation of thinking to existence. Reduplication is defined by the editors of the third Danish edition as the actualizing of a theory in practice (*S.V.* 20:175). This recalls the definition offered by Anti-Climacus: "to reduplicate is to exist in what one understands" (*TC*, 133; *S.V.* 16:130), which echoes his earlier reference to reduplication as existing in what one teaches (*TC*, 123; *S.V.* 16:121). Elsewhere Kierkegaard characterizes reduplication as a dialectical "godly effort" to counteract one's own effort, in contrast to the direct or worldly effort "to strive in immediate continuity with an actually given condition" (*PV*, 147n; *S.V.* 18:67). In short, the idea is generally that of the duality and opposition between thought/possibility and existence/actuality,

but the particular nuances vary as much as Kierkegaard's spelling of the word (the *d* can be single or double, and the *k* is sometimes replaced by *c*).

26. I agree with Taylor that the aesthetic stage cannot be characterized exclusively in terms of either immediacy or reflection but embraces both within its dialectic. See his discussion in *Authorship*, pp. 156ff. I would add to his analysis only that this bipolar contradiction—so typical of the aesthetic stage—is actually overcome in the movement of deception, which is a reflected immediacy or immediate reflection.

27. The existence of this systematic structure demonstrates that Victor's claim that he "let chance determine the order" of A's essays (*E/O*,I, 7) is ironical. This conclusion is also supported by Kierkegaard's two Journal entries on the subject: one says that *"Either/Or* has a plan from the first word to the last," and the other explicitly denies that it is merely "a collection of loose papers I had lying in my desk" (*JP*, no. 5627, 5628 [IV A 214, 215]). Malantschuk respects the order of the essays without attempting to explain or interpret it. His discussion is particularly helpful for setting *E/O*, I, in its historical context as a critique of Romanticism (*Thought*, pp. 216-225).

CHAPTER THREE
The Ethical as a Stage

1. I refrain from referring to Volume I as *"Either"* and Volume II as *"Or,"* since that practice could inadvertently encourage looking at the aesthetic primarily through the eyes of Judge William.

2. The Judge denies that he is a dialectician (*SLW*, 99), a judgment that Louis Mackey, for one, shares in *Kierkegaard: A kind of Poet* (Philadelphia: University of Pennsylvania Press, 1971), p. 124.

3. Robert L. Perkins prefers to call it a "striving." See "Kierkegaard and Hegel: The Dialectical Structure of Kierkegaard's Ethical Thought" (Ph.D. dissertation, Indiana University, 1965), p. 162.

4. As Emanuel Hirsch did in *Kierkegaard-Studien*, 2 vols. (Gütersloh: C. Bertelsmann, 1933), 2:613-615.

5. Mackey suggests that this is an allusion to the wedding ring (*Kierkegaard*, p. 73).

6. *E/O*,II, 181; *S.V.* 3:166. The Danish word, *Øiblikket*, can be translated by "instant" or "moment." However, it is important not

to confuse the temporal and dialectical uses of the term. See Stephen Crites, *In the Twilight of Christendom: Hegel vs. Kierkegaard on Faith and History*, AAR Studies in Religion, no. 2 (Chambersburg, Pa.: American Academy of Religion, 1972), p. 83.

7. In *Stages on Life's Way*, Judge William credits Socrates with the aphorism, "Marry or do not marry, you will rue them both" (*SLW*, 154).

8. On the Hegelian concept of necessity, see the Introduction, note 11.

9. *E/O*,II, 120; *S.V.* 3:113. The Danish for "lifted up" is *indoptaget*, not *ophævet*, yet the dialectical implication is clear.

10. *E/O*,II, 185; *S.V.* 3:170. Danish, like German, has one word that can mean either spirit or mind (*Aand*, cf. *Geist*; here *aandeligt*, cf. *geistig*).

11. The Judge stresses that all movements of the aesthetic are both immediate and external (*E/O*,II, 184). This second movement, however, introduces a social dimension and is thereby both more external and less immediate.

12. Thus Stephen Crites concludes that there are four stages in the Judge's analysis of the aesthetic; see "Pseudonymous Authorship as Art and as Act," in *Kierkegaard: A Collection of Critical Essays*, ed. Josiah Thompson (Garden City, N.Y.: Doubleday Anchor, 1972), p. 202n. Reidar Thomte actually finds five "modes" here; see *Kierkegaard's Philosophy of Religion* (Princeton: Princeton University Press, 1948), pp. 43-45.

13. A few of the scholars who have discussed the Judge's Hegelianism are: Crites, *Twilight*, p. 11; Mackey, *Kierkegaard*, pp. 70, 76; and Perkins, who summarizes the ways in which the Judge is and is not Hegelian in "Kierkegaard and Hegel," p. 135. Whereas Perkins interprets much of Kierkegaard as a Kantian reply to Hegel, George Schrader sees the Judge as a Hegelian critic of Kant: "Kant and Kierkegaard on Duty and Inclination," in *Kierkegaard: A Collection of Critical Essays*, ed. Josiah Thompson (Garden City, N.Y.: Doubleday Anchor, 1972), pp. 328-332. See also N. H. Søe, "The Period up to The Postscript," in *Kierkegaard's View of Christianity*, ed. Niels Thulstrup and Maria Mikulova Thulstrup, Bibliotheca Kierkegaardiana, vol. 1 (Copenhagen: C. A. Reitzel, 1978), pp. 110-111.

14. Mark C. Taylor, *Kierkegaard's Pseudonymous Authorship: A Study of Time and the Self* (Princeton: Princeton University Press,

1975), pp. 185-197, follows Climacus in emphasizing the Judge's existentialist side and virtually ignoring his traditionalist statements.

15. Josiah Thompson, "The Master of Irony," in *Kierkegaard: A Collection of Critical Essays*, ed. Josiah Thompson (Garden City, N.Y.: Doubleday Anchor, 1972), p. 135.

16. Mackey, *Kierkegaard*, pp. 85, 124, 131. Climacus, too, politely accuses the Judge of oversimplifying the difficulties involved in marriage (*CUP*, 161).

17. To my knowledge, no one has proposed that the Judge's prolixity is either *his* "incognito" or *his* sense of irony (although, in relation to Kierkegaard, it is no doubt both).

18. Crites, *CLA*, p. 43.

19. Gregor Malantschuk, *Kierkegaard's Thought*, ed. and trans. Howard V. Hong and Edna H. Hong (Princeton: Princeton University Press, 1971), p. 226. Irony, of course, marks the transition from the aesthetic to the ethical (*CUP*, 473n).

20. Alasdair MacIntyre, *After Virtue: A Study in Moral Theory* (Notre Dame: University of Notre Dame Press, 1981), pp. 40-41.

21. Although they locate this attitude in various parts of the Judge's writings, most interpreters mention it at one point or another. See Crites, *Twilight*, p. 12; Mackey, *Kierkegaard*, p. 61; Perkins, "Kierkegaard and Hegel," p. 138; and Taylor, *Authorship*, pp. 232-234.

22. *E/O*,II, 98; *S.V.* 3:94. The Danish for "overcome" is *overvundet*.

23. *E/O*,II, 113; *S.V.* 3:107. Lowrie's "self-repression" seems too strong for *Betvingelse af sig selv*.

24. See *CUP*, 263n. Climacus consistently offers a less equivocal and more "existential" understanding of the ethical than does Judge William.

25. This passage is not quite as Hegelian as it might sound, for the verb translated by "overcome" is *overvinde*, to defeat or overcome, not *ophæve*, to annul and preserve. See *S.V.* 3:98.

26. This inversion should not be confused with the "inverted dialectic" associated with religiousness A (see Chapter Six, pp. 193-213).

27. This absence accounts for the Judge's use of conditional verb forms throughout his description of the putative objections to marriage. Climacus refers ironically to the fact that the Judge "cannot be supposed to know" the plan of "In Vino Veritas" (*CUP*, 264).

28. This is the opinion expressed by Gregor Malantschuk in *Kierkegaard's Way to the Truth*, trans. Mary Michelsen (Minneapolis: Augsburg, 1963), p. 50.

29. *SLW*, 147; *S.V.* 7:133. The redundancy is in the Danish: *med en dæmonisk Beslutning beslutter*.

30. *SLW*, 107-108; *S.V.* 7:93. The Danish for "taken up" is *optagen*; that for "reflection" is *Overveielse*, which seems in this passage to be synonymous with *Reflexion*.

31. These last two quotations are from *SLW*, 126, 154. I have altered the translation in the former (*S.V.* 7:112).

32. These words are Mackey's in *Kierkegaard*, p. 61.

33. Thus Josiah Thompson, *The Lonely Labyrinth: Kierkegaard's Pseudonymous Works* (Carbondale: Southern Illinois University Press, 1967), p. 170.

34. This interpretation was first suggested by Frater Taciturnus in *SLW*, 430. Taylor seems to follow him in *Authorship*, pp. 76, 236.

35. This is why "a man's nature cannot harmoniously reveal itself" (*E/O*,II, 166).

CHAPTER FOUR
Approaches to the Religious Stage

1. Gregor Malantschuk makes this point in *Kierkegaard's Thought*, ed. and trans. Howard V. Hong and Edna H. Hong (Princeton: Princeton University Press, 1971), p. 243.

2. This is not so much to disagree with Stephen Crites (*In the Twilight of Christendom: Hegel vs. Kierkegaard on Faith and History*, AAR Studies in Religion, no. 2 [Chambersburg, Pa.: American Academy of Religion, 1972], p. 83), who understands repetition as rebirth, as it is to put the accent in a different place. In Christian thought, resurrection and rebirth are correlative concepts. Brita K. Stendahl makes a helpful observation about repetition in *Søren Kierkegaard* (Boston: Twayne, 1976), p. 197: the Danish (*Gentagelse*), she writes, "has a very special nuance, which the English equivalent is too general to catch. It means 'retake'—in the sense that a film director can order a retake. The scene is going to be played again, but the positions, the lighting, the accents are changed; it becomes not just a dull repetition but a 'double take' on the situation. . . ." André Clair suggests that repetition refers to the existential ap-

propriation of a thought by an individual; *Pseudonymie et paradoxe: La pensée dialectique de Kierkegaard* (Paris: J. Vrin, 1976), pp. 65-75.

3. *R*, 130; *S.V.* 5:179. The category of ordeal (*Prøvelse*) is examined below, pp. 120-122.

4. This is Malantschuk's observation, *Thought*, p. 273.

5. On the relation between this letter and Kierkegaard's learning of Regina's engagement to Schlegel, see Peter P. Rohde, "Søren Kierkegaard: The Father of Existentialism," in *Essays on Kierkegaard*, ed. Jerry H. Gill (Minneapolis: Burgess Publishing Co., 1969), pp. 16-18. It is unclear from the young man's letter just how "spiritual" his experience of repetition really is. It is occasioned by news of the girl's marriage, not by something inward. It does free him from his ethical concerns, but whether he reverts to an aesthetic viewpoint (as Constantin thinks) or experiences an "infinite resignation," like that discussed in *Fear and Trembling*, cannot be ascertained from the text of the last letter. As André Clair points out, there is a striking contrast between the young man and Job. The latter's repetition is a restoration to his prior ethical situation; the former's leads away from the ethical and the temporal, thereby showing that "repetition in its ethical form is . . . always incomplete." See Clair, "Kierkegaard et l'acte dialectique," in *Analogie et Dialectique, Lieux Theologiques* no. 3 (1982), p. 194.

6. For example, Walter Lowrie in *Kierkegaard* (London: Oxford University Press, 1938), p. 168, n. 83.

7. *R*, 137. Undoubtedly, this aesthetic concept of death and rebirth, and the notion of "consciousness raised to the second power" (*R{L}*, 156), are ironical allusions to Hegel's concept of *Aufhebung*.

8. Josiah Thompson claims that Constantin also reaches "the plateau of resignation" in *The Lonely Labyrinth: Kierkegaard's Pseudonymous Works* (Carbondale: Southern Illinois University Press, 1967), p. 162. This view lacks support in the text and conflicts sharply with the portrayal of Constantin as advocating cruelty toward the girl in the interests of self-cultivation.

9. *Repetition* and *Fear and Trembling* were both published on October 16, 1843. Their "reunion" in one volume in *Kierkegaard's Writings* is most welcome.

10. Quoted by Robert L. Perkins in *Kierkegaard's "Fear and Trembling": Critical Appraisals*, ed. Robert L. Perkins (University: University of Alabama Press, 1981), p. x.

11. Louis Mackey, *Kierkegaard: A kind of Poet* (Philadelphia: University of Pennsylvania Press, 1971), p. 206.

12. The suggestion is Malantschuk's in *Thought*, pp. 236-243. Admittedly, this interpretation is intriguing, both in its own right and in psychobiographical terms, however dubious it may be as a reading of *Fear and Trembling*. Malantschuk's argument is, in brief, that *Fear and Trembling* is Kierkegaard's effort to explain to Regina that he had sacrificed her only because he himself had already been sacrificed by his father. Thus Isaac, as the sacrificial victim, displaces Abraham as the focal point of interest, and the problem of the paradoxical nature of Abraham's faith virtually disappears. The connection between Abraham and Kierkegaard's father is also drawn by Johannes Hohlenberg, *Sören Kierkegaard*, trans. T. H. Croxall (New York: Pantheon Books, 1954), pp. 118-119. For the standard view, see Lowrie, *Kierkegaard*, p. 256, for whom Abraham is the central figure and the psychobiographical problem is that of having to sacrifice a loved one (Isaac = Regina) in obedience to God.

13. This is the view of Mackey in *Kierkegaard*, p. 221. See also Mackey, "The View from Pisgah: A Reading of *Fear and Trembling*," in *Kierkegaard: A Collection of Critical Essays*, ed. Josiah Thompson (Garden City, N.Y.: Doubleday Anchor, 1972), pp. 394-428.

14. Of course, the real target here is Hegel, who tried (somewhat inconsistently) to make the method of doubt an absolute principle of his philosophy. See Robert L. Perkins, "Beginning the System: Kierkegaard and Hegel," in *Akten des XIV Internationalen Kongresses für Philosophie* (Vienna: Herder, 1968), pp. 480, 485. For a discussion of *Fear and Trembling* as a critique of Hegel, see Merold Westphal, "Abraham and Hegel," in *Kierkegaard's "Fear and Trembling": Critical Appraisals*, ed. Robert L. Perkins (University: University of Alabama Press, 1981), pp. 62-80. Perkins's own essay in that volume, "For Sanity's Sake: Kant, Kierkegaard, and Father Abraham," pp. 43-61, explores the extent to which that critique can be characterized as Kantian.

15. On this distinction between faith as a way of life and faith as mental assent, see Jerry H. Gill, "Faith Is as Faith Does," in *Kierkegaard's "Fear and Trembling": Critical Appraisals*, ed. Robert L. Perkins (University: University of Alabama Press, 1981), pp. 204-217; and "Kant, Kierkegaard and Religious Knowledge," in *Essays on Kierkegaard*, ed. Jerry H. Gill (Minneapolis: Burgess Publishing Co., 1969), pp. 58-73.

16. Gill discusses this issue, with reference to William Barrett's famous advocacy of "irrational man," in "Faith Is as Faith Does," p. 204. One of the best-known attacks on Kierkegaard on this point is by Walter Kaufmann. See Crites's Introduction to *CLA*, p. 38n, for the references and a rebuttal. Interesting defenses of Kierkegard's "irrationalism" are presented by Alastair McKinnon, "Kierkegaard: Paradox and Irrationalism," in *Essays on Kierkegaard*, ed. Jerry H. Gill (Minneapolis: Burgess Publishing Co., 1969), pp. 102-112; and N. H. Søe, "Kierkegaard's Doctrine of the Paradox," trans. Margaret Grieve, in *A Kierkegaard Critique*, ed. Howard A. Johnson and Niels Thulstrup (Chicago: Henry Regnery Company, 1962), pp. 207-227.

17. A communication about the incommunicability of faith is not a communication of faith as such. De Silentio, as Gill points out ("Faith Is as Faith Does," pp. 205-206), is not at all silent about faith as *he* understands it. As I shall show, however, this characterization is not an ironic ploy within the context of an actual analysis of faith. On the contrary, *Fear and Trembling* attempts to demonstrate that faith really does elude all efforts at human understanding, including those of de Silentio.

18. Josiah Thompson points out that *Tvivl* and all words with *tv* signal a "doubling of consciousness." See "The Master of Irony," in *Kierkegaard: A Collection of Critical Essays*, ed. Josiah Thompson (Garden City, N.Y.: Doubleday Anchor, 1972), p. 124. The Danish word *Tvende* means two or the twain.

19. For a thorough discussion of problem I as Kierkegaard's treatment of the issue of categorical imperatives in relation to Kant and Hegel, see Robert L. Perkins, "Kierkegaard and Hegel: The Dialectical Structure of Kierkegaard's Ethical Thought" (Ph.D. dissertation, Indiana University, 1965), pp. 82-102. Perkins offers similar analyses of problems II and III in relation respectively to transcendence and language (pp. 102-128).

20. John Donnelly's ingenious effort to argue against this claim, and thereby to deny that there can be a teleological suspension of the ethical, overlooks the fact that ethical duty, as "the expression for God's will" (*FT*, 60), is no less ordained by God than Abraham's terrible assignment. See Donnelly, "Kierkegaard's Problem I and Problem II: An Analytic Perspective," in *Kierkegaard's "Fear and Trembling": Critical Appraisals*, ed. Robert Perkins (University: University of Alabama Press, 1981), pp. 115-140.

21. For example, Malantschuk identifies the merman with Kierkegaard's own view as one who seriously confronts the problem of sin (*Thought*, p. 240). Certainly the figure of the merman does shift attention from the category of trial (Abraham, Job) to that of repentance as that which takes the individual out of the universal, thereby breaking through what Louis Dupré aptly calls "the self-enclosed ethical sphere"; *A Dubious Heritage: Studies in the Philosophy of Religion after Kant* (New York: Paulist Press, 1977), pp. 39-40. However, the main point of this discussion is not repentance; it is the impossibility of communicating the religious paradox.

22. This is Mackey's term in "The View from Pisgah," p. 417.

23. "Ordeal" avoids some of the confusion created by Lowrie's use of "trial" for *Prøvelse* (*FT{L}*, 36, 62). See note 2 to *FT*, 9.

24. *CUP*, 410-411; *S.V.* 10:142-144. See Walter Lowrie, *FT{L}*, 267, n. 47.

25. Donnelly thinks that these two terms can be clearly distinguished from one another ("Kierkegaard's Problem I and Problem II," p. 134) and that to understand the text one must simply analyze carefully the words in it. Fortunately, he also recognizes that Kierkegaard was not always careful or consistent in his use of language.

26. *FT*, 31. The Danish for this sentence is: "Men elskede han ikke som Abraham, saa var jo enhver Tanke om at offre Isaak en Anfaegtelse" (*S.V.* 5:31).

27. See *S.V.* 5:65.

28. For example, Stephen Crites denies that the knight of faith in *Fear and Trembling* represents religiousness B as it appears in *Postscript*, but he implies that there is a correspondence between the knight of infinite resignation in *Fear and Trembling* and religiousness A in *Postscript*, of which resignation is the initial expression; Crites, "Pseudonymous Authorship as Art and as Act," in *Kierkegaard: A Collection of Critical Essays*, ed. Josiah Thompson (Garden City, N.Y.: Doubleday Anchor, 1972), pp. 201-202. Mackey's claim that *Fear and Trembling* is not really about the relation of religion to ethics is based in part upon the dual identifications of infinite resignation with religiousness A and ethics with conventional morality (*Kierkegaard*, p. 221). Malantschuk's overemphasis on the merman is part of his argument that Johannes de Silentio has arrived at religious guilt, which is the decisive expression of religiousness A (*Thought*, 239-241). Finally, Mark C. Taylor states that "religion A makes its first appearance in *Fear and Trembling*"; *Kierkegaard's Pseudonymous*

Authorship: A Study of Time and the Self (Princeton: Princeton University Press, 1975), p. 244.

29. The incommensurability of inner and outer in the resignation of religiousness A is discussed in Chapter Six, pp. 190-193.

30. See the comment to this effect by Virgilius Haufniensis, *CA*, 17n.

31. In the third edition, " 'Guilty?'/'Not Guilty?' " is volume 8 and runs to 280 pages, whereas "In Vino Veritas" and "Various Observations" constitute volume 7, which is only 160 pages. Thompson, *Labyrinth*, p. 170, reports that Kierkegaard had considered publishing them separately.

32. Even Lowrie complains (*R*, 167, n. 66).

33. *CUP*, 256-257. Climacus then offers some interesting remarks on the similarities and differences between this diary and the one in *Repetition*.

34. My translation; cf. *SLW*, 183. The Danish is: "Saaledes indadvendt er Indesluttetheden altid" (*S.V.* 8:13). *Indesluttethed* has caused translators no little difficulty. In ordinary Danish, it means "reserve" or "reticence." In English translations, it has been rendered "morbid reserve" (Lowrie), "enclosing reserve" (Hong), "isolation" (Thompson), and "encapsulation" (Kirmmse). I prefer to use "withdrawnness," in part because it, like the Danish, is an ordinary word with a technical (psychological) application, not a technical phrase unrelated to ordinary speech. It also emphasizes the inner aspect: *Indesluttethed* is compounded from *inde* (in, within) and *sluttet* (closed, concluded). In contrast, Judge William writes about an individuality that is "shut" (*lukket, lukkede*), by which he means an external development that lacks, at this point, any "internal process of blossoming" (*E/O*,II, 137; *S.V.* 3:128).

35. The Danish translated as "morbid reflection" is *Reflexionssyge* (*S.V.* 8:71), literally, "sick from reflection." Quidam's denial that this is an accurate description of his situation is further evidence that Lowrie's use of "morbid reserve" for *Indesluttethed* is too strong.

36. It is true that Quidam says he enjoys inferring internal states from external appearances (*SLW*, 337), but this "diversion" is ironic, not a confession of belief in inner/outer commensurability. Indeed, it is only the incommensurability of inner and outer that makes such a pastime diverting.

37. Taciturnus remarks (*SLW*, 389; *S.V.* 8:226): "To illuminate his withdrawnness, I have introduced into the diary a few passages

in which he gropes as it were after an expression for his own with-drawnness." These passages prompted Aage Henriksen to write that a psychobiographical interpretation is legitimate only when a literary one is impossible; *Methods and Results of Kierkegaard Studies in Scandinavia: A Historical and Critical Survey* (Copenhagen: Ejnar Munksgaard, 1951), p. 86. The ambiguous relation between Quidam and Taciturnus is discussed on pp. 138-139.

38. Compare Quidam's boast that he did not initially deceive the girl (*SLW*, 198-200) with his later use of deception, allegedly to spare her feelings (*SLW*, 230-232, 310).

39. The Danish is *Prøve-Menneske; S.V.* 8:170.

40. In Danish, as in German, the words for suffering and passion are closely related: *Lidelse/Lidenskab* and *Leiden/Leidenschaft*. Crites comments that "in Kierkegaard's usage these two terms are like sympathetic musical chimes" (*Twilight*, p. 88).

41. The italics are mine.

42. Quidam provides what may be the clearest statement of Kierkegaard's conception of the demonic: "every individual is demonic who through himself alone, without any middle term . . . stands in relation to the idea; if the idea is God, the individual is religious, if the idea is the evil, the individual is in the stricter sense demonic" (*SLW*, 219; *S.V.* 8:50-51). See also Chapter Five, pp. 157-162.

43. The Danish for "resolves" is *opløser* (*SLW*, 398; *S.V.* 8:235). The complete sentence is: "If the object of faith is the absurd, it is not the historic which is believed, but faith in the ideality which resolves an *esse* into a *non posse*—and then *will* believe it."

44. *SLW*, 400; *S.V.* 8:237-238. The Danish for "to test" is *at friste*, while "a test can be made" is *kan forsøges*.

45. *SLW*, 430; *S.V.* 8:267. The Danish for "jerk" is *Ryk*.

46. Crites writes of "the sheer dialectical bones" of Kierkegaard's thinking (*Twilight*, p. 66).

CHAPTER FIVE
Varieties of Religious Dialectic

1. Vincent A. McCarthy explores some of the Hegelian elements in " 'Psychological Fragments': Kierkegaard's Religious Psychology," in *Kierkegaard's Truth: The Disclosure of the Self*, ed. Joseph H. Smith, Psychiatry and the Humanities, vol. 5 (New Haven: Yale University Press, 1981), p. 253. See also in the same volume Paul

Ricoeur's "Two Encounters with Kierkegaard: Kierkegaard and Evil; Doing Philosophy after Kierkegaard," pp. 313-342. Kresten Nordentoft observes that some passages in *The Concept of Anxiety* are "almost word-for-word identical with some introductory observations in a book to which he himself refers later in *The Concept of Anxiety*, namely, the German philosopher Karl Rosenkranz' *Psychologie*. The similarity does not mean that Kierkegaard is simply plagiarizing this German pupil of Hegel, but it shows that Kierkegaard is taking his point of origin in views which were well-known in his time, while he continues his analysis in a completely original way." Nordentoft, *Kierkegaard's Psychology*, trans. Bruce Kirmmse (Pittsburgh: Duquesne University Press, 1978), p. 21. *The Concept of Anxiety* also resembles Rosenkranz's work in that both have systematically dialectical structures, perfectly obvious and intentional in the latter, but quite obscure in the former. Although there are occasional parallels within those structures, Nordentoft's point about Kierkegaard's originality is well taken. See Karl Rosenkranz, *Psychologie, oder die Wissenschaft vom subjectiven Geist* (Königsberg: Bornträger, 1837).

2. Gregor Malantschuk, *Kierkegaard's Thought*, ed. and trans. Howard V. Hong and Edna H. Hong (Princeton: Princeton University Press, 1971), p. 244.

3. Reidar Thompte, in his historical introduction to *The Concept of Anxiety*, p. xii.

4. An earlier version of this analysis of *The Concept of Anxiety* appears in *Kierkegaard's "Concept of Anxiety": Critical Appraisals*, ed. Robert L. Perkins (Macon, Ga.: Mercer University Press, forthcoming).

5. Malantschuk writes that Haufniensis treats "the eternal *outside of man*" but ignores "the eternal *in man*." See *Thought*, p. 340. Vincent A. McCarthy agrees in *The Phenomenology of Moods in Kierkegaard* (The Hague: Martinus Nijhoff, 1978), p. 89.

6. *The Concept of Anxiety* is almost like a mirror, reflecting to each interpreter what interests that interpreter most. It is certainly one of the best examples of those dialectical structures that so fascinate me. Josiah Thompson, with his psychobiographical approach, reads it as a statement about Kierkegaard's personal experiences of anxiety and despair. In *The Lonely Labyrinth: Kierkegaard's Pseudonymous Works* (Carbondale: Southern Illinois University Press, 1967), pp. 150-164, he appropriately deals with it within the context of discussing the aesthetic stage. See also "The Master of Irony" in *Kierkegaard:*

A Collection of Critical Essays, ed. Josiah Thompson (Garden City, N.Y.: Doubleday Anchor, 1972), pp. 127-129. McCarthy also places it in the aesthetic, due to Haufniensis's emphasis upon withdrawnness and the demonic, although the latter category seems to me to be primarily religious (see *Moods*, pp. 45, 52). Mark C. Taylor's fascination with the process of decision by which the self moves into the ethical stage and then goes on to Christianity leads him to include *The Concept of Anxiety* in his treatments of both the ethical and the religious stages in *Kierkegaard's Pseudonymous Authorship: A Study of Time and the Self* (Princeton: Princeton University Press, 1975), pp. 217ff., 269ff. My claim that it belongs preeminently to the religious is based upon my analysis here, although I happily cite a supporting remark by Johannes Climacus: "anxiety represents [the individual's] state of mind in the desperate emancipation from the task of realizing the ethical" (*CUP*, 240; *S.V.* 9:225).

7. "Psychology" in the nineteenth century was the general study of human nature, which today might be called "philosophical anthropology." See *R*, xxix.

8. A note on the translation of *Angest* (German, *Angst*) is necessary. Lowrie (*CD*, x) confesses the impossibility of finding an English word that captures both the present painfulness (anguish) and the orientation toward the future (dread) that are implied in Kierkegaard's use of this word. He settles on "dread," a decision that some leading contemporary scholars still support (for example, Taylor, *Authorship*, p. 219n). However, the general consensus now is to follow Swenson and Capel in using "anxiety," which reduces the intensity of the pain but preserves the future orientation (see *E/O*,I, 152-153, and *CI*, 432). This is Hong's decision for *Kierkegaard's Writings* (thus Thomte in *CA*), and I shall follow it, more to avoid confusion than out of firm conviction that "anxiety" is preferable to "dread."

9. The Danish is: "den kun kan ophaeves ved Skyld" (*S.V.* 6:130).

10. *CA*, 41; *S.V.* 6:136. I have employed "determination" for *Bestemmelse* throughout this chapter, since it, rather than "qualification," is the normal equivalent for *Bestimmung* in works by Hegel. Note the structural parallel between dreaming anxiety and dreaming desire, as set forth in Chapter Two, pp. 35-38.

11. It is the same with "the irony of nature." See *CI*, 271n.

12. *CA*, 68; *S.V.* 6:159.

13. *CA*, 80; *S.V.* 6:169. On the identity of male and female in Christianity, see Gal. 3:28.

14. This analysis makes clear how appropriate Haufniensis's treatment of objective anxiety is within the context of the total dialectical development of anxiety. Cf. McCarthy, *Moods*, pp. 40-41.

15. This is obviously not a historical progression, or Christendom could not precede paganism and Judaism. Gregor Malantschuk nonetheless implies that it might be. See *Kierkegaard's Way to the Truth*, trans. Mary Michelsen (Minneapolis: Augsburg, 1963), chap. 2, and also *Thought*, pp. 265-266.

16. In order to distinguish the Moment when eternity enters time from both dialectical moments and moments in a temporal series, I shall capitalize it.

17. The use of "Christendom" here for what Haufniensis calls Christian paganism is justified insofar as both refer to a situation where Christianity has been abandoned in substance but not in name. Of course, Kierkegaard developed a rich and complex critique of Christendom in his later writings, which is adumbrated but not encompassed by this section of *The Concept of Anxiety*.

18. The Danish for this bit of technical Hegelian jargon is *ophævet Mulighed* (*CA*, 113; *S.V.* 6:198). From a comment by Johannes Climacus about guilt-consciousness (*CUP*, 474; *S.V.* 10:205), it is clear that this state is an actuality in which the development is from abstract to concrete. See also the editor's note to that passage, *S.V.* 10:303, and Chapter Six, note 32. For another systematically dialectical analysis of guilt and sin, but one that reverses their order, see Paul Ricoeur, *The Symbolism of Evil*, trans. Emerson Buchanan (Boston: Beacon Press, 1969), pp. 47-150. I have analyzed that dialectical structure in "History and Phenomenology: Dialectical Structure in Ricoeur's *The Symbolism of Evil*," *Harvard Theological Review* 76, no. 3 (July 1983), pp. 343-363.

19. *CA*, 115; *S.V.* 6:199. The Danish word translated "cancel" is *haeve*.

20. The object of this barb is presumably not only Hegel but also Immanuel Kant, who defines schema as a "mediating representation" between logical categories. See *Critique of Pure Reason*, trans. Norman Kemp Smith (New York: St. Martin's Press, 1965), p. 181 (B 177/A 138). For a definition of "demonic," see Chapter Four, note 42.

21. On "withdrawnness" as a translation of *det Indesluttede*, see Chapter Four, note 34.

22. *CA*, 133-134; *S.V.* 6:216.

23. *CA*, 151; *S.V.* 6:231. To declare that one who refuses to repent is ipso facto demonic presupposes that the self is both created by God (and therefore essentially dependent) and also fundamentally free (and therefore responsible for choosing itself). As Louis Dupré remarks, "Kierkegaard is the first philosopher to place man's relation to God in the very heart of the self." *A Dubious Heritage: Studies in the Philosophy of Religion after Kant* (New York: Paulist Press, 1977), p. 49.

24. One example can be found in the Historical Introduction to *SD*, xxii.

25. This is Louis Mackey's observation in *Kierkegaard: A kind of Poet* (Philadelphia: University of Pennsylvania Press, 1971), p. 138. Johannes was a sixth-century Byzantine monk and author of a work on mystical theology, *Scala Paradisi*.

26. The translators' capitalization of "System" raises a very complex problem. Danish, like German, capitalizes all nouns. Translators of philosophical texts frequently capitalize technical nouns in English for the sake of emphasis. That is especially the case in *Philosophical Fragments*. I have restored the lower case for all words except "Moment" (when it refers to the meeting of eternity and time; see above, note 16), primarily for the sake of consistency. Names for the divine pose a particularly difficult problem. I capitalize them only when they are proper nouns (that is, personal names). In *Philosophical Fragments*, Climacus writes of *Guden*, the god, in a way that "consciously abstracts from the historical given" (editors' note, *S.V.* 6:328).

27. *PF*, 16; *S.V.* 6:18, which reads: "fordi det Evige, som for ikke var, blev til i dette Øieblik." A literal translation would be as follows: "for the eternal, which was not, became in this Moment."

28. I agree with Taylor, *Authorship*, p. 330n, that "rebirth" is the closest equivalent of *Gjenfødelsen* (*S.V.* 6:23).

29. In his rereading of *Philosophical Fragments*, Louis Mackey argues that it is "obsessed with alterity" and that its dialectic is an "interminable dialectical oscillation of the same and the other." See "A Ram in the Afternoon: Kierkegaard's Discourse of the Other," in *Kierkegaard's Truth: The Disclosure of the Self*, ed. Joseph H. Smith, in Psychiatry and the Humanities, vol. 5 (New Haven: Yale University Press, 1981), pp. 193, 204. According to Mackey, sameness is represented by the Socratic dialectic, otherness by the Christian. However, the semiotic categories of this analysis exact their own

toll, for "interminable dialectical oscillation" does not leave much room for the paradoxical unities that are so evident in the text. In this respect, Mackey's discussion of *Fragments* in *Kierkegaard* is more satisfying. See also note 33 below.

30. The Danish for "poetic" is *digterisk* (*S.V.* 6:26), which is synonymous with *poetisk* (*E/O*,I, 301; *S.V.* 2:283), although, as with all germanic/latinate synonyms in Danish (as in English), their connotations differ, a difference that Kierkegaard is certainly exploiting. "Imagination" is normally used for *Inbildning* or *Fantasi*, and may be used here by Swenson/Hong in order to avoid confusion with the aesthetic category of the poetic. While discussing matters of translation, I should point out that "God's anxiety" (*PF*, 37) translates *Gudens Bekymring* (*S.V.* 6:32), a phrase that also occurs in the previous sentence, where Swenson/Hong render it "God's solicitude." In both sentences, "God's concern" would be best—but certainly not "God's anxiety," given the role that anxiety plays in Kierkegaard's thought!

31. *PF*, 59; *S.V.* 6:47. Once again, I am using "sublate" to capture the satirical flavor of the passage. See Chapter Two, note 18. From a Hegelian perspective, of course, there can never be any "absolute unlikeness," just as "absolute likeness" is impossible for a dialectic of opposition. Another ironical reference to Hegel in this passage is the claim that the god's self-revelation implies that he wants humans to "understand him fully." Occurring as it does within an argument against the capacity of reason to grasp the divine, the irony is an attempt to turn Hegel's own logic against him and to show that there can be no understanding of that which is beyond the grasp of reason. For an interesting discussion of a Hegelian schema in *Fragments* (namely, immediacy, negativity, and paradoxical unity), see Henry E. Allison, "Kierkegaard's Dialectic of the Religious Consciousness," *Union Seminary Quarterly Review* 20 (March 1965), pp. 225-233.

32. *PF*, 64-65; *S.V.* 6:50. "An Acoustic Illusion" is the subtitle to the Appendix.

33. Because of this, it is understandable that Mackey concentrates upon chapter III in his article on alterity (see note 29 above), but ignores chapter II, where the opposite poles are so clearly (if paradoxically) united. In this regard, it is interesting to compare this article with his earlier discussion of *Fragments* (*Kierkegaard*, pp. 155-159), where chapter II is analyzed in detail, but chapter III is treated as a digression (which Climacus himself also implies, *PF*, 68).

34. This is Mackey's distinction in *Kierkegaard*, p. 165.

35. On the distinction between a development that is systematic and one that is also logically necessary, see the Introduction, note 11. The issue here may be less Kierkegaard's relation to Hegel himself than his reaction against the rigid system building of the Danish Hegelians. For a defense of Hegel along these lines, see Robert C. Whittemore, "Pro Hegel, Contra Kierkegaard," *Journal of Religious Thought* 13, no. 2 (1956), pp. 131-144.

36. Mackey sees a bit of Hegelian thinking here that even I have trouble accepting, although the suggestion is an intriguing one. In this part of "Interlude," he argues, "faith conquers doubt . . . by including it within itself as a constantly *aufgehoben* moment" (*Kierkegaard*, p. 60). I find more plausible the claim that faith and doubt are taken up together into an attitude of faith in God and simultaneous doubt toward the autonomously rational self. Climacus does insist that belief (= faith; Danish *Tro*) and doubt are "opposite passions" (*PF*, 105).

37. See the Hongs' Historical Introduction to *SD*, xiii. André Clair also uses the term in *Pseudonymie et paradoxe: La pensée dialectique de Kierkegaard* (Paris: J. Vrin, 1976), p. 21.

38. If *The Concept of Anxiety* is to serve in such a capacity, it must be by casting the dialectical structure in terms of the development of freedom. The role of Ariadne's thread that I have claimed for the inner/outer dialectic is assigned by Malantschuk to the dialectic of freedom; see *Kierkegaard's Way*, p. 113, and Louis P. Pojman, "The Dialectic of Freedom in the Thought of Søren Kierkegaard" (Th.D. dissertation, Union Theological Seminary, 1972).

CHAPTER SIX
The Dialectic of Religious Inwardness

1. A version of this chapter appears as "Rhetoric and Reality in Kierkegaard's *Postscript*," *International Journal for Philosophy of Religion* (forthcoming). Gregor Malantschuk argues that *Postscript* combines the abstract concerns of *Anxiety* and *Fragments* with the concrete investigations of *Either/Or, Repetition, Fear and Trembling*, and *Stages*. However, he seems to limit the concrete line in *Postscript* to Climacus's long commentary on the other concrete literature. Malantschuk, *Kierkegaard's Thought*, ed. and trans. Howard V. Hong and Edna H. Hong (Princeton: Princeton University Press, 1971), pp.

281-282. I, on the contrary, would include within the concrete material Climacus's own systematic description of religious inwardness. The issue is the status to be granted to Climacus's axiom, "no system of existence can be given" (*CUP*, 99, 107). Malantschuk lets this doctrine guide his entire interpretation, whereas I treat it as a belief that stands in tension with Climacus's own analysis of religious inwardness, an analysis that in fact presents a systematic account of the existence of the religious individual.

2. Climacus claimed to be a humorist rather than a Christian (*CUP*, 431, 545). The irony in the title is perhaps unintended for the first two words: Kierkegaard did intend to *conclude* his pseudonymous authorship with *Postscript*, and he was presumably unaware of the extent to which the book is susceptible to *systematic* analysis in the Hegelian sense of the term. However, the idea that it is a *postscript* is certainly ironic, since *Fragments* is in no sense a letter, and *Postscript* is more than six times its length.

3. On the difference between the ditches of Climacus and Lessing, see G. E. Michalson, Jr., "Lessing, Kierkegaard, and the 'Ugly Ditch': A Reexamination," *Journal of Religion* 59, no. 3 (July 1979), pp. 324-334.

4. "Double reflection" and "reduplication" seem to be used synonymously, at least by Anti-Climacus (*TC*, 132) and Walter Lowrie in *Kierkegaard* (London: Oxford University Press, 1938), p. 627. On reduplication, see Chapter Two, note 25.

5. This is Josiah Thompson's claim in *The Lonely Labyrinth: Kierkegaard's Pseudonymous Works* (Carbondale: Southern Illinois University Press, 1967), p. 148. A more penetrating critique of Kierkegaard's attitude toward thought is that he affirms it in such a way as to undermine its role and importance for determining truth. Thus Malcolm Diamond argues that Kierkegaard defends a position that is "meaningless" ("Kierkegaard and Apologetics," *Journal of Religion* 44, no. 2 [April 1964], pp. 122-132); and Michael Levine maintains that Climacus's emphasis upon subjectivity as the guarantor of truth eliminates the "risk" from all claims for truth ("Kierkegaard: What Does the Subjective Individual Risk?" *International Journal for Philosophy of Religion* 13, no. 1 [1982], pp. 12-22). For another view, see E. D. Klemke, "Some Misinterpretations of Kierkegaard," *Hibbert Journal* 57, no. 3 (April 1959), pp. 259-270.

6. Conversely, Hegelians are fond of pointing out that Kierkegaard's theory that truth is subjectivity is stated as an objective truth!

See, for example, Joachim Ringleben, *Hegels Theorie der Sünde* (Berlin: Walter de Gruyter, 1976), p. 110. Kierkegaard himself was well aware of this paradox: "But the task is to relate objectively to one's own subjectivity" (*JP*, no. 4571 [XI² A 97]). That task may be impossible to fulfill; but it is not, like Heiberg's conversion story, comical.

7. The critique of mediation in this chapter turns on Climacus's discussion of *Aufheben* (to perish *and* to preserve, in Hegelian usage) as a self-contradictory concept. It is indicative of Climacus's (Kierkegaard's?) reading of Hegel, however, that he thinks that this preservation occurs without alteration (*CUP*, 199), whereas for Hegel the whole point is transformation. The main puzzle that Hegel is trying to solve is the historical fact of identity-within-difference, not the logical definition of identity versus difference.

8. The Danish here is *haever* (*S.V.* 15:10).

9. See Chapter Four, note 40, on suffering.

10. The italics are mine. The validity of *concrete* thought is stressed frequently (for example, *CUP*, 377, 537).

11. Climacus does not use this term until after his analysis is complete (*CUP*, 493). The word "religiousness" first occurs in the discussion of suffering, where *Religieusiteten* is initially rendered "religiosity" by Lowrie (*CUP*, 568), with no explanation as to why he feels obligated to follow Swenson's translation. Lowrie clearly realizes that "religiosity" in English implies a shallow conventionality that is just the opposite of the Danish *Religieusitet* (cf. German *Religiosität*), but he does not switch over to "religiousness" until the "Immediate Clause between A and B."

12. The text has: "The pathetic factor is represented in the first part above" (*CUP*, 345). Lowrie's "above" is confusing as well as missing in Danish (*S.V.* 10:80); it probably refers to the superscription. The Danish mentions only the first and second parts, which I understand as religiousness A and B respectively. This interpretation is compatible with Lowrie's. See also the note by Hans Martin Junghaus to his German translation of the text, *Abschliessende unwissenschaftliche Nachschrift*, pt. 2, vol. 16 in Sören Kierkegaard, *Gesammelte Werke* (Düsseldorf: Eugen Diederichs Verlag, 1958), p. 366, n. 277.

13. Climacus does not introduce the word "resignation" until p. 352, where Lowrie finds it surprising (note, p. 568). Yet the connection between resignation and respect, which is the subject of the heading for this section, is indicated on p. 366. Note this difference

between Climacus and Anti-Climacus: the latter denies that there can ever be absolute respect without sin-consciousness (*TC*, 72), whereas the former places absolute respect in religiousness A, before sin-consciousness, which first enters in religiousness B. Throughout this section, resignation (*Resignation*) and renunciation (*Forsagen*) are used synonymously, and Lowrie is generally consistent in translating them that way (although *at forsage Alt* [*S.V.* 10:98] becomes "resigning everything" [*CUP*, 363]).

14. Even though both Judge William and Climacus discern a continuum between the ethical and the religious, a fundamental distinction between them must be noted. As Louis Mackey points out, the Judge's continuum involves an ethical and religious reconciliation with the external world, whereas that of Climacus is inward and nonhistorical; *Kierkegaard: A kind of Poet* (Philadelphia: University of Pennsylvania Press, 1971), pp. 174, 201. For the "ethico-religious" as the ethics of religion, see Robert L. Perkins, "Kierkegaard and Hegel: The Dialectical Structure of Kierkegaard's Ethical Thought," (Ph.D. dissertation, Indiana University, 1965), pp. 294-303.

15. This discussion is one of the few places where the absolute *telos* is explicitly identified with God (*CUP*, 359). That identification occurs at the end of a paragraph that has a translation problem in the middle, where Lowrie has "principle of resignation" for "absolute *telos*": "In the moment of resignation, of deliberation, of choice, the individual is assumed to honor the absolute *telos*—but afterwards comes the time for mediation" (*CUP*, 358; *S.V.* 10:93).

16. Mackey sees here an implied criticism of Romantic theology, especially of Schleiermacher's doctrine of the feeling of absolute dependence as the union of finite and infinite (*Kierkegaard*, pp. 203-204). This criticism became, of course, one of the major Kierkegaardian elements in twentieth-century "dialectical" theology.

17. This incognito distinguishes the resignation of religiousness A from that of the knight of infinite resignation in *Fear and Trembling*. See Chapter Four, pp. 123-124, and note 28.

18. *CUP*, 387; *S.V.* 10:120. Both of the last two quotations have been altered, the second being particularly important, since Lowrie appears to have reversed "positive" and "negative" in his rendering: "the positive is the index of the negative." The Danish reads: "det viser sig atter her, hvad der er Kjendet paa den religieuse Sphaere, at det Positive er kjendeligt [lit. "recognizable"] paa det Negative."

19. On the inverted dialectic of negative and positive, see Sylvia Walsh Utterback, "Kierkegaard's Inverse Dialectic," *Kierkegaardiana* 11 (1980), pp. 34-54, and *JP*, no. 760 (VIII¹ A 492).

20. Climacus also points out (*CUP*, 414) that this impotence before God must be distinguished from masochism, in which self-torture is an expression of one's power over oneself.

21. To annul one's suffering in religious joy is to revert to an aesthetically foreshortened perspective (*CUP*, 395-396), for it is either an attempt to transcend the suffering or an effort to recall it in a deceptive manner.

22. *CUP*, 405; *S.V.* 10:138. Here Lowrie translates *trygt* as "secure," which echoes nicely the theme of suffering as a "guarantee" (*Sikkerheden*) on p. 397 (*S.V.* 10:129). Notice, however, that *Sikkerhed* is also used for the security that comes externally and can cause one to cease to suffer religiously (*CUP*, 406; *S.V.* 10:138).

23. This is Mackey's phrase in *Kierkegaard*, p. 202.

24. See Chapter Four, pp. 120-122, on spiritual trial.

25. *CUP*, 410; *S.V.* 10:142.

26. See Chapter Five, p. 172, on acoustic illusion.

27. The Danish lacks "to the finite" (*S.V.* 10:155), but Lowrie's interpolation is apt.

28. By extension, it could be argued that the ironist exploits the contradiction between inner and outer without being fully committed to ethical inwardness.

29. Mackey also interprets resignation, suffering, and guilt as "three moments . . . each of which presumes and subsumes its predecessors" (*Kierkegaard*, p. 199).

30. Mackey, *Kierkegaard*, p. 203.

31. Admittedly, there are those who would maintain that such contradictions remain nonsensical even *in* a dialectical context. The question of criteria for judging the value of paradoxical assertions is no less problematic in Kierkegaard's thought than it is in contemporary philosophical hermeneutics. Hans-Georg Gadamer, for example, ultimately appeals to the "harmony of all the details with the whole" as "the criterion of correct understanding." See *Truth and Method*, trans. edited by Garrett Barden and John Cumming (New York: Continuum, 1975), p. 259. For an example of a (dialectically) guiltless guilt, see the discussion of Antigone in Chapter Two, p. 40.

32. One indication of this concreteness is that Climacus treats

guilt as an "annulled possibility" (*CUP*, 474), that is, as a consciousness of actuality, whereas Haufniensis restricts it to the level of consciousness of possibility. See Chapter Five, p. 156, and note 18.

33. The identity of subject and object in guilt-consciousness is implied by Paul Ricoeur in *The Symbolism of Evil*, trans. Emerson Buchanan (Boston: Beacon Press, 1969), pp. 143ff.

34. John Elrod summarizes this debate in *Being and Existence in Kierkegaard's Pseudonymous Works* (Princeton: Princeton University Press, 1975), p. 101n. Paul Sponheim writes: "It seems hard to deny the appropriateness of the category of development"; *Kierkegaard on Christ and Christian Coherence* (London: SCM Press, 1968), p. 35.

35. On Kierkegaard's affirmation of the external in his early works, see Utterback, "Kierkegaard's Inverse Dialectic," pp. 53-54.

36. *CUP*, 505-508; *S.V.* 10:237-240. The terminology here, especially in Lowrie's translation, is more confusing than it needs to be. Each existence-communication (sphere) has a particular understanding of life. Climacus's word for understanding is *Opfattelse*, which Lowrie translates sometimes as "interpretation" and other times as "apprehension." Note also that Lowrie has omitted a phrase from a sentence in the middle of p. 506 (*S.V.* 10:238), which should read (restored clause is italicized): "For speculative philosophy, existence has vanished and only pure being is; *for religiousness A, only existence is actuality*, and yet the eternal is constantly concealed in it and as concealed is present."

37. Climacus first indicates that speculative philosophy does not belong to either the aesthetic or the ethical sphere of existence when he asserts that its principle is the identity of inner and outer (*CUP*, 123), a principle that neither A nor Judge William would affirm.

38. Mackey, *Kierkegaard*, p. 205, where he develops this point nicely. Mackey also sees a similar relation between the three moments of religiousness A and the " 'three godly discourses' on the lilies of the field and the birds of the air" (p. 236).

39. Mackey, *Kierkegaard*, p. 205.

40. *CUP*, 509. The italics are mine.

41. *CUP*, 513; *S.V.* 10:245. Stephen Crites has already drawn attention to Lowrie's substitution of A for B in this passage; *In the Twilight of Christendom: Hegel vs. Kierkegaard on Faith and History*, AAR Studies in Religion (Chambersburg, Pa.: American Academy of Religion, 1972), p. 79, n. 43. The identity of theology and

anthropology is argued by Ludwig Feuerbach in *The Essence of Christianity*, trans. George Eliot (New York: Harper & Row, 1957), p. xxxvii.

42. The Danish for "smart" is *Smerte* (*S.V.* 10:251); cf. German *Schmerz*.

43. The final chapter of *Postscript* recapitulates the subjectivity/objectivity issue without advancing the dialectic of religious inwardness.

CHAPTER SEVEN
The Dialectical Structure of Consciousness

1. See, for example, Bruce Kirmmse, "Psychology and Society: The Social Falsification of the Self in *The Sickness unto Death*," in *Kierkegaard's Truth: Disclosure of the Self*, ed. Joseph H. Smith, Psychiatry and the Humanities, vol. 5 (New Haven: Yale University Press, 1981), pp. 167-192. There is an interesting symmetry between *The Concept of Irony* and the works by Anti-Climacus that, to my knowledge, has not been discussed in the secondary literature: Kierkegaard's master's thesis is, in the view of some interpreters (for example, Capel, *CI*, 357), ironical to the point of being his first "pseudonymous" work; whereas *Sickness unto Death*, at the other end of his authorship, is held to be pseudonymous in name only.

2. *Indøvelse* is translated "Training" by Lowrie and "Practice" by the Hongs in their translation of Gregor Malantschuk, *Kierkegaard's Thought* (Princeton: Princeton University Press, 1971), pp. 347ff. The basic meaning of the word is "drilling," as when soldiers or athletes drill in preparation for the real contest. Both English words connote this idea, although "practice" has the added advantage of alluding to the idea of religious practice, which in turn accords well with Kierkegaard's emphasis in his later writings upon the need to express in Christian works the inwardness of faith. Thus I shall follow the Hongs' translation for the full title, although page references must be to Lowrie's version (thus, *TC* rather than *PC*).

3. *JP*, no. 6446 (X^1 A 548), 6517 (X^2 A 147), and 6518 (X^5 B 206).

4. John Elrod credits Robert L. Perkins with this phrase in *Kierkegaard and Christendom* (Princeton: Princeton University Press, 1981), p. xi.

5. The relation between non-Christian Climacus and Christian

Anti-Climacus has traditionally been understood as one of direct opposition. See Lowrie's Preface to *TC*, p. xxii; Malantschuk, *Thought*, pp. 334-338; and Louis Mackey, *Kierkegaard: A kind of Poet* (Philadelphia: University of Pennsylvania Press, 1971), p. 60. This view is based upon Kierkegaard's own remarks in *JP*, no. 6349 (X^6 B 48) and 6433 (X^1 A 517). Recently the Hongs have suggested that "Anti-Climacus" means "before" (as in "anticipate") rather than "against" Climacus (*SD*, xxii), but they do not explain this claim in relation to the Journal entries cited above.

6. Thus John Elrod, *Being and Existence in Kierkegaard's Pseudonymous Works* (Princeton: Princeton University Press, 1975), and Mark C. Taylor, *Kierkegaard's Pseudonymous Authorship: A Study of Time and the Self* (Princeton: Princeton University Press, 1975).

7. See *JP*, no. 6271 (XI A 390).

8. The extent to which Anti-Climacus's works contain dialectical structures is noted by Malantschuk: "The structure of *The Sickness Unto Death* embodies a very clearly designed progressive dialectical movement; of all the authorship this work most obviously carries through the development of a theme. *Practice in Christianity* came about through the joining together of some separate pieces, but Anti-Climacus manages to give this work, too, a dialectical, cohesive structure." Malantschuk, *Thought*, p. 339. See also Vincent A. McCarthy, *The Phenomenology of Moods in Kierkegaard* (The Hague: Martinus Nijhoff, 1978), pp. 83, 96. Johannes Sløk has also contributed to the understanding of Kierkegaard's dialectics of the self in *Die Anthropologie Kierkegaards* (Copenhagen: Rosenkilde und Bagger, 1954). For Sløk, the dialectic in *Sickness unto Death* is to be found in the definition of the self as a self-relating synthesis of opposites, whereas for Malantschuk and McCarthy it is also a matter of the organization of the text. No one has previously noticed the systematic nature of that dialectical organization, although Paul Ricoeur examines *Sickness unto Death* for "the immanent structure of a true dialectic," by which he means one in which every opposition is resolved in a third term. All he finds there, however, is "a sort of grimacing simulacre of Hegelian discourse." See "Two Encounters with Kierkegaard: Kierkegaard and Evil; Doing Philosophy after Kierkegaard," in *Kierkegaard's Truth: The Disclosure of the Self*, ed. Joseph H. Smith, Psychiatry and the Humanities, vol. 5 (New Haven: Yale University Press, 1981), p. 320.

9. The social dimension of *Sickness unto Death* has recently been

discussed by Kirmmse (in "Psychology and Society") in terms of its sociopolitical critique. John Elrod, in "Climacus, Anti-Climacus and the Problem of Suffering," *Thought* 55, no. 218 (September 1980), pp. 306-319, explores the social nature of Christian suffering in both *Postscript* and *Sickness unto Death*.

10. *SD*, 44. Cf. *CA*, 95-96.

11. I cannot agree with Malantschuk that *Sickness unto Death* is a continuation of *The Concept of Anxiety* that arrives at the concept of "the eternal *in man*" whereas *Anxiety* deals only with "the eternal *outside of man*" (*Thought*, p. 340). See Chapter Five, p. 155.

12. See George J. Stack's comment in *Kierkegaard's Existential Ethics* (University: University of Alabama Press, 1977), p. 141: "Consciousness cannot be an 'object' for itself since it is that which is the condition for the possibility for comprehending anything as object."

13. Kierkegaard was very fond of this sort of typological method and could be fruitfully compared with such twentieth-century writers as Max Weber. Cf. Kirmmse, "Psychology and Society."

14. It may be that "the pragmatist" for *Spidsborgerlighed* (*S.V.* 15:97) departs too far from ordinary Danish usage, and it is certainly offensive to pragmatic American ears to hear this term used in a derogatory manner, but I wonder if it is not closer to Anti-Climacus's meaning than the alternatives. He certainly seems less concerned here with philistinism (pomposity, hypocrisy, etc.) than with triviality and lack of imagination. The Hongs' "philistine-bourgeois" (*SD*, 41) and Kirmmse's "bourgeois philistine" ("Psychology and Society," p. 177n) aim at this something more, yet decades of Marxist use have added to "bourgeois" associations of political and economic class consciousness rather than an individual sense of selfhood grounded in trivial practicality. In this regard, Lowrie's rendering of *beroliger sig i det Trivielle* ("tranquilizes itself with the trivial") is just right (*SD*[L], 174; *S.V.* 15:98). For Kierkegaard's criticism of Xenophon's portrayal of Socrates as a pragmatist, see Chapter One, p. 13. Elswhere, Kierkegaard does use *spidsborgerlig* with the sense of "bourgeois" (*E/O*,I, 374; *S.V.* 2:350).

15. The Danish (*S.V.* 15:98) is *Fortvivlelse seet under Bestemmelsen: Bevidsthed*, which means literally: despair seen as a determination (or qualification) of consciousness.

16. *SD*, 47; cf. *CA*, 95.

17. Kirmmse suggests that the direction in *Sickness unto Death* is "away from self-realization and the affirmation of the God-relation-

ship," and that *Practice in Christianity* "follows the development in the opposite direction" ("Psychology and Society," p. 175).

18. Kirmmse takes this position, pointing to the fact that Anti-Climacus describes both as the most common forms of despair. See "Psychology and Society," pp. 183-184, and *SD*, 45, 57.

19. Anti-Climacus explains in this footnote that, although all despair is *of* the eternal, the objects *over* which one despairs vary (something earthly, the earthly as such, or oneself).

20. On "withdrawnness" for *Indesluttethed*, see Chapter Four, note 34.

21. Kirmmse relates these respectively to the social types of the Romantic genius (defiance), the philistine bourgeois (spiritlessness), and Kierkegaard's "ideal intended reader" (weakness). He sees in the last type "a mediating or middle position between these two extremes," for he is both respectable and aware of "the hollowness of his respectability." "Psychology and Society," pp. 185-186.

22. Thus McCarthy, *Moods*, pp. 97-98.

23. *SD*, 86, *SD*(L), 217; *S.V.* 15:139. The Danish is *Menneske* in both phrases. The Hongs' change of "man" to "men" would appear to increase its gender specificity unnecessarily.

24. H. L. Martensen was a leading Danish Hegelian with whom Kierkegaard studied for several years and whom he later criticized at every opportunity. The paragraph in which this argument is spelled out becomes intelligible if its third sentence is deleted: "But if this is true, then sin is a negation" (*SD*, 97, *SD*[L], 227; *S.V.* 15:149). The point of this paragraph, however, is that comprehension negates sin, not that sin is a negation. It is in the next paragraph that sin is treated as a negation, for there Anti-Climacus makes the point that a speculative definition of repentance as the negation of negation assumes that sin is a negation rather than a position.

25. "Continuance" is such an uncommon and awkward word in English that the Hongs' choice of it for *Fortsættelse* seems odd (*S.V.* 15:156).

26. *SD*, 109; *S.V.* 15:159-160. The Danish for "withdrawn into itself" is *slutte sig inde med sign selv*.

27. See *SD*, 60n, and note 19 above, on the difference between despair "of" and despair "over."

28. Compare the third version of the Abraham story, *FT*, 13.

29. *SD*, 113, *SD*(L), 244; *S.V.* 15:163. The Danish here is *maa være at henføre*.

30. Another possible solution is McCarthy's suggestion that *Purity of Heart* represents the cure for despair (*Moods*, p. 83).

31. Lowrie's choice of "totalitarian" for *et hele* (*TC*, 92; *S.V.* 16:93) is typical of the simplistic view of Hegel that has characterized so much Kierkegaard scholarship. Hegel's holistic philosophy of freedom bears almost no resemblance to "totalitarianism," and Anti-Climacus is certainly not claiming that it does.

32. Although Mark C. Taylor criticizes this position, his own Hegelian conclusion seems in some ways quite close to it; *Journeys to Selfhood: Hegel and Kierkegaard* (Berkeley: University of California Press, 1980), pp. 18-19, 271. Of course, if the concept of sin is omitted or rejected, as it effectively is by Hegel, then Kierkegaard has no defense against the charge that he sets up the "unhappy consciousness" as his ideal.

33. See Chapter One, p. 12, on the use of "point" for the lowest or most minute structural layer.

34. I have avoided assigning despair to a particular stage because it so obviously occurs in all three stages. Thus, in a very rough sense, despair without regard to consciousness recalls the consciousness of contradiction in the aesthetic stage; despair as consciousness bears some similarity to the quest for reconciliation in the ethical stage; and despair as sin is the religious *Aufhebung* of contradiction (within the self and between the self and God) and reconciliation (with oneself and with God). The parallelism is too weak to press very far, but it does clear up a question that worries Louis Dupré: How, if despair is sin, can there be such a thing as aesthetic despair? Dupré, *Kierkegaard as Theologian: The Dialectic of Christian Existence* (New York: Sheed and Ward, 1963), pp. 42ff., 68. The answer is that aesthetic despair is appropriate to despair in-itself, but the full revelation of despair in-and-for-itself (namely, sin) occurs only in the religious stage.

WORKS CITED

Agacinski, Sylviane. *Aparté: Conceptions et morts de Sören Kierkegaard.* Flammarion: Aubier, 1977.

Adorno, Theodor. *Kierkegaard: Konstruktion des Asthetischen.* Tübingen: J.C.B. Mohr, 1933.

Allison, Henry E. "Kierkegaard's Dialectic of the Religious Consciousness." *Union Seminary Quarterly Review* 20 (March 1965), pp. 225-233.

Anz, Wilhelm. *Kierkegaard und der deutsche Idealismus.* Tübingen: J.C.B. Mohr, 1956.

Bense, Max. *Hegel und Kierkegaard: Eine prinzipielle Untersuchung.* Cologne: Staufen-Verlag, 1948.

Broudy, Harry S. "Kierkegaard's Levels of Existence." *Philosophy and Phenomenological Research* 1, no. 3 (March 1941), pp. 294-310.

Buber, Martin. "The Question to the Single One." In Buber, *Between Man and Man.* Translated by Ronald Gregor Smith, with an Introduction by Maurice Friedman. New York: Macmillan, 1965. Pp. 40-82.

Capel, Lee M. Historical Introduction, Translator's Notes, and Glossary to *The Concept of Irony*, by Søren Kierkegaard. Bloomington: Indiana University Press, 1965. Pp. 7-41, 351-434.

Cavell, Stanley. "Kierkegaard's *On Authority and Revelation.*" In *Kierkegaard: A Collection of Critical Essays.* Edited by Josiah Thompson. Garden City, N.Y.: Doubleday Anchor, 1972. Pp. 373-393.

Clair, André. "Kierkegaard et l'acte dialectique." *Analogie et Dialectique, Lieux Theologiques*, no. 3 (1982), pp. 161-204.

————. *Pseudonymie et paradoxe: La pensée dialectique de Kierkegaard.* Paris: J. Vrin, 1976.

Collins, James. "Kierkegaard's Imagery of the Self." In *Kierkegaard's Truth: The Disclosure of the Self.* Edited by Joseph H. Smith. Psychiatry and the Humanities, vol. 5. New Haven: Yale University Press, 1981. Pp. 51-84.

————. *The Mind of Kierkegaard.* Chicago: Henry Regnery Company, 1953.

Crites, Stephen. *In the Twilight of Christendom: Hegel vs. Kierkegaard on Faith and History.* AAR Studies in Religion, no. 2. Chambersburg, Pa.: American Academy of Religion, 1972.

―――. Introduction to *Crisis in the Life of an Actress and Other Essays on Drama*, by Søren Kierkegaard. New York: Harper Torchbooks, 1967.

―――. "Pseudonymous Authorship as Art and as Act." In *Kierkegaard: A Collection of Critical Essays.* Edited by Josiah Thompson. Garden City, N.Y.: Doubleday Anchor, 1972. Pp. 183-229.

Croxall, T. H. "Assessment." In *Johannes Climacus or, De Omnibus Dubitandum Est*, by Søren Kierkegaard. Stanford: Stanford University Press, 1958. Pp. 15-97.

―――. *Kierkegaard Studies.* London: Lutterworth Press, 1948.

Davis, Russell H. "Kierkegaard and Community." *Union Seminary Quarterly Review* 36, no. 4 (Summer 1981), pp. 205-222.

Deuser, Hermann. *Sören Kierkegaard: Die paradoxe Dialektik des politischen Christen.* Munich: Kaiser Verlag, 1974.

Diamond, Malcolm L. "Kierkegaard and Apologetics." *Journal of Religion* 44, no. 2 (April 1964), pp. 122-132.

Diem, Herman. *Kierkegaard's Dialectic of Existence.* Translated by Harold Knight. Edinburgh: Oliver and Boyd, 1959.

―――. "Methode der Kierkegaardforschung." *Zwischen den Zeiten* 6 (1928), pp. 140-171.

―――. *Philosophie und Christentum bei Sören Kierkegaard.* Munich: Kaiser Verlag, 1929.

Donnelly, John. "Kierkegaard's Problem I and Problem II: An Analytic Perspective." In *Kierkegaard's "Fear and Trembling": Critical Appraisals.* Edited by Robert L. Perkins. University: University of Alabama Press, 1981. Pp. 43-61.

Dunning, Stephen N. "The Dialectic of Contradiction in Kierkegaard's Aesthetic Stage." *Journal of the American Academy of Religion* 49, no. 3 (September 1981), pp. 383-408.

―――. "History and Phenomenology: Dialectical Structure in Ricoeur's *The Symbolism of Evil.*" *Harvard Theological Review* 76, no. 3 (July 1983), pp. 343-363.

―――. "Kierkegaard's 'Hegelian' Response to Hamann." *Thought* 55, no. 218 (September 1980), pp. 259-270.

―――. "Kierkegaard's Systematic Analysis of Anxiety." In *Kierkegaard's "Concept of Anxiety": Critical Appraisals.* Edited by Robert L. Perkins. Macon, Ga.: Mercer University Press, forthcoming.

————. "Rhetoric and Reality in Kierkegaard's *Postscript.*" *International Journal for Philosophy of Religion* (forthcoming).

Dupré, Louis. *A Dubious Heritage: Studies in the Philosophy of Religion after Kant.* New York: Paulist Press, 1977.

————. *Kierkegaard as Theologian: The Dialectic of Christian Existence.* New York: Sheed and Ward, 1963.

Elrod, John W. *Being and Existence in Kierkegaard's Pseudonymous Works.* Princeton: Princeton University Press, 1975.

————. "Climacus, Anti-Climacus and the Problem of Suffering." *Thought* 55, no. 218 (September 1980), pp. 306-319.

————. *Kierkegaard and Christendom.* Princeton: Princeton University Press, 1981.

Fenger, Henning. *Kierkegaard, The Myths and Their Origins: Studies in the Kierkegaardian Papers and Letters.* Translated by George C. Schoolfield. New Haven: Yale University Press, 1976.

Feuerbach, Ludwig. *The Essence of Christianity.* Translated by George Eliot. New York: Harper & Row, 1957.

Findlay, J. N. *The Philosophy of Hegel: An Introduction and Re-examination.* New York: Collier, 1962.

Foulquié, Paul. *La dialectique.* Paris: Presses Universitaires, 1969.

Gadamer, Hans-Georg. *Truth and Method.* Translation edited by Garrett Barden and John Cumming. New York: Continuum, 1975.

Gill, Jerry H. "Faith Is as Faith Does." In *Kierkegaard's "Fear and Trembling": Critical Appraisals.* Edited by Robert L. Perkins. University: University of Alabama Press, 1981. Pp. 204-217.

————. "Kant, Kierkegaard and Religious Knowledge." In *Essays on Kierkegaard.* Edited by Jerry H. Gill. Minneapolis: Burgess Publishing Co., 1969. Pp. 58-73.

Harper, Ralph. *The Seventh Solitude: Man's Isolation in Kierkegaard, Dostoevsky, and Nietzsche.* Baltimore: Johns Hopkins University Press, 1965.

Heiss, Robert. *Hegel, Kierkegaard, Marx: Three Great Philosophers Whose Ideas Changed the Course of Civilization.* Translated by E. B. Garside. New York: Delta, 1975.

Henriksen, Aage. *Methods and Results of Kierkegaard Studies in Scandinavia: A Historical and Critical Survey.* Copenhagen: Ejnar Munksgaard, 1951.

Hirsch, Emanuel. *Kierkegaard-Studien.* 2 vols. Gütersloh: C. Bertelsmann, 1933.

Hohlenberg, Johannes. *Sören Kierkegaard*. Translated by T. H. Croxall. New York: Pantheon Books, 1954.

Holmer, Paul L. "Kierkegaard and Kinds of Discourse." *Meddelelser fra Søren Kierkegaard Selskabet* 4, no. 4 (1954), pp. 1-5.

————. "Kierkegaard and Religious Propositions." *Journal of Religion* 35, no. 3 (July 1955), pp. 135-146.

————. "On Understanding Kierkegaard." In *A Kierkegaard Critique*. Edited by Howard A. Johnson and Niels Thulstrup. Chicago: Henry Regnery Company, 1962. Pp. 40-53.

————. "Post-Kierkegaard: Remarks about Being a Person." In *Kierkegaard's Truth: The Disclosure of the Self*. Edited by Joseph H. Smith. Psychiatry and the Humanities, vol. 5. New Haven: Yale University Press, 1981. Pp. 3-22.

Joest, Wilfried. Review of *Hegel und Kierkegaard*, by Max Bense. In *Sören Kierkegaard*. Edited by Heinz-Horst Schrey. Darmstadt: Wissenschaftliche Buchgesellschaft, 1971. Pp. 81-89.

Johnson, Howard A. "Kierkegaard and Politics." In *A Kierkegaard Critique*. Edited by Howard A. Johnson and Niels Thulstrup. Chicago: Henry Regnery Company, 1962. Pp. 74-84.

Junghaus, Hans Martin. Translator's Notes to *Abschliessende unwissenschaftliche Nachschrift*, pt. 2. In Sören Kierkegaard, *Gesammelte Werke*, vol. 16. Düsseldorf: Eugen Diederichs Verlag, 1958. Pp. 345-419.

Kainz, Howard P. "Kierkegaard's 'Three Stages' and the Levels of Spiritual Maturity." *Modern Schoolman* 52 (May 1975), pp. 359-380.

Kant, Immanuel. *Critique of Pure Reason*. Translated by Norman Kemp Smith. New York: St. Martin's Press, 1965.

Kirmmse, Bruce. "Kierkegaard's Politics: The Social Thought of Søren Kierkegaard in Its Historical Context." 2 vols. Ph.D. dissertation, University of California, 1977.

————. "Psychology and Society: The Social Falsification of the Self in *The Sickness unto Death*." In *Kierkegaard's Truth: The Disclosure of the Self*. Edited by Joseph H. Smith. Psychiatry and the Humanities, vol. 5. Hew Haven: Yale University Press, 1981. Pp. 167-192.

Klemke, E. D. "Some Misinterpretations of Kierkegaard." *Hibbert Journal* 57, no. 3 (April 1959), pp. 259-270.

Kroner, Richard. "Kierkegaard or Hegel?" *Revue internationale de Philosophie* 6, no. 1 (1952), pp. 79-96.

————. "Kierkegaard's Understanding of Hegel." *Union Seminary Quarterly Review* 31, no. 2, pt. II (January 1966), pp. 233-244.

Levine, Michael. "Kierkegaard: What Does the Subjective Individual Risk?" *International Journal for Philosophy of Religion* 13, no. 1 (1982), pp. 13-22.

Lowrie, Walter. *Kierkegaard.* London: Oxford University Press, 1938.

————. "Translators and Interpreters of S. K." *Theology Today* 12, no. 3 (October 1955), pp. 312-327.

McCarthy, Vincent A. *The Phenomenology of Moods in Kierkegaard.* The Hague: Martinus Nijhoff, 1978.

————. " 'Psychological Fragments': Kierkegaard's Religious Psychology." In *Kierkegaard's Truth: The Disclosure of the Self.* Edited by Joseph H. Smith. Psychiatry and the Humanities, vol. 5. New Haven: Yale University Press, 1981. Pp. 235-266.

McInerny, Ralph. "Ethics and Persuasion: Kierkegaard's Existential Dialectic." *Modern Schoolman* 33 (May 1956), pp. 219-239.

MacIntyre, Alasdair. *After Virtue: A Study in Moral Theory.* Notre Dame: University of Notre Dame Press, 1981.

Mackey, Louis. *Kierkegaard: A kind of Poet.* Philadelphia: University of Pennsylvania Press, 1971.

————. "The Loss of the World in Kierkegaard's Ethics." In *Kierkegaard: A Collection of Critical Essays.* Edited by Josiah Thompson. Garden City, N.Y.: Doubleday Anchor, 1972. Pp. 266-288.

————. "A Ram in the Afternoon: Kierkegaard's Discourse of the Other." In *Kierkegaard's Truth: The Disclosure of the Self.* Edited by Joseph H. Smith. Psychiatry and the Humanities, vol. 5. New Haven: Yale University Press, 1981. Pp. 193-234.

————. "The View from Pisgah: A Reading of *Fear and Trembling.*" In *Kierkegaard: A Collection of Critical Essays.* Edited by Josiah Thompson. Garden City, N.Y.: Doubleday Anchor, 1972. Pp. 394-428.

McKinnon, Alastair. *The Kierkegaard Indices.* 4 vols. Leiden: E. J. Brill, 1970.

————. "Kierkegaard: Paradox and Irrationalism." In *Essays on Kierkegaard.* Edited by Jerry H. Gill. Minneapolis: Burgess Publishing Co., 1969. Pp. 102-112.

————. "Kierkegaard's Irrationalism Revisited." *International Philosophical Quarterly* 9, no. 2 (June 1969), pp. 165-176.

———. "Kierkegaard's Pseudonyms: A New Hierarchy." *American Philosophical Quarterly* 6, no. 2 (April 1969), pp. 116-126.

Malantschuk, Gregor. *The Controversial Kierkegaard.* Translated by Howard V. Hong and Edna H. Hong. Waterloo: Wilfrid Laurier University Press, 1980.

———. *Kierkegaard's Thought.* Edited and translated by Howard V. Hong and Edna H. Hong. Princeton: Princeton University Press, 1971.

———. *Kierkegaard's Way to the Truth.* Translated by Mary Michelsen. Minneapolis: Augsburg, 1963.

Mesnard, Pierre. "The Character of Kierkegaard's Philosophy." *Philosophy Today* 1, no. 2/4 (June 1957), pp. 84-89.

———. *Le vrai visage de Kierkegaard.* Paris: Beauchesne, 1948.

Michalson, G. E., Jr. "Lessing, Kierkegaard, and the 'Ugly Ditch': A Reexamination." *Journal of Religion* 59, no. 3 (July 1979), pp. 324-334.

Mooney, Edward F. "Understanding Abraham: Care, Faith, and the Absurd." In *Kierkegaard's "Fear and Trembling": Critical Appraisals.* Edited by Robert L. Perkins. University: University of Alabama Press, 1981. Pp. 100-114.

Nordentoft, Kresten. *Kierkegaard's Psychology.* Translated by Bruce Kirmmse. Pittsburgh: Duquesne University Press, 1978.

Perkins, Robert L. "Beginning the System: Kierkegaard and Hegel." In *Akten des XIV Internationalen Kongresses für Philosophie.* Vienna: Herder, 1968. Pp. 478-485.

———. "For Sanity's Sake: Kant, Kierkegaard, and Father Abraham." In *Kierkegaard's "Fear and Trembling": Critical Appraisals.* Edited by Robert L. Perkins. University: University of Alabama Press, 1981. Pp. 43-61.

———. "Hegel and Kierkegaard: Two Critics of Romantic Irony." In *Hegel in Comparative Literature.* Edited by Frederick G. Weiss. Jamaica, N.Y.: St. John's University Press, 1970. Pp. 232-254.

———. "Kierkegaard and Hegel: The Dialectical Structure of Kierkegaard's Ethical Thought." Ph.D. dissertation, Indiana University, 1965.

Plekon, Michael. " 'Anthropological Contemplation': Kierkegaard and Modern Social Theory." *Thought* 55, no. 218 (September 1980), pp. 346-369.

———. " 'Other Kierkegaards'—New Views and Reinterpretations

in Scholarship." *Thought* 55, no. 218 (September 1980), pp. 370-375.

Pojman, Louis P. "The Dialectic of Freedom in the Thought of Søren Kierkegaard." Th.D. dissertation, Union Theological Seminary, 1972.

Ricoeur, Paul. *The Symbolism of Evil.* Translated by Emerson Buchanan. Boston: Beacon Press, 1969.

———. "Two Encounters with Kierkegaard: Kierkegaard and Evil; Doing Philosophy after Kierkegaard." In *Kierkegaard's Truth: The Disclosure of the Self.* Edited by Joseph H. Smith. Psychiatry and the Humanities, vol. 5. New Haven: Yale University Press, 1981. Pp. 313-342.

Ringleben, Joachim. *Hegels Theorie der Sünde.* Berlin: Walter de Gruyter, 1976.

Ritschl, Dietrich. "Kierkegaards Kritik an Hegels Logik." *Theologische Zeitschrift* 11 (1955), pp. 437-465.

Rohde, Peter P. "Søren Kierkegaard: The Father of Existentialism." In *Essays on Kierkegaard.* Edited by Jerry H. Gill. Minneapolis: Burgess Publishing Co., 1969. Pp. 6-30.

Rosenkranz, Karl. *Psychologie, oder die Wissenschaft vom subjectiven Geist.* Königsberg: Bornträger, 1837.

Sannwald, Adolf. *Der Begriff der "Dialektik" und die Anthropologie.* Munich: Kaiser Verlag, 1931.

Sartre, Jean-Paul. *Critique of Dialectical Reason.* Translated by Alan Sheridan-Smith. London: Verso, 1982.

Schmuëli, Adi. *Kierkegaard and Consciousness.* Translated by Naomi Handelmann. Princeton: Princeton University Press, 1971.

Schrader, George. "Kant and Kierkegaard on Duty and Inclination." In *Kierkegaard: A Collection of Critical Essays.* Edited by Josiah Thompson. Garden City, N.Y.: Doubleday Anchor, 1972. Pp. 324-341.

Schröer, Henning. *Die Denkform der Paradoxicalität als theologisches Problem: Eine Untersuchung zu Kierkegaard und die neueren Theologie als Beitrag zur theologischen Logik.* Göttingen: Vandenhoeck & Ruprecht, 1960.

Sløk, Johannes. *Die Anthropologie Kierkegaards.* Copenhagen: Rosenkilde und Bagger, 1954.

Søe, N. H. "Kierkegaard's Doctrine of the Paradox." Translated by Margaret Grieve. In *A Kierkegaard Critique.* Edited by Howard A.

Johnson and Niels Thulstrup. Chicago: Henry Regnery Company,
1962. Pp. 207-227.

———. "The Period up to The Postscript." In *Kierkegaard's View
of Christianity*. Vol. 1 in *Bibliotheca Kierkegaardiana*. Edited by
Niels Thulstrup and Maria Mikulova Thulstrup. Copenhagen: C.
A. Reitzel, 1978. Pp. 107-130.

Sponheim, Paul. *Kierkegaard on Christ and Christian Coherence*. London: SCM Press, 1968.

Stack, George J. *Kierkegaard's Existential Ethics*. University: University of Alabama Press, 1977.

———. "On the Notion of Dialectics." *Philosophy Today* 15, no. 4/
4 (Winter 1971), pp. 276-290.

Stendahl, Brita K. *Søren Kierkegaard*. Boston: Twayne, 1976.

Swenson, David F. "The Anti-Intellectualism of Kierkegaard." *Philosophical Review* 25, no. 4 (1916), pp. 567-586.

———. *Something About Kierkegaard*. Edited by Lilian Marvin Swenson. Minneapolis: Augsburg Publishing House, 1956. Reprinted,
Macon, Ga.: Mercer University Press, 1983.

Taylor, Charles. *Hegel*. Cambridge: Cambridge University Press,
1975.

Taylor, Mark C. "Aesthetic Therapy: Hegel and Kierkegaard." In
Kierkegaard's Truth: The Disclosure of the Self. Edited by Joseph H.
Smith. Psychiatry and the Humanities, vol. 5. New Haven: Yale
University Press, 1981. Pp. 343-380.

———. *Journeys to Selfhood: Hegel and Kierkegaard*. Berkeley: University of California Press, 1980.

———. *Kierkegaard's Pseudonymous Authorship: A Study of Time and
the Self*. Princeton: Princeton University Press, 1975.

———. "Sounds of Silence." In *Kierkegaard's "Fear and Trembling":
Critical Appraisals*. Edited by Robert L. Perkins. University: University of Alabama Press, 1981. Pp. 165-188.

Theunissen, Michael. "Kierkegaard's Negativistic Method." In *Kier-
kegaard's Truth: The Disclosure of the Self*. Edited by Joseph H.
Smith. Psychiatry and the Humanities, vol. 5. New Haven: Yale
University Press, 1981. Pp. 381- 423.

Thomasson, James W. "Concepts: Their Role, Criteria and Correction in the Thought of Søren Kierkegaard." Ph.D. dissertation,
Yale University, 1968.

Thompson, Josiah. *The Lonely Labyrinth: Kierkegaard's Pseudonymous
Works*. Carbondale: Southern Illinois University Press, 1967.

————. "The Master of Irony." In *Kierkegaard: A Collection of Critical Essays*. Edited by Josiah Thompson. Garden City, N.Y.: Doubleday Anchor, 1972. Pp. 103-163.

Thomte, Reidar. *Kierkegaard's Philosophy of Religion*. Princeton: Princeton University Press, 1948.

Thulstrup, Niels. *Kierkegaard's Relation to Hegel*. Translated by George L. Stengren. Princeton: Princeton University Press, 1980.

————. *Kierkegaards Verhältnis zu Hegel: Forschungsgeschichte*. Stuttgart: Verlag W. Kohlhammer, 1969.

————. "Theological and Philosophical Kierkegaardian Studies in Scandinavia, 1945-1953." Translated by Paul Holmer. *Theology Today* 12, no. 3 (October 1955), pp. 297-311.

Traub, Friedrich. "Zum Begriff des Dialektischen." *Zeitschrift für Theologie und Kirche* 37 (1929), pp. 380-388.

Tzavaras, Johann. *Bewegung bei Kierkegaard*. Frankfurt am Main: Peter Lang, 1978.

Utterback, Sylvia Walsh. "Kierkegaard's Dialectic of Christian Existence." Ph.D. dissertation, Emory University, 1975.

————. "Kierkegaard's Inverse Dialectic." *Kierkegaardiana* 11 (1980), pp. 34-54.

Wahl, Jean. *Études Kierkegaardiennes*, 4th ed. Paris: J. Vrin, 1974.

Westphal, Merold. "Abraham and Hegel." In *Kierkegaard's "Fear and Trembling": Critical Appraisals*. Edited by Robert L. Perkins. University: University of Alabama Press, 1981. Pp. 62-80.

————. "Kierkegaard and the Logic of Insanity." *Religious Studies* 7, no. 3 (September 1971), pp. 193-211.

————. "Kierkegaard's Politics." *Thought* 55, no. 218 (September 1980), pp. 320-332.

————. "Kierkegaard's Sociology." Forthcoming in the International Kierkegaard Commentary on *Two Ages*. Edited by Robert L. Perkins. Mercer University Press.

Whittemore, Robert C. "Pro Hegel, Contra Kierkegaard." *Journal of Religious Thought* 13, no. 2 (1956), pp. 131-144.

Zuurdeeg, William F. "Some Aspects of Kierkegaard's Language Philosophy." In *Atti del XII Congresso Internazionale di Filosofia, (1958)*, vol. 12. Florence: Sansoni Editore, 1961. Pp. 493-499.

INDEX

A, 33-58, 75, 78-80, 84, 92, 95, 101, 119, 267-270
Abelard, 130
Abraham, 113-125, 247, 255, 267, 275-277
abrogate, 10, 24, 27, 187, 265, 269. *See also aufheben*
absolute, 11, 32, 59, 64, 152; choice of self, 78-79; consciousness, 226; contradiction, 47, 69, 73; deception, 44, 47, 53-59, 68-73; demonic, 118; dependence, 288; desire, 37, 58, 64-65, 72; difference between divine and human, 172-173, 178; duty toward God, 116, 121; fact, 177-178, 208; = God, 117, 288; grief, 44-47, 58; indifference, 243, 251; inwardness, 56, 58, 73, 235; love (parental), 44, 72; = man, 65; method (Hegel's), 264, 284; negativity, 20-26; paradox, 171, 173, 178, 251; poetry, 57; relation to the absolute, 118-119, 122, 190, 192-194; respect (resignation), 190, 192, 199, 202-203, 234, 288; self-consciousness, 236; subjectivity, 20, 27, 31; *telos*, 190-193, 199, 202, 288; venture (religion), 192, 198
abstract, 9-11, 14, 24, 179, 263, 282; thought, 72, 142-143, 183, 187-188, 285
absurd, 48, 98, 110, 114, 172, 175-176, 193, 207-208, 246, 254, 279
accidental, 14-15, 33, 47-50, 53, 85, 153, 169, 174, 185
acoustic illusion, 172-173, 196
active, 10-11, 36-37, 41, 44-46, 50-59, 68, 70, 160, 191, 232
actuality, 14-17, 22-31, 48, 50, 106, 111-112, 119, 127, 130-134, 143-146, 156-157, 163, 165, 175-176, 206, 209, 243, 263-265, 269, 282, 290
Adam, 144-148
ad hominem, 84, 93
Adorno, T., 263
aesthete, 48, 54, 95, 100-101, 105, 112, 128, 179, 184, 243-244
aesthetic, 4, 7, 32-112, 116-120, 124-125, 128-130, 133-143, 153, 179, 188, 190-197, 200, 205-206, 242-247, 270-274, 280-281, 284, 289-290, 295
"Aesthetic Validity of Marriage," 74-91
Afham, William, 60-63, 71, 268
Agacinski, S., 259
Agnes, 118-119
algebraic, 179, 245, 250-251, 263
alienation, 21, 45, 128-129, 150, 155, 225-226, 233, 236-241
Allison, H. E., 284
alterity, 178, 283-284
"Ancient Tragical Motif," 39-41, 73
Ånd (Aand), 271. *See also* spirit

LIBRARY OF CONGRESS CATALOGING IN PUBLICATION DATA

Dunning, Stephen N. (Stephen Northrup), 1941-
Kierkegaard's dialectic of inwardness.

Bibliography: p.
Includes index.
1. Kierkegaard, Søren, 1813-1855.   2. Dialectic—
History—19th century.   3. Religion—Philosophy—
History—19th century.   I. Title.
B4378.D5D86   1985   198.9   85-3443
ISBN 0-691-07299-X (alk. paper)